LEFT TO THE WOLVES: IRISH VICTIMS
OF STALINIST TERROR

In memory of
Louis Bennett (1953–1991)

LEFT TO THE WOLVES

IRISH VICTIMS OF STALINIST TERROR

BARRY McLOUGHLIN

IRISH ACADEMIC PRESS
DUBLIN • PORTLAND, OR

First published in 2007 by
IRISH ACADEMIC PRESS
44 Northumberland Road, Dublin 4, Ireland

and in the United States of America by
IRISH ACADEMIC PRESS
c/o ISBS, Suite 300, 920 NE 58th Avenue
Portland, Oregon 97213-3786

Website: www.iap.ie

British Library Cataloguing in Publication Data
An entry can be found on request

ISBN 978-0-7165-2914-9 (cloth)
ISBN 978-0-7165-2915-6 (paper)

Library of Congress Cataloging-in-Publication Data
An entry can be found on request

Typeset in 11pt on 13pt Sabon
by FiSH Books, Enfield, Middx.
Printed by MPG Books Ltd., Bodmin, Cornwall

Contents

Photographs and Illustrations

1. Pat Breslin, Lenin School, 1928.
2. Pat Breslin, Moscow, 1930.
3. Jack Carney, c. 1928.
4. Jim Larkin at 5th Comintern Congress, Moscow, 1924.
5. Sean Murray, Moscow, 1935.
6. Peadar O'Donnell, Berlin, March 1930.
7. Pat Breslin and Irina on holidays, July 1936.
8. Pat Breslin, Lubianka, December 1940.
9. Prisoners beginning the journey to the Gulag, Moscow, October 1941.
10. Henry Löwenstein, Moscow 1935.
11. Henry Löwenstein, 1956, after release from the Gulag.
12. Genrikh Kreitser, Katya's father.
13. Olga, Katya's mother.
14. Katya, c. 1926.
15. Katya in kimono, c. 1924.
16. Irina with grandmother and mother, 1934.
17. Katya, Genrikh and Irina, ca. 1948.
18. Daisy McMackin as schoolgirl, c. 1915.
19. Daisy McMackin, Belfast BA graduation 1919.
20. Daisy McMackin, Jacob Miller and an unknown woman, Moscow 1936.
21. Mairead Breslin, 1955.
22. Hamilton Frederick Stuart Goold-Verschpyle in court dress, 1890s.
23. Hamilton Frederick Stuart Goold-Verschoyle ('Tim'), Brian's father.
24. Sibyl Goold-Verschoyle and her children 1914, from left to right: Eileen, Sheila, baby Brian, Dennis and Neil.
25. Willi Münzenberg of the KPD at the 5th Congress of the Comintern, Moscow 1924.
26. The Goold-Verschoyle family in their limousine, c. 1920.

Preface and Acknowledgements

An article I read in the summer of 1989 at my home in Vienna was the starting point for this book, the stories of three Irishmen who died in Soviet confinement during the Stalin era. The piece by Paula Garb in *Moscow News* summarised the history of the popular weekly's predecessor, *Moscow Daily News*, and what had happened to its staff during the Great Terror of the 1930s. One name stood out – Patrick Breslin.

At the time I was extremely interested in Gorbachev's attempts to reform the Soviet system, especially his reassessment of the Soviet past. The tentative moves to disclose facts about the crimes of Stalinism, commenced by Khrushchev and stopped by Brezhnev, were restricted in the Gorbachev era to the rehabilitation of prominent Bolsheviks. But when the USSR imploded in 1991, the policy of the Russian state towards the victims of communism changed radically. The Rehabilitation Law, signed by President Boris Yelzin on 18 October 1991, enabled the families of the victims to examine the prosecution files of their loved ones, and granted the survivors of Stalin's Gulags social and material benefits.

Any foreigner interested in the fate of somebody who had 'disappeared' in the USSR could also gain access to such documentation, providing he or she had a letter-of-attorney from a near relative of the victim. I found my first victim family because of the persistence of James (Shay) Courtney of Kilmashogue, County Dublin. I had discussed the Breslin case on many occasions in Shay and Mary's house in the Dublin Mountains but our joint musings (Breslin is a fairly common name in Ireland) produced no results. That all changed in April 1992, when Shay telephoned me to say that he had located Pat Breslin's daughter, Mairead Breslin Kelly, in Dublin. With Mairead's letters, I received her father's files in Moscow and within a year had also found her Russian family, Genrikh and Irina, the children of Breslin's first marriage.

Through Mairead I gained access to the family of the second Irish victim, Brian Goold-Verschoyle from Dunkineely, County Donegal. David Simms, former Professor of Mathematics at Trinity College Dublin, is the nephew of Brian. With David's accreditation, I was allowed to view Goold-Verschoyle's dossiers in Moscow and made the acquaintanceship of Pyotr Guberov, David's Russian first cousin. Pyotr is the son of Brian Goold-Verschoyle's eldest brother, Neil.

I came across the third victim, Seán McAteer, purely by chance, by reading his pseudonym David Twist and his nationality (*irlandets*) in a volume published in Odessa by the human rights association Memorial. It took me years to crack the coded name and place him in his political context. Unfortunately I could not locate his daughter Maria, and the Ukrainian Red Cross could offer me no information on her whereabouts. But the long interruptions between one bout of writing and the next were a blessing in disguise. In the intervals I learned Russian and completed books on the Austrian victims of the Great Terror, and with my friend Kevin McDermott (Sheffield Hallam University), co-edited a volume of contributions on the mass repression launched by Stalin's Politburo in the summer of 1937.

Needing time to complete one research programme before returning to the Irish cases was also opportune because I benefited from the release of secret service 'subversion' files by the British Public Record Office in London. During my sojourns in London, I was fortunate to meet another person who, like Mairead Breslin Kelly and David Simms, had a personal interest in my archival excavations: Merilyn Moos. Merilyn is the daughter of Lotte Moos, Brian Goold-Verschoyle's companion.

Without their help, this book would not have been written. All three gave generously of their time and hospitality, providing me with family letters, photographs and manuscripts. They commented on what I had written about the tragic fate of their relatives. I have desisted from continuing the narrative to include accounts of how the families dealt with the loss of the victim, feeling that this was a task for those immediately involved. Furthermore, in keeping a balance between 'academic credibility' and a popular style, I also refrained from outlining the book's contents in detail at the outset, as in the case of an introduction to a strictly academic volume. Of more importance, perhaps, I also chose to place the main characters in their historical context and consciously refrained from passing personal judgement, preferring to leave the readers to come to their own conclusions. And since none of the Irish protagonist-victims were famous, they left no personal papers, nor can their contemporaries, long deceased, bear witness. That is the main reason why the narrative oscillates constantly between definite historical backgrounds and the individual's place in them.

A special debt of thanks is due to Dr Emmet O'Connor, who commented on the text. Emmet and I spent two longer periods in Moscow during the mid-1990s, working on Irish material in the Comintern archive RGASPI. Over the years he has sent me books, photocopies and good advice. Another friend, the professional editor Christina O'Shaughnessy, deserves my special gratitude. Her meticulous reading of the manuscript at an early stage was of great value and saved me from many pitfalls.

My dealings with post-Soviet officialdom were greatly facilitated by assistance generously afforded by the Irish Embassy in Moscow, by the Ambassadors Patrick McCabe and David Donoghue and their capable staff, especially Richard Fallon, Tom Russell, Damien Coyle, Brian Earles, Julian Clare and James C. O'Shea. Aidan O'Hara of the Irish Embassy in Prague was instrumental in smoothing my path to the archive of the Ukrainian secret service in Kiev, where Seán McAteer's prosecution dossier is kept.

In the course of research in Dublin, London, Berlin, Moscow and Kiev, I corresponded with historians, archival employees, linguists and friends who answered my never-ending stream of queries by providing information, good sense, pieces of their own research, rare books and translations:

Ireland: Eunan O'Halpin, Bill Sheeran, Theresa Moriarty, Commandant Peter Young (decd.), Anton MacCaba, Lara Kelly, Katie Donovan

Britain: John Halstead, Duncan Forbes, Alan Campbell, John McIlroy, Andy Flinn, Richard Kirkwood, Andy Croft, Kevin Morgan, Julian Hendy, Wolf Suschitzky

Germany: Reinhard Müller, Slawa Hedeler, Meinhard Stark

Spain: Guillermo Casan

USA: Paula Garb, Brian O'Neill, Penny Fernquist

Austria: Berthold Unfried, Martin Grünberg, Vitaly Bodnar, Verena Moritz, Wolfgang Neugebauer, Gerhard Ungar

Russia: Henry Löwenstein (decd.), Aleksandr Vatlin, Nataliia Mussineko, Sergei Zhuravlev, Lina Rozovskaya, Oleg Tsarev and Asja Steiner (decd.)

Ukraine: Yuri Shapoval, Natalia Makovska and the 'Black Admiral'.

For their forbearance and cooperation over a period of twelve years I am grateful to Svetlana Rozental and Ludmilla Karlova of RGASPI, and to Ina Shchekotova and her assistants in the library of the Sakharov Centre in Moscow. The staffs at the Bundesarchiv in Berlin, the Public Record Office in Kew, the British Library Newspaper Collection at Colindale, the National Archives of Ireland and the Irish National Library were unremittingly cheerful and helpful. In London, Joyce Rathbone and Pegeen O'Flaherty shared with me recollections of their father, Liam O'Flaherty.

Research trips abroad from Vienna were made memorable by the kindness and hospitality of friends and relatives: Aideen and Joe in Monasterevin; Tom Arnold, Bríd and Brendan O'Rourke, and Mairead in Dublin; Slawa and Meinhart in Berlin; Svetlana Bartels, Séamus Martin, Vadim and Rita Levitsky in Moscow; Genrikh and Tamara in Pushchino.

A grant funded jointly by the Royal Irish Academy and the Austrian Academy of Sciences enabled me to spend July 2003 in Ireland to continue research. Eunan O'Halpin of the Department of Contemporary Irish History at Trinity College Dublin provided me with the use of an office in the new penthouse over the library with its spectacular vista. Emmet O'Connor ferried me around the home country of Seán McAteer, and David and Anngret Simms entertained us at their cottage near the Goold-Verschoyle home in Dunkineely.

The later stages of the writing were overshadowed by the deaths of Genrikh and Irina Breslin in Russia. They both visited the land of their father, Patrick, before ill-health curtailed their movements. They were excellent cooks and good company. During the making of the RTE documentary 'Amongst Wolves' in Kazan in September 2000, I finally had the opportunity to meet Henry Löwenstein in person. I had read his two volumes of Gulag memoirs and he kindly presented me with his drawings (from memory) of the camp hell. Henry died in October 2004 and I regret very much that we did not meet again.

The manuscript was shepherded through the refining process by the literary agent Jonathan Williams. He has taught me a lot about editing and I thank him for keeping faith in my project for over a decade. It was also a pleasure to work with Lisa Hyde of Irish Academic Press, who, with enthusiasm and persistence, made sure that the book could be prepared for publication in a relatively short period.

The photograph of Jim Phelan in the *Liverpool Echo* of 28 June 1923 was reproduced by permission of the British Library. The group photograph of the Rotunda occupation (*The Freeman's Journal*, Friday, 20 January 1922, p.3) is reproduced by courtesy of the National Library of Ireland.

Finally, I thank Susanne for bearing with me, the text and its characters for so long. The book is dedicated to the memory of a dear friend, Louis Bennett of Drimnagh, a true Dublin wit and great singer. *Friede seiner Asche.*

Barry McLoughlin
August 2006

Abbreviations and Acronyms

AOH: Ancient Order of Hibernians
CI: Communist International, or Comintern
CP: Communist Party
CPGB: Communist Party of Great Britain
CPI: Communist Party of Ireland
CPSA: Communist Party of South Africa
CPUSA: Communist Party of the United States of America
ECCI: Executive Committee of the Communist International
GB: State Security (Soviet)
Gosplan: Soviet state planning agency
GPU: Soviet secret police, 1922–27
GRU: Main Intelligence Administration of the Red Army
GUGB: Main Administration of State Security (central) of the NKVD
ICA: Irish Citizen Army
ILP: Independent Labour Party (Britain)
ILS: International Lenin School (Moscow)
INO: Foreign Department of the Soviet secret service
INSNAB: Shops for foreigners at reduced rouble rates
Intourist: Soviet tourist agency for foreign visitors
IPK: International Propaganda Committees of the Transport Workers
IRA: Irish Republican Army
IRB: Irish Republican Brotherhood
ITGWU: Irish Transport and General Workers' Union
ITIR: Russian acronym for Co-operative Publishers for Foreign Workers in the USSR
ITUC: Irish Trade Union Congress

IWL: Irish Worker League

IWW: Industrial Workers of the World

Komsomol: Youth section of the Soviet CP

KPD: Communist Party of Germany

KPÖ: Communist Party of Austria

Krestintern: Communist International of Peasants

KRTD: Russian acronym for 'counter-revolutionary Trotskyist activity'

LSE: London School of Economics

MDN: *Moscow Daily News*

MI5: British secret service (UK operations)

MI6: British secret service (foreign operations)

MOPR: International Red Help

MP: Member of Parliament

NKVD: People's Commissariat of Internal Affairs (including secret police)

OGPU: Soviet secret police, 1927–34

OMS: Department of International Communications in the Comintern

OSO: Special Board (secret sentencing instance in the NKVD)

OTC: Officer Training Corps

PCE: Communist Party of Spain

POUM: Workers' Party of Marxist Unification (Spain)

Profintern: Communist Trade Union International

PSOE: Spanish Socialist Workers' Party

PSUC: Unified Socialist Party of Catalonia (communist)

RIC: Royal Irish Constabulary

ROP: Russian Oil Products

RUC: Royal Ulster Constabulary

RWG: Revolutionary Workers' Groups (Ireland)

SIM: Military intelligence service of the Spanish Republican Government

SLON: Solovetsky Special Camps

SOE: 'Socially dangerous element' (Russia)

Sovtorgflot: Soviet Merchant Marine

SPD: Social Democratic Party of Germany

SPI: Socialist Party of Ireland

TASS: Soviet news agency

TORGSIN: Soviet trade outlets dealing only in foreign currency

TUC: Trades Union Congress (Britain)

UCD: University College Dublin

UGB: Administration of State Security of the NKVD (local)

VKP(b): Soviet CP, 1925–52

VOKS: All Union Association for Cultural Affairs with Abroad (USSR)

Wobbly: Member of the Industrial Workers of the World (IWW)

WPI: Workers' Party of Ireland

WUI: Workers' Union of Ireland

YCL: Young Communist League (of Great Britain)

ARCHIVES

GARF: State Archive of the Russian Federation, Moscow

NAI: National Archives of Ireland

ÖSTA: Austrian State Archives, Vienna

PRO: Public Record Office, London

RGASPI: Russian State Archive for Social and Political History, Moscow

SAPMO: Stiftung Archiv der Parteien und Massenorganisation der DDR, Bundesarchiv, Berlin

RUSSIAN ARCHIVAL SYSTEM

f., *fond* (archival stock)

o., *opis* (registry)

d., *delo* (file)

l. or ll. (page numbers)

Glossary of Russian Terms

antisovetchik: person held to be against the regime

apparat: personnel of an influential Soviet institution

balanda: watered-down soup

bania: bath house

bedkom: acronym for 'committee of the poor'

bilet: ticket; here, Party membership-card

byvshie liudi: the former middle class

cheka: popular phrase for the Soviet secret police and its acronym, 1917–22

chekist: member of the Soviet secret police

chistka: purge of Party organisations

dacha: rural holiday home, usually with a vegetable patch

dom terpimosti: euphemism for brothel

elektrichka: electrified suburban railway.

etap: stretch of the long rail journey to the Gulag

glasnost: openness

kartser: punishment cells in prison or camp

khoziain: literally proprietor; Stalin's nickname within the Soviet higher bureaucracy

komandirovka: work assignment in another city, region or abroad

kombinat: here, comprehensive third-level educational college

kommunalka: communal apartment

konveier: round-the-clock interrogation

kulturnost: cultivation of manners and a more civilised way of life

lavochka: literally huckster's shop, shady concern, gang

makhorka: inferior kind of tobacco

meshochniki: literary 'bagmen', speculators

miasorubka: mincing-machine, synonym for interrogation and torture

militsiia: normal, as opposed to secret, police

nomenklatura: holders of high positions entitled to privileges

opravka: here, being led out of the cell to a sit-down lavatory

paika: thick heel of rationed bread loaf

parasha: open toilet bucket in a communal prison cell

partorg: organiser of Party sub-organisation

pedtechnikum: teacher training college for technical subjects

praktika: 'practical' work carried out by students, usually in a factory

Pravda: daily newspaper of the Central Committee of the VKP(b)

proforg: shop steward in ILS

propusk: pass for entry to a building

proverka: review of Party cadres during a purge

rezident: commanding officer of Soviet secret service in a large city, spymaster

rezindentura: foreign agency of a Soviet secret service

seksot: police informer

sharashka: scientific work carried out by an inmate in prison or camp

sledovatel: NKVD officer investigating a prosecution case

sobachnik: box in prison, confinement space for incoming prisoners

sovetnik: adviser

spetskorpus: special building within a complex

stazh: length of service

tarakany: cockroaches

troika: three-man sentencing board

udarnichestvo: attempts to raise productivity

urki: professional criminals

valenki: felt boots for winter wear

zek: abbreviation for *zakliuchënnyi* (prisoner)

Introduction

Nothing befitted the communist movement more than the manner of its passing. Nobody outside Russia demonstrated for its retention. Not a shot was fired in its defence. Soviet communism collapsed not only because of the arms race and because its economies did not function. It disappeared almost soundlessly because it was also morally compromised – by its omnipresent secret police, by its work camps, by its bureaucratic obtuseness and ideological rigidity, and, perhaps more importantly, by the mortgage of its crimes. The immanent violence of the communist movement, the millions (in double figures) of victims it had produced, had long since delegitimised it.

The heyday of communism in the English-speaking world, where it never established a bridgehead in parliamentary, as distinct from trade union, politics, was between 1935 and 1945. Fear of the fascist powers made an alliance with the Soviet Union attractive for many in the shameful years of 'appeasement'; and the enormous losses incurred by the Soviet peoples in the struggle against the Axis invaders boosted sympathy for Stalin and his plucky Russians.

Ireland, as is often the case in comparative history, is an exception. Since the Bolsheviks were avowedly 'godless' and persecuted religious believers and their priests, the Papacy was vociferously anti-Communist. Irish Catholics followed this lead, especially after the publication of the encyclical Quadragesimo Anno (1931) by Pius XI, which condemned the class struggle, socialism and communism. While communism was making strides on the continent in the second half of the 1930s, Ireland was in the grip of religious fervour and it chose to be neutral during World War II. Moscow's interest in Ireland, and prospects for the admirers of Bolshevism on the island, seemed greatest when the Irish conflict with imperialist Britain peaked – in the revolutionary years 1919/23 and in the first half of the 1930s, when Eamon de Valera's administration tried to break constitutional and economic constraints imposed by London. Communism in Ireland, then, was always linked to the national struggle ('The National Question') and its adherents were generally ex-IRA members.[1]

The Irish labour movement was traditionally weak. In European terms a comparative late-comer, it entered the political limelight shortly before World War I. The occasion was the first successful attempt to organise the unskilled, in an uneven fight forced upon the Irish Transport and General Workers' Union (ITGWU) during the Dublin Lock-Out of 1913. Labour militancy was therefore trade-union based and suspicious of politics. Arguably, the outbreak of the war intervened before a strong political wing could be established.

During the international armed conflict, the leaders associated with the upsurge of Irish labour were sadly missed: James Larkin went to the United States in 1914, James Connolly was executed in the aftermath of the 1916 Easter Rising. Sympathy for the New Russia was high during the War of Independence in 1919–21. But the anti-militarist strikes, the occupation of factories and creameries ('Soviets') or the struggle of agricultural labourers for a decent wage owed little to Marxist agitation. That social struggle running parallel to the armed one soon petered out because it was essentially a reaction against the economic retrenchment (wage-cuts) of the post-war slump.

In the revolutionary years the Irish Labour Party existed as an election machine, not as a movement of paying members, whom it did not begin to recruit on an individual basis until 1930. There was therefore no organised left-wing organisation of any great size in Ireland between 1919 and 1921 which would have supplied a nucleus of experienced cadres when the Communist International (Comintern) began to establish national sections. Setting up a Communist Party in Ireland was compounded by another problem – the double fission of radical ranks in 1922/23. The first centred on the rejection of the Anglo-Irish Treaty, signed in London in December 1921. When the Civil War broke out in June 1922, almost all Communists and the majority of trade-union militants sided with the Republicans.

The second split concerned the return of James Larkin to Ireland at the close of the Civil War in May 1923. Larkin had been secretary of the ITGWU until he embarked on what was thought to be a short tour of the United States. On returning after nine years' absence, he believed he could now resume where he had stopped in 1914. The incumbents in the ITGWU rejected his take-over and Larkin founded his own trade union, The Workers' Union of Ireland (WUI). The split between Larkin and William O'Brien of the ITGWU debilitated the Irish labour movement for decades, just as the Civil War poisoned party politics. One asset that Larkin still had in the first years of the Irish Free State was his international reputation. He had been imprisoned in America because of communist activities, and the Comintern hoped to use him, the fire-eating orator in Dublin and America, to rebuild a communist group in Ireland. In deference to him and on the advice of the British Communist Party (CPGB), the Comintern dissolved the original Communist Party of Ireland (CPI) in early 1924.

The arrangement did not work. Larkin was a one-man operation. He resented advice and, being a nationalist, would not countenance being bridled by CPGB emissaries. They were acting out their part in the typical role drafted by Moscow, so that representatives from a larger party would supervise a smaller one. Larkin's relationship with Moscow went downhill because he failed to deliver what the Russians wanted, a pliant section of the International, and owing to this sin of omission, they were reluctant to give him the funds he demanded. Larkin wanted money for his union, the withdrawal of British unions from the Irish Free State and a portion of the profits from the only Russian franchise in Ireland – Russian Oil Products in the Dublin docks.[2]

James Larkin broke with Moscow in 1929. A new departure initiated by the CPGB and Irish graduates of the International Lenin School (ILS) eventually led to the formation of the (second) Communist Party of Ireland in June 1933. Until its self-dissolution eight years later, following a deadlock on the neutrality issue after the German invasion of the Soviet Union, the CPI was subject to British supervision to an increasing degree.

Anyone who became a communist in the Irish Free State had usually been somewhere else before politically, in organisations as diverse as the IRA, the Orange Order, the Labour Party (north or south) or de Valera's Fianna Fáil. The recruitment base for the Left in southern Ireland was exceptionally narrow, for there were no more than 100,000 industrial workers in the 1920s in a country where most people were still engaged in agriculture. The divisions of continental communism, armies of metal workers and miners, did not exist in Ireland.

All communist parties in the inter-war period experienced a high turnover of membership. Communist activity often led to imprisonment, discrimination, dismissal and, as in Ireland, pressure from the Catholic clergy. Being a communist meant commitment, making sacrifices. Nonetheless, the international nature of Soviet communism, a world-within-a-world, a transcontinental fraternity (women, largely, did not count), had appeal because of its universality as regards presence, practice and application. For Irish radicals, the USSR was also attractive because it was anti-imperialist, the gravest threat to the British Empire until the rise of Hitler. Communism also offered an alternative when the world economy was collapsing; its simplified brand of Marxism under Lenin and Stalin seemed to have an answer for every problem. Given the narrow industrial base of the Irish Free State and the anti-communist propaganda, which reached crescendo levels during the Spanish Civil War, it is not surprising that the core of Irish communism comprised activists who were accustomed to being outlawed by Church and State – Red Republicans.

The three biographies in this book conform to this motivation model to a limited degree. One aspect which characterises all three lives is disparity – in social origin, politicisation and profession. Their only common attributes were Irish nationality and a belief in communism – the poet-translator (Patrick Breslin), the radio expert (Brian Goold-Verschoyle) and the Larkinite revolutionist (Seán McAteer). They probably never met, either in Ireland or in Russia. Breslin and McAteer were activists of the first CPI (1921–24), but Goold-Verschoyle joined the communist movement in Britain. He was from an upper-class Protestant background, Breslin from the lower middle class of northside Dublin. Neither had been active in a Republican organisation. McAteer was a Republican socialist from the hilly country between Dundalk and Newry.

In the USSR all three were very much on their own, individuals, and not part of an immigrant community like the Italians, Germans or Bulgarians, who had fled to the Soviet Union because they were persecuted in their own countries. The three Irishmen became disillusioned to varying degrees with the Stalinist system, but their insights into the true nature of the communist tyranny came relatively late, too late.

What did they know, what could they have known, about Russia before going there? Over generations, millions of communists in the

West shrugged off negative pictures of Soviet reality. Before World War II, communists believed or tried to convince themselves that the sources of anti-communist propaganda were not credible: capitalist governments unwilling to tackle social problems at home or free their colonial subjects overseas; or the Catholic Church, which promoted the corporate state and fascist dictators. Since the empire of Lenin and Stalin was hermetically sealed off from the outside world, one was forced to speculate on what was said to have happened there.

Foreign communists living in the Soviet Union began to question the Stalinist system when it turned against them during the latter half of the 1930s. A decade earlier, the Bolshevik administration had stabilised after the ruinous Civil War and accompanying famine. Private industry and trade flourished, but most Bolsheviks hated the *nouveaux riches* and the prosperous peasants, regarding them as a temporary plague. In 1928, the second revolution was proclaimed: the transformation of industry and agriculture. The peasants were withholding grain because there were too few industrial products to buy with their surplus cash. Stalin decided to break the peasant village because he needed its wealth (grain for the cities and for export) to finance his gigantic industrialisation programme. The workers contributed to the building costs of the giant factory complexes by being forced to subscribe to national loans and saw their own wages plummet in value because of a high turnover tax on foodstuffs.

Farming folk were driven off the land, transported to the far north or executed. Since the new collective farms in the devastated countryside could produce only a fraction of what the free peasantry had previously yielded, the food shortage became so acute that rationing was introduced (bread 1929, meat 1932).

For the Bolsheviks, who ignored the famine in the Ukraine and southern Russia caused by grain requisitions, the worst was over by February 1934, the month of their 17th Party Congress. They called it the 'Congress of Victors', having beaten the rich peasant (kulak) and laid the foundations for a planned economy, the basis for an arms industry to repel any repetition of the capitalist armed intervention of the preceding decade. The orchestration of the Party assembly, however, went awry. Over a hundred delegates (one-twelfth) struck Stalin's name off the proposed list of candidates for the Central Committee, which elected the Politburo, the highest Party forum and inner cabinet running the country. Stalin's closest henchmen, Molotov and Kaganovich, received a similar tally of deletions, but Kirov, the Leningrad Party secretary, had only a handful of negative ballots. A minority of the assembled had not forgiven Stalin and his nearest cohorts for the gratuitous brutality of the war on the peasantry and the famine it had caused.

The vote for Kirov was proof that he was popular among the Party activists (if not in the population) and it sealed his fate. His assassination on 1 December 1934 was the opening shot for an orgy of violence as yet unparalleled in modern history. Libraries have been written about this 'Great Terror'. Western scholars now agree that Stalin and his circle initiated and monitored the mass arrests, but many of the repressive measures ordered by the Politburo seem, in retrospect, to have been ad hoc, i.e. reactions to current developments. There was no 'master plan' for the Great Terror. The 'what' has been provided by archival material and can be read in editions of documents compiled by Russian historians. The 'why?', however, is a real conundrum, a weighing of arguments.

A key to a partial understanding of the bloodbath lies in the mentality of the Bolsheviks. They saw themselves as 'hard men', using the military vocabulary they had acquired in the Civil War and reverting again and again to the violent measures learned at the front. Their policies were highly voluntarist, which had two disastrous consequences. First, since their policies of collectivising agriculture or stamping giant industries out of the bare earth were not planned or carried through on the basis of any scientific rationale, they ran into trouble. And since the Politburo could not be apportioned blame for the mishaps, the 'guilty' had to be found lower down the hierarchy. Hence the constant scapegoating of managers, engineers, agronomists and scientists. Second, as the revolution on the land or in the factories was not thought out to a logical conclusion, 'unforeseen circumstances' followed as night follows day.

Such disquieting phenomena, the result of utopian megalomania, faced Stalin's Politburo in 1937. The Kremlin leaders felt threatened. The peasants, who had been exiled during the collectivisation campaign, had done their five-year stretch in the frozen wastes and were back in the home village 'causing trouble'. Some even wanted their land back. The new (1936) Constitution allowed non-Party candidates at elections, and the Supreme Soviet was to be elected towards the end of 1937. It became known that some rural communities wanted their Orthodox priests to stand. These were the signals coming 'from below', from the regional Party organisations afraid of losing power, or their lives, at the hands of the discontented peasantry.

Equally disquieting were the preliminary results of the January 1937 Census, and therefore never published, that two-thirds of all adults in the USSR described themselves as 'believers'. Two final considerations were behind the further enlargement of the victim spectrum: the drop in industrial output and the international situation. In the Manichean world of the Stalin loyalists, economic problems were caused by the self-satisfied Party and industrial elites in the provinces, not by faulty or unrealistic planning goals. So, the regional leaders, too, were to be removed. The state of foreign affairs was also alarming, with the war in Spain going badly and the Japanese advancing in China. Ethnic minorities were seen as a potential fifth column in the major war everybody was expecting. Non-Russian ethnics were thus another targeted segment. They were decimated in 1937/38, especially the Poles, Germans and Latvians.

Within this huge mass of victims, ranging from petty criminals to local potentates, the three Irish cases stand out. Most of the indictments the secret police (NKVD) drew up in 1937/38 were crude fantasies, such as espionage for a foreign power (non-Russian ethnics) or membership in an armed kulak insurrectionist conspiracy (peasants, priests, believers). In contrast, the charges against the Irishmen were based on what they had actually done or said. Furthermore, they were not seized primarily on the basis of prescribed 'arrest quotas', nor on the basis of their nationality.

Judging from the files that their tormentors and murderers compiled on them, Patrick Breslin, Brian Goold-Verschoyle and Seán McAteer had minds of their own. That was their ultimate undoing. They were able to identify and offer reasons for their disappointment with the Soviet experiment. In the atomised totalitarian society that the USSR had become by 1937, thinking along those lines was treasonable. Arguing against Soviet policies, even in coded language, was taken as proof of guilt. Notably, all three victims, despite the physical and mental torment they underwent, refused to admit to the fantastic charge of espionage, which was a capital offence. They held out for as long as they could endure against the charges of 'anti-Soviet agitation'. Since expressing one's point of view or telling a joke about Stalin sufficed for such an indictment, the interrogators had few problems framing a charge. The ubiquitous corps of informers provided the 'evidence'.

Irish history is bloody, but it was never totalitarian. It is therefore difficult to comprehend what the three Irish victims endured. Had they survived, they might have underwritten the sentiments of Lazar Brankov, a Yugoslav diplomat given a life sentence during the Rajk show trial in Hungary (1949):

> In this extreme situation, where the prisoner is confronted by the secrets of life and death, many things lose their meaning. But should this person survive by chance, he will have an indistinguishable feeling, the only possible attitude to the world: not hatred in the political sense of the word, but loathing, an organic and psychological loathing for all kinds of coercion, a loathing for everything which is inhumane and tyrannical.[3]

NOTES

1. See the recent and exhaustive study based on Russian documents: Emmet O'Connor, *Reds and the Green, Ireland, Russia and the Communist Internationals 1919–43* (Dublin 2004).
2. Idem, *James Larkin* (Cork 2002).
3. Lazar Brankov, 'Ein Augenzeugenbericht zum Rajk-Prozeß', in Wolfgang Maderthaner, Berthold Unfried and Hans Schafranek (eds), *'Ich habe den Tod verdient'. Schauprozesse und politische Verfolgung in Mittel- und Osteuropa* (Vienna 1991), p. 36 (Trans. BMcL).

PART I
Patrick Breslin

Youth in Dublin

Patrick Breslin was born on 16 June 1907 in London and was baptised two days later at Holy Trinity Church in Hammersmith. His father Francis, still using the more Gaelic form of his name, O'Breslin, hailed from Ardara in County Donegal. Born in 1864 as one of ten children to a small farmer-cum-tailor, Frank O'Breslin had an English mother. His father, when in Britain to buy suit-lengths, fell in love with an English Protestant girl, Maria, and brought her back to the fastness of County Donegal. She converted to Catholicism but, being genteel, was laughed at in the small-farm neighbourhood. Like three of his brothers, Frank emigrated to America as a young man. There he tried his hand at a variety of jobs, even opening a jewellery shop before re-emigrating, this time to Britain. While working as a buyer for Harrods, he spent time in Cork, dealing with the Munster Arcade drapery store and staying in digs with the Linehan family, who had moved from Kanturk to the big city.

Frank was forty, and twenty years older than his bride, when he married Christina, the daughter of his Cork landlord, in Killarney. Patrick Emmet was their first child, Marie the second. The third child, Noreen, died in infancy and Paul ('Danny') completed the quartet. Frank's job as a travelling salesman meant that the family moved often – to Cork and Dublin for some months in 1911, then back to London until 1919, before settling for good in Dublin in early 1920. Frank Breslin bought a house with a small garden at 150 North Strand for £500, installing a grocery shop in the front parlour. He still worked occasionally as a travelling clothes salesman but was no longer well off, not least because of his penchant for gambling on horses.[1]

His eldest son, Pat, never lost his English accent and had to confront his teasing classmates on many occasions in O'Connell Schools. In 1921, at the end of the War of Independence, young Breslin left secondary school and received an apprenticeship, presumably through his father's connections, with the drapers Gleeson's. He later worked for McCabe outfitters in North Earl Street, where he was employed until his departure from Ireland in 1928. The introduction of the fourteen-year-old to the world of work was accompanied by a political awakening. As a child his 'first tastes were for the ascetic life of the religious recluse',[2] and later for Republican Socialism, after reading a pamphlet by James Connolly in 1917. Pat Breslin supported the Republicans in the guerrilla war against the British, but their parents forbade both Pat and 'Danny' to join the Fianna, the youth section of the IRA. Father and mother were basically apolitical, Christina's background being rising middle-class with affection for the British royal family. Both subsequently blamed Uncle John, Frank's brother, for introducing their eldest son to socialism.

John Breslin had been a trade union activist in America and, after returning to Ireland, took his nephew Pat to political street meetings in Dublin. They probably heard Liam O'Flaherty, the veteran of the Western Front and future literary figure, haranguing the jobless on Sundays at Beresford Place, one of the first public appearances of the Communist Party of Ireland (CPI). Its leading founding figure was Roddy Connolly, the son of the executed 1916 leader.

Around that time Patrick Breslin (P.E. O'Breslin) joined the fledgling CPI and, although only fifteen, was given a weekly column in *The Workers' Republic*, the Party's broadsheet. His first article, published on 5 August 1922, announced the foundation of the Young Communist League of Ireland for workers under 24. His contributions are remarkably succinct, if flowery, for someone of his age; they were fired by class rather than nationalistic rhetoric, attacking slum conditions, low wages, lack of education for the poor, and especially the absence of secular schools. Breslin admitted that the emergency situation of the Civil War (June 1922–May 1923) hindered effective propaganda, since the new government had interned several prominent communists. His column of 26 August 1922 demonstrated his rejection of the vicious tit-for-tat killings in Dublin, a point of view at odds with Roddy Connolly's uncon-ditional underwriting of the Anti-Treaty stance:

> There is one particular mode of warfare that they adopt which calls for condemnation. I refer to the bomb throwing and the ambushing in the public streets during the daytime when the children of the workers are wont to gather and play. Looked at from a military, strategical, as well

as from a humane point of view, no real tactical advantage is gained. Not only is a considerable amount of sympathy and support lost, but the ambushers rarely, if ever, attain their objective. Let it be hoped that in future the I.R.A. will make provision for the workers and their families during the fight against their renegade former comrades.

On 2 September, however, Pat Breslin regurgitated crude Marxist social analysis that definitely did not correspond to Irish realities:

[Apart from the propertyless workers] there is another class, the middle-class, which does not interest us now and is made up of the small shopkeeper and the medium farmer, or semi-bourgeois as it is often so styled, but it is growing smaller and smaller each year, as the industrial administration of the capitalist state becomes slowly, yet surely, merged into two or three large trusts or corporations.

Breslin conceded on 23 September that calls to join the youth section of the CPI were 'getting a very feeble response'.

In his lengthy report to the Executive Committee of the Communist International (ECCI) on the activities of the first year of the CPI, Roddy Connolly wrote that the youth section was 'progressing favourably', its secretary being 'a young worker of Dublin some fourteen years old'.[3] This was Breslin, who, together with the eighteen-year-old apprentice Michael Deegan, reported on the youth work of the Party at the first CPI congress held in Dublin in late January 1923. There was some criticism that Connolly, the sitting president and editor of *The Workers' Republic*, had 'left the path of Communism for that of Republicanism'. Connolly lost his seat on the permanent executive, as well as his editorship of the Party newspaper.[4] An increase in membership and a more public presence were enhanced by the return to class, as against civil war, politics. This change was pronounced in the directive of the Comintern, published in *The Workers' Republic* on 24 February 1923: 'to concentrate the activity of the Party on the work among the urban proletarian masses and the rural proletarian and semi-proletarian workers'.

The youth section was allotted a room in Exchequer Street, Dublin, where a debating society and a sports club were inaugurated. One of the debates was entitled 'Education under Capitalism'. A 'Labour Day Céilidh' was organised, and in the summer months rambles to the Pine Forest in the Dublin Mountains, dances at the

Galway Arms Hotel in Parnell Square and cycling tours in the countryside to sell Party literature.

The spurt of activity had spent itself by the end of 1923. Breslin's last known statement on the state of internal CPI affairs is a testimony to the split between the more nationalist and the 'class warrior' elements in the tiny sect. According to an informer's report concerning a closed CPI meeting on 12 November 1923, Breslin gave 'a disjointed sort of speech', advocating a break with the Republicans. Following his remark that Eamon de Valera and his supporters were 'flag-waving fools', Roddy Connolly demanded that Breslin apologise, but was howled down by most of the twenty-seven members in attendance.[5] The leaders of the British Communist Party (CPGB), given a supervisory role in Ireland, recommended to Moscow that the CPI be dissolved. Arthur McManus, the leading Scottish communist, for example, visited Dublin and Galway and found that the members knew little of communism but were republicans, that the leaders in Dublin had either resigned or had gone to work for de Valera, and that the constant in-fighting and expulsions had discredited the movement. Furthermore, the paper was losing £10 a week and had collapsed in October with debts of £200. Moscow agreed in the hope that Big Jim Larkin, who had returned to Ireland from his American prison ordeal as the Civil War ended in May, would provide the mass base for starting a new Comintern section.[6]

The official dissolution of the first Communist Party of Ireland in January 1924 also marked the beginning of the end of Pat Breslin's political activities in the strictly political party sense. Although Larkin Snr set up the Irish Worker League (IWL) in 1923 and had it recognised by the Comintern, it never became a truly Marxist-Leninist party. Larkin hoped that Moscow could persuade the British labour movement, through the CPGB, to withdraw British unions from Ireland. This would have left him with a sound financial base for the WUI should the National Union of Railwaymen, for instance, close down its Irish operations. He also needed money to run or relaunch the vituperative weekly *The Irish Worker* (1923–25), his main propaganda weapon against the hated ITGWU and the Labour Party it controlled.[7] The activities of the IWL in its early phase centred on social events such as train excursions, or collecting money for Republican prisoners. Its only memorable foray into politics was the September 1927 general election, when it polled remarkably well.

Not all ex-members of the CPI had drifted away from the socialist fold, despite their rejection of Larkin's League as a social club or election machine. Some gathered around the Connolly Workers' Club and its educational programme. Breslin, always interested in bettering himself intellectually, attended the classes and was involved in helping the unemployed. The club members seemed to have mainly belonged to the short-lived Workers' Party of Ireland (WPI), a rallying point for former members of the CPI frustrated by Jim Larkin's sulphurous polemics. During the summer of 1926 the WPI held open air meetings on Burgh Quay, with Breslin, Roddy Connolly and Captain Jack White as the speakers.[8] Breslin had been a member of the Union of Distributive Workers and Clerks since 1922, but moved to Larkin's union (WUI) in 1926, where he was again active in political education. He joined the Irish Worker League that same year but remained politically inactive throughout 1927.

Apart from his political persona, what kind of a person was Patrick Breslin? It is evident from family tales that the atmosphere in the household was tolerant, possibly because his father had travelled widely or on account of the large age-gap between husband and wife. Culture, especially music and reading, was held in high regard. Pat's foibles were the source of family jokes. He was dubbed 'Handy Andy' because of his inclination to drop and break things, or was teased for his voracious reading, even on the street, when accompanying his sister Marie (who later worked in a music shop) to her piano lessons. He also took a correspondence course in Esperanto, getting up at six to study before breakfasting at nine. Most of his friends were older, and from a political, intellectual or artistic background. Liam O'Flaherty, enjoying the first fruits of literary fame, used to collect Pat Breslin from the draper's shop for high tea in a Dublin hotel; Breslin also remained on good terms with Roddy Connolly, despite their political differences.

Sympathy for the Russian Revolution in Dublin of the 1920s was not uncommon in republican and bohemian circles, a situation that was to change radically in the following decade, following de Valera's accession to power and when, owing to the untrammelled propaganda of the triumphalist Catholic Right, being 'Irish' and 'a good Catholic' became synonymous. Still, in September 1927, Jim Larkin Snr was elected to Dáil Éireann as a communist and there was considerable support for left-wing policies in the trade unions, especially in Dublin.[9]

The interest in the New Russia among Dublin intellectuals is testified by a now forgotten episode. In October 1925, the poet and theatre manager F.R. Higgins, together with Dr W. Pilger, a medical practitioner in Hume Street, set up the Radical Club at 21 Dawson Street. Its statutes, now in a Moscow archive, suggest that it was the kind of free-spirited community that would have appealed to the eighteen-year-old Pat Breslin:

1. To provide a centre of intercourse for Irish intellectual workers.

2. To encourage all forms of progressive cultural activity in Ireland.

3. To fight for the freedom of cultural expression in Ireland.

4. To promote solidarity among artists, writers, scientists, and all people engaged in intellectual pursuits in Ireland.

Higgins and Pilger contacted VOKS, the Soviet umbrella organisation for cultural relations with capitalist countries, and subsequently received the weekly bulletin of the British branch in London. There were also negotiations to build up a library of reference books from Moscow at the Dawson Street address. However, as so often in Irish politics, a 'split' ensued. The last letter in the file (from Pilger) informed Madame Kameneva, the VOKS president (wife of Lev Kamenev, the Soviet Minister for Trade), that 'the most revolutionary elements' were involved in a struggle they might win or lose.[10]

Breslin's closest friend and mentor was an older man from an upper middle-class background. Cyril Fagan (1896–1970) worked in the Patents Office of the Department of Industry and Commerce until his retirement in 1956. He was a colourful figure in post-independence Dublin, a tall, flamboyantly dressed man with a booming voice. Scarlet fever as a child had left him partially deaf, thus hindering him from studying medicine, the career of his father, a well-known Dublin doctor. Today, Fagan is known only in the esoteric community, as a famous astrologer who caused a schism in the American Federation of Astrologers by stressing the importance of Babylonian, as against Hellenistic, influences in the history of astrology. His best-known works are *Zodiacs Old and New* (1950) and *Astrological Origins* (1969). Fagan took up astrology in 1916, shortly after he had left Castleknock College, and founded the Irish Astrological Society, where W.B. Yeats befriended him. The society,

also known as Hermes Lodge, was affiliated to the Irish Theosophical Society, which had rooms in South Frederick Street.[11]

Breslin's attachment to non-Marxist philosophical questions and
psychic phenomena began in the mid-1920s. He resigned from the
Connolly Club in disgust because some of its leading members
supported de Valera, and began attending the twice-monthly
meetings of the theosophists in South Frederick Street. He rapidly
came under the influence of Fagan, whom he met regularly over the
next three years. Because Pat often quoted Fagan's phrase of 'the
other world around us' to his family, Mrs Breslin invited Cyril Fagan
to the family home for tea. The visit was not a success. Fagan stated
that he could move objects when in a trance or foresee a person's
future on the basis of their date of birth. This was too much for a
Catholic family, no matter how liberal, and Frank Breslin warned his
son to desist from involvement with such arcane practices.

Whereas Pat continued to consort with the eccentric civil servant,
he may have moved away from astrology towards theosophy. In any
case, the family reaction was now benign, with his mother teasing
him about 'Christy Murphy', i.e. Krishnamurti. Theosophy – the
attempt to integrate Eastern philosophical traditions into European
thought – had chosen Krishnamurti as a new Messiah. Set up in New
York by the Russian aristocrat Madame Blavatsky in 1875, the
Theosophical Society sought to promote universal brotherhood
regardless of race and creed. The movement's headquarters subsequently moved to Britain and gained increasing public coverage
because of the movement's leading personality, the Fabian socialist,
suffragette and feminist, Annie Besant. After a crisis of conscience,
she had left her clergyman husband to become an advocate of
socialism and birth control. She found her spiritual home in India,
where she established an extensive complex for the Society on the
banks of the river Adyar in Madras. There she found, in 1909, her
avatar, or world teacher, in the thirteen-year-old son of her employee
Jiddu Narayaniah, an orthodox Brahmin who had joined the
Theosophical Society in 1882.

The boy Krishnamurti (Krishna incarnate) and his brother were
whisked off to Britain by Mrs Besant in 1911, against the will of
their widower father. The Order of the Star in the East was the
vehicle used by Besant to propagate the young redeemer's coming,
but the boys were unhappy in their British environment, surrounded
by aristocratic ladies, tutors and butlers. After 1923 Krishnamurti,

an ethereally beautiful, slim youth, travelled the globe in the commission of the Order. He acquired cult status in a world seeking answers after the armed cataclysm. Pat Breslin would have learned of the Indian mystic from the daily press and, we may assume, from the bulletin of the Order, which had 50,000 adherents in over fifty countries at its inception in 1911. Following his brother's death in 1925, Krishnamurti, who had grown to detest the jargon of his Western esoteric disciples, their organisations and their fawning adoration, detached himself gradually from the mother-figure Annie Besant.[12] Two years before he officially broke with the Order, Krishamurti wrote a passage in *Who Brings the Truth?* (1927) that could equally have described Pat Breslin's intellectual quest in all its phases:

> It has been a struggle all the time to find the truth because I was not satisfied by the authority of another, or the imposition of another, or the enticement of another: I wanted to discover for myself, and naturally, I had to go through sufferings to find out.[13]

Whether or not Krishnamurti, who acquired influential supporters such as George Bernard Shaw, Anita Loos, Aldous Huxley and the American novelists Henry Miller and Howard Fast and left a thriving philosophical movement after his death in 1986, influenced Breslin's thinking to a great degree is a matter for speculation. While the philosophical attitude of the Indian – one has to find the truth oneself – is attractive, it presupposes personal self-transformation. That is a common characteristic of religious movements and quasi-religious sects, but it does not change existing social conditions, or purport to do so. Political ideologies like Soviet Communism claimed to offer more down-to-earth solutions for the world's problems, but Bolshevik dogma ignored psychology and the spiritual side of human experience.

The decision to send Breslin for Party schooling in the USSR came out of the blue in a double sense. Breslin was not active in the Irish Worker League and therefore knew nothing about its internal deliberations; and Larkin Snr could not make up his mind until the last moment how many League members he should 'delegate' to the International Lenin School (ILS). The offer, first made in January 1925 by the ECCI at the behest of the Scottish Communist William Gallacher, read: 'A group of young Republicans should (in agreement with Larkin) be invited to Moscow.'[14] The Comintern leadership reserved two places for the IWL at the ILS in August 1927.[15] Larkin held back because he disliked being advised on the basis of Moscow's collaboration with the CPGB, but also because of the political situation at home. Fianna Fáil entered the Dáil in August 1927 and, in the run-up to the snap elections one month later, there was a furious burst of activity at the Marlborough Street headquarters of the WUI and the IWL. Present there to advise Larkin was a Comintern emissary, Christian Hilt, the Norwegian representative at the headquarters of the Communist International. Less than at Hilt's urgings, but rather more in order to set up an effective electoral machine for the coming polls, Larkin reactivated the IWL. The meeting of its most loyal cohort in late July, with Larkin Snr in the chair, decided on a parcel of measures, some in line with general Comintern policy (setting up a youth section and a bookshop, relaunching *The Irish Worker*) but mostly in connection with the elections. However, even in this close circle of Larkinite loyalists there was no unanimity, with Seán Shelly, later Breslin's classmate at the ILS, arguing against participation in parliamentary politics – that politicians always left the workers 'in the lurch'.[16]

Similarly, the programme of the IWL, sanctioned at a conference one month later (four years after the founding of the League), was that of a broad left-wing movement and could hardly have passed muster in Moscow: references to the Comintern, Marxism or to Marxist-Leninist tenets (dictatorship of the proletariat) were absent from the slim document, which was more of a compilation of contemporary demands than a blueprint for the road to power. The repeal of the 1927 Public Safety Act was given pride of place, as was Larkin's long-term and most cherished goal, namely 'the withdrawal of the machinery of British Unions from Ireland'.[17]

Since Breslin heard of the invitation to study in Moscow only on 8 March 1928, five days before he left Dublin, and the 9th Plenum of the ECCI which Larkin Snr attended had ended on 25 February, it seems likely that the composition of the student delegation was decided by Big Jim personally on his return, after consulting with his right-hand man, Jack Carney. Carney, due in Moscow for the 4th Congress of the Profintern, the Trade Union International, in March, organised Pat Breslin's departure. They met twice in Carney's office, mainly to complete the application form for an Irish passport, which Breslin received on the day of departure, 13 March. Breslin travelled to Moscow via London, with Carney and the other WUI delegates to the Profintern congress.[18] On their arrival in London, the group took the Dover train and the boat crossing to Ostend. Travelling overland to Germany, Carney and his charges, including Breslin, waited two days in Berlin for Soviet entry visas. They crossed the Russo-Polish border after five days' travel, entering the Soviet Union through the beflagged wooden arch at Negoreloe, where they changed trains, and to the wider Russian rail gauge, for the last leg to Moscow. Two Irish members of the ILS class, Jim Larkin Jnr and Seán Murray, had travelled to Moscow the previous November; the remainder, Bill Denn, Seán Shelly, Dan Buckley and Charlie Ashmore, followed in April.

Not knowing of the 'conspiratorial' nature of the school, Breslin had told his closest friends and family of his great adventure, which he and Carney considered to be an educational opportunity without great political import. His sister Marie and mother Christina, fearing they would cry, did not accompany him to the North Wall boat in Dublin. Frank Breslin, now of pension age, accompanied his son to the night ferry.

NOTES

1. Details about Breslin's early years were provided by his daughter Mairead Breslin Kelly, and his sister Marie, since deceased. A further source is Pat Breslin's interrogation file held in the Russian State Archive (GARF), Moscow.
2. Russian State Archive for Social and Political History (RGASPI), f. 17, o. 98, d. 4565, l. 5 (autobiography, n.d. [March 1928]).
3. RGASPI, f. 495, o. 89, d. 16, l. 61.
4. RGASPI, f. 495, o. 89, d. 21, ll. 1–5.
5. UCD Archives, Richard Mulcahy Collection, file P7a/87.
6. RGASPI, f. 495, o. 18, d. 210, ll. 52–55.
7. For the best accounts to date of Larkin Senior's links to the Comintern and Profintern, see Emmet O'Connor, 'Jim Larkin and the Communist Internationals', *Irish Historical Studies*, xxxi, no. 123, May 1999, pp. 357–72; Emmet O'Connor, *James Larkin* (Radical Irish Lives) (Cork 2002).
8. *The Irish Hammer and Plough* (Official Organ of the Workers' Party of Ireland), 19, 26 June 1926. I am indebted to Dr Emmet O'Connor for this reference.
9. Séamus Cody, John O'Dowd and Peter Rigney, *The Parliament of Labour. 100 Years of the Dublin Council of Trade Unions* (Dublin 1986), pp.139–47.
10. GARF, f. 528, o. 3, d. 11, ll. 3, 62–73.
11. For details of Cyril Fagan's biography, I thank Mr Bill Sheeran, Naas, Co. Kildare.
12. Evelyne Blau, *Krishnamurti. 100 Years* (New York 1995), pp. 3–83.

13. Ibid, p. 53.
14. RGASPI, f. 495, o. 89, d. 28, l. 24.
15. RGASPI, f. 495, o. 7, d. 3, Sitzungen der Ständigen Kommission des EKKI, 1. und 8. August 1927.
16. RGASPI, f. 495, o. 89, d. 42, ll. 18–19.
17. RGASPI, f. 495, o. 89, d. 47, *Irish Worker League. Founded by Jim Larkin. Programme, Constitution and Rules. Adopted by I.W.L. in Dublin, 30th August 1927, The Fodhla Printing Co., Dublin* (pamphlet).
18. RGASPI, f. 534, o. 1, d. 106, ll. 100–104 (questionnaires of the Irish delegates).

The International Lenin School, 1928–30

Patrick Breslin's expectations of what awaited him in Moscow were not specific. Just before his departure, Carney had informed him that he would be going to a workers' university to receive general and political education for two years. At that time the Executive Committee of the Communist International (ECCI) managed four main centres of learning for foreign revolutionaries in Moscow.[1]

Breslin and his fellow Irishmen, however, were destined for the most distinguished institute of learning under ECCI control – the International Lenin School, the cadre forge for future leaders of the national sections of the Communist International. The primary function of the ILS was to transform revolutionaries into party functionaries, who on their return home would implement the 'Soviet line'. The schooling of promising cadres from abroad was also a long-term investment, designed to destroy the tradition of dissension which had become apparent during the first congresses of the Communist International. Not until the late 1920s did Moscow succeed, mainly by expulsions and demotions, in deposing the first generation of communist leaders, experienced labour figures who came from the syndicalist movement, social democratic parties and disparate left-wing groups. The Soviet assumption was that only Moscow-trained leaders of the communist parties would underwrite policies that had little to do with the development of international capitalism but were dictated primarily by the exigencies of the power-struggle within the Soviet Politburo and Stalin's emergence as uncontested leader in 1928/29.

All official attempts to ensure that the communist parties adhered to Russian directives were summarised under the heading 'Bolshevisation'. This concept was introduced as the main political task of the international movement at the 5th Comintern Congress (July–August 1924). A 'course permeated by the ideas of Leninism' was deemed necessary for cadres from abroad, and the Agitation and Propaganda (Agitprop) Department of the ECCI called, in October 1924, for the organisation of such courses in Moscow. The Lenin School, however, did not open its portals until May 1926. Owing to the severe housing shortage in Moscow, it took a considerable time to find a suitable building and to adapt it for classes and student accommodation. The house chosen was at Ulitsa Vorovskogo (Vorovsky Street) No. 25A, a town palace built for Prince Gagarin, Director of Imperial Theatres in the 1820s, and used as a girls' boarding school before the Revolution. The building was without heating or electricity and all structural changes had to be implemented in compliance with the strict norms set down for historical monuments. The second main factor that delayed the school's inauguration was the dearth of suitable teaching staff. Prospective lecturers and tutors were expected to be polyglot 'authorities in their special subjects' and have undergone 'sound Marxist-Leninist training'. Since Western communist parties were loath to release any of their own intellectuals for this work, the ILS Board had to make do with native or naturalised Russians who had some knowledge of a foreign language. A further workload was thus imposed on a relatively small circle of learned Party members who also taught in other Soviet institutions.

Seventy-five places (eight for British communists) were allocated for the first intake. The students, it was hoped, would have knowledge of Marxism-Leninism, have spent some time in industrial employment and have been Party members for at least three years.[2] In a review of the school's first academic year, the leading British communist and member of the ILS Board, J.T. Murphy, noted that the low level of theoretical knowledge displayed by the first students necessitated prolonging the course beyond the envisaged twelve months. Another drawback was that few of Lenin's works had been translated by 1927. One of the subjects to be studied was 'Party construction', which gave the students an insight into how the All-Union Communist Party (Bolsheviks), known by its Russian acronym VKP(b), ruled the vast country through a hierarchy starting from the factory cell. Students observed the all-pervasive 'leading role' of the Party during visits to factories or in the course of their practical work (*praktika*) during the spring and summer months, when they studied working and living conditions in Siberia, Leningrad and Tashkent. In addition to the heavy academic workload during school term, the students also had to write reports on the practical side of their education.[3]

The new, 1927–28, enrolment entered a school still beset by teething difficulties. An order from the ECCI to set up separate 'semester' courses at short notice threw the organisational plans for the main intake into confusion. Teaching began two months late, in early 1928, so that the late Irish arrivals of March 1928 were not unduly disadvantaged.[4] The postponed start of the academic year was also attributable to disruption caused by the students: the French refused *partout* to stay at the school 'under the present material conditions'.[5] The ILS leadership was also disappointed by the attitude of the communist parties, which had sent only seventy-eight cadres, although the allotment was 125; after written exams and a medical check, this figure was further reduced to fifty-four.[6] ECCI issued an appeal to the Comintern sections to send students without the usual formalities, and the Irish contingent, originally set at two,[7] was raised to seven. Towards the end of the three-year course, which ended in June 1930, class numbers had grown to eighty-nine.[8]

The expectations of the school board were unrealistic about the educational levels of the undergraduates. Before leaving for the USSR, English-speaking students were supposed to have read volumes by Marx, Bukharin, Kautsky, Engels, Lenin and Stalin, and to have familiarised themselves with the statutes of the Soviet Party and the congress minutes of the Comintern. Some advance knowledge of the Russian language was recommended.[9] The British party pointed out that 'some of the books mentioned by you in your reference letter are either not available, or too expensive for some of our most active workers to procure'.[10] It transpired that only 2–3 per cent of the total intake had read the prescribed literature before departure.[11] The school management structure militated against streamlined learning, since the composition of school staff (ninety-four in October 1928) was weighted heavily in favour of administration or security personnel, with only thirty-nine persons, including five translators, involved directly in teaching. This was typical of Soviet enterprises, especially the emphasis on maintenance staff and guards, who constituted just under a third of all school employees.[12] Instruction and study totalled seventy-two hours, or twelve hours daily:

Instruction: 15.5 hrs.

Study: 27.5 hrs.

Practical and Party work: 29 hrs. (Party and school meetings, work in the Communist International and with the Moscow Party organisation)[13]

The students enrolled at the ILS in the late 1920s were divided, first, into language sectors (English, German, French and Russian 'Land Groups'), and, secondly, into study circles. Since students were attributed pseudonyms and were forbidden to use their own names, it is difficult to identify all students in any one school year. At least twenty-two candidates of Irish birth were proposed for instruction at the Lenin School in the years 1927 to 1935. The Irish proposed for ideological schooling in the Soviet metropolis were sent in groups in 1928, 1930, 1931, 1933, 1934 and 1935. The first group, the largest ever sent from Ireland, consisted of James Larkin Jnr (Lawlor), Pat Breslin (Brennan), Bill Denn (King), Charlie Ashmore (Donn), Dan Buckley (Brien) and Seán Shelly. Another Irishman in the circle, Seán Murray (Black), was a member of the CPGB.[14]

The two most prominent Irish cadres in the 1928 class were Larkin Jnr. and Seán Murray. Larkin, born in 1904 in Liverpool as the eldest of Big Jim's sons, received his secondary education at St Enda's, the school founded by Patrick Pearse in Rathfarnham, Co. Dublin. Before leaving for the Soviet Union in November 1927, young Jim had served as assistant editor of the Larkinite *Irish Worker* (1923–25). During his father's absence at gatherings in Moscow, Jim edited and managed the broadsheet. Larkin *fils* was also a member of the IWL Executive Committee and a candidate for the League at the September 1927 Dáil general election.[15]

While Larkin Jnr took a backstage role in Irish Communist politics from 1936 onwards and concentrated his energies on building up the WUI, Murray served as secretary of the Communist Party of Ireland from 1933 to 1941. His status as Moscow's most important and trusted representative in Ireland was due to his long Party record and links with those British emissaries who supervised Comintern business in Ireland. Born into poor farming stock in Cushendall, Co. Antrim, in 1899, Murray worked on the land as a child, left school at eleven and became interested in socialism by reading the pamphlets of James Connolly. He was imprisoned in the Curragh for IRA membership, but released when the Truce was declared in the summer of 1921. Elected as a delegate to the IRA conventions in 1922 and an active officer until 1923, Murray joined the IWL before emigrating to Britain in 1925. He worked there at a variety of unskilled jobs and was employed by Soviet enterprises, including Russian Oil Products. He was a delegate of the Distributive Workers' Union on the London Trades Council, the organiser of the Islington Branch of the CPGB and a member of the Party's London District Committee.[16] The nine other members of the CPGB contingent at the school included two of declared Irish nationality: Max Goldberg, a railway stoker from Cardiff, and the Scottish steel worker Bob McIlhone. The only woman was Maggie Jordan, a Yorkshire textile worker from a strict Catholic background.[17]

The 1927–30 class of the English-speaking group was initially accommodated four to a room, but moved subsequently into double rooms with study facilities in a modern block beside the old Gagarin palace. Situated on Vorovsky Street, the ILS was within walking distance of the city centre and also near the recently built Lenin Library and the Institute of Marxism-Leninism, both of which the students visited when researching their projects. Then, as now, Vorovsky Street was a 'good address', but the presence of foreign embassies, including the British and the German, on this road parallel to Gorky Street, Moscow's main shopping thoroughfare, should have precluded locating the school in this built-up area. In the mid-1930s, by which time security regulations at the school had been significantly tightened, the ILS was moved to the suburbs. From the city end of the Ulitsa Vorovskogo, it was but a short walk to the headquarters of the Comintern, situated between the Kremlin walls and the Lenin Library. On handing in their passports, the students were given passes to the Comintern building, where they were allowed to take part in sittings of the Anglo-American Secretariat of the ECCI or to work in the office as probationers during their *praktika*.

In the early years of the school's existence, the students were not restricted in their movements outside the ILS compound and, being candidate-members of the VKP(b), they mixed socially with Russian communists and were invited to meetings and conferences. Students also called on Irish and British delegates to Comintern or Profintern meetings who were staying at the legendary Hotel Lux in Gorky Street. They probably also dropped in next door, to a popular beer-hall with a gypsy orchestra.[18] The school's self-service canteen served three meals a day. A small allowance of sixty roubles was paid to cover the extra-curricular expenses and, if the students (all unmarried) had been the main breadwinner at home, the family was given a weekly sum that corresponded to the national minimum wage. From the outset the school authorities were concerned about the students' well-being: a thorough medical examination took place which included embarrassing questions about the neophytes' sex life.

The sports programme on offer had strong military connotations since it was carried out within the framework of Ossoaviakhim (Society for the Promotion of Defence, Chemistry and Flying), a form of workers' self-defence corps. ILS students were expected to reach proficiency on the rifle-range, attaining the 'Voroshilov-Rifleman' badge, first and second class, named in honour of Stalin's long-term Defence Minister, Marshal Klim Voroshilov. Apart from arms training, the students took part in war games. The insurrections studied in simulation included Ireland's Easter Rising and the abortive Hamburg uprising of the German Communists in October 1923. First Aid and locomotive driving courses were organised as well.[19] Riding was the form of physical exercise promoted at the school. Many students never mastered the skills imparted by the bandy-legged instructor, owing to their reluctance to practise at first light at a time of year when they were preoccupied with completing seminar papers. In the spring, rides into the countryside were *de rigueur*. The striking spectacle of ILS students, some obviously foreign, cantering through Moscow's early morning streets was another breach of security which made nonsense of the school's much-vaunted policy of conspiratorial secrecy.

The first rector, that is, nominal head, of the Lenin School courses was Nikolai Bukharin, who fell from favour in 1928/29 and was replaced by the Hungarian Communist Béla Kun. The day-to-day management of the school was in the hands of Klavdiia Kirsanova, an old Bolshevik and Civil War veteran.

The teaching staff monitored the students' progress attentively and endeavoured to involve them in the management of the school. A statement of income and expenditure was circulated to the study circles, as was the school journal, in which students could note organisational deficiencies of the course. Critical remarks emanating from the student body related, in the main, to the heavy academic workload. While such statements gained a hearing at least, the teachers did not tolerate any levelling down of standards, but told the students to keep their rooms at the right temperature and their desks tidy. Proceeding from the belief that the young proletarians from abroad had to learn how to learn, teaching staff placed much emphasis on individual tutoring and written projects. In the ECCI guidelines for instruction at the ILS, conventional lectures were discouraged in favour of group work in seminars and 'laboratory tasks'. This was a direct adaptation from the curriculum of Soviet secondary schools, where project-orientated teaching was popular until 1931.

The Laboratory or Dalton Plan, first introduced by Helen Parkhurst at a high school in Dalton, Massachusetts, in 1918, required that students sign a work agreement for every subject, each focusing attention on a single overarching theme:

> Groups of pupils completed assignments at their own pace, roving about rooms or laboratories, each designed for a particular discipline irrespective of grade. Teachers responded as friends when needed and more advanced students helped their younger or slower colleagues.[20]

The English 'Land Group' consisted of Irish, English, Welsh, Scottish, American and Canadian students. The group was further divided into circles of ten to fifteen students, and then into sub-units of four or five for individual subjects. Circle leaders distributed the themes, and essays had to be completed in three weeks. In addition, all circle members had to read a minimum amount of recommended literature for each subject. 'Laboratory tasks' consisted of consulting literature in the school library or the Marx-Engels-Lenin Institute.[21] Intensive discussions in the sub-groups accompanied research work in the libraries. Sometimes the compulsory half-yearly project essays were presented to the Land Group. Despite the favourable pupil–teacher ratio,[22] the sheer bulk of the curriculum proved too much for some of the 1927–30 class:

> Russian revolutionary politics from the Decembrists (1825) onwards
>
> Marxist economics based on *Das Kapital*
>
> Philosophy starting with Locke and Hume, through Hegel to dialectics and dialectical materialism
>
> History of the European labour movement

Consultations with the students also took place on a more political plane. The students of the English Land Group elected a representative – *partorg* – to the school branch of the VKP(b), which was headed by officials of the ILS Party Bureau. The tasks of the *partorg*, according to Harry Wicks, who replaced Jim Larkin Jnr in this post in 1929, included ensuring that the colleagues attended their classes and regular Party meetings. Each sector also elected a *proforg*, a shop steward who sat on the school's trade union committee, which supervised the students' living conditions.[23] Heads of departments were often graduates of the Red Professors' Academy. Ivan Mints, a historian and co-editor of the early four-volume history of the Bolshevik Party, held the chair for studies of Leninism. Lajos Rudas, a fugitive from fascist Hungary, was pro-rector and in charge of the history department. He had studied philosophy at Heidelberg and taught that subject, as well as British labour history, to the English Land Group.

Since Kirsanova was directly responsible to the Central Committee of the VKP(b), instruction at the school was strongly coloured by the harsh polemics that accompanied Stalin's consolidation as Party leader – removing Trotsky (Left Opposition) and Bukharin ('Right Deviation') from the Politburo and writing them out of the history of the Russian Revolution. For the British and Irish students, this introduction to Soviet political reality must have been a bracing experience, not least because of the virulence of the debates. The induction course that followed the written entrance examination in early 1928 was almost entirely about the 'errors' of Trotsky. Stewart Smith, who taught the Canadians and the Americans, proposed during the induction course a resolution denigrating Trotsky as 'objectively counter-revolutionary'. An amendment from the floor deleting these words was supported by only two of the English Land Group, Harry Wicks and a comrade from the USA. Kirsanova addressed the school assembly twice or three times a week, apprising the students of Stalin's 'Great Leap Forward' in the industrialisation and collectivised agricultural programmes.

Surviving records of some of the Irish students show that they had adapted well to academic work and displayed a remarkable aptitude, considering the scanty formal education they had received in Ireland. The yearly report on Seán Murray read: 'Very capable, very active, shows independence of thought and has succeeded well. Shows a good grasp of Marxist-Leninist methods.'[24] Charlie Ashmore gained average grades and was recommended for a 'subordinate function' in the Irish movement.[25] Pat Breslin was awarded good marks regarding 'activity', 'capabilities' and 'academic progress'.[26]

James Larkin Snr in Dublin, by contrast, had a petulantly dismissive opinion of the Irish at the ILS. At the suggestion of Harry Wicks, Larkin, in Moscow for an international conference, visited the old palace in Vorovsky Street. He addressed the English Land Group as 'little Lenins', described the decline of trade union strength in the Irish Free State and discounted the notion that a communist party could ever take root there. More disappointing for Wicks, however, were his negative comments about James Connolly:

> What stuck in my gullet most was that, for some reason or other, he was very critical of James Connolly. Emphasising the stranglehold of the Catholic Church, he went out of his way to note that even Connolly had died in its arms. Now, that may well have been. But Larkin was loading the blame for his current difficulties onto Connolly. That seemed to me worse than silly.[27]

How the Irish colleagues reacted to Larkin's small-minded outburst is unknown, but they would hardly have supported attempts to tarnish Connolly's reputation. In fact, they organised a meeting in the school on the thirteenth anniversary of Connolly's execution and had material sent over from Dublin especially for the event. Bill Denn wrote to his trade union colleague J. J. Moore shortly afterwards:

> I received all in time, in fact three or four days before the time. It was a great success. In the evening we had a fine concert [with] some of the best singers in Moscow and Connolly's photo over the stage.[28]

Big Jim Larkin was also critical of what he had heard about Breslin's progress at the school, alleging in a letter of 24 April 1928 that the twenty-year-old was showing 'the least signs of promise of all students'. His teacher Lajos Rudas sent a spirited reply, stating his belief that Breslin was 'promising'. He advised Larkin to draw his information in future from the school administration in order to avoid 'gossip'.[29]

In a letter to Bukharin, Larkin requested financial assistance for the families of Ashmore and Breslin. He then went on, in his rambling fashion, to give subjective pen-portraits of his quintet at the ILS, Shelly having returned home in the meantime:

> One of them, I regret to say, from reports reaching me from sources

here, has not got the conscious sense of responsibility to his class, of which he gave an undertaking on leaving. I am informed that he is communicating with a group of petty bourgeois politicians. I have been unable at this time to secure any written document. *I think steps should be taken to watch any correspondence passing out* [...] This chap's name is Ashmore. I thought he would make better timber. Then there is a chap called Breslin. He is a keen student with an irritating personality [...] Then there is Denn. He would be a tremendously useful fellow upon the completion of his training and his return to industrial life. I think he is really in earnest.

Big Jim expected that his students would put the IWL case forcefully at meetings of the Anglo-American Secretariat of the ECCI. He terminated his controversial career with Moscow in 1929 and, by virtue of default, cleared the way for the CPGB to refound communist groups in the Irish Free State. This new departure was concomitant with a major turn-about in Comintern policy, the so-called 'Third Period'. According to the new Stalinist interpretation of international politics, the communist movement, having failed to seize power in Central Europe in 1918–23 or win substantial gains in the ensuing period of 'capitalist stabilisation', was now entering a third phase. The new era was to be marked by mounting 'contradictions', which would lead to the collapse of capitalism and a rise in revolutionary consciousness among workers. Although the Wall Street Crash of October 1929 seemed a portent that might support such political expectations, there was little sociological evidence in 1928/29 to underpin the basically voluntarist tenets of the 'Third Period'. The redirection in Comintern strategy was rather a transposition of the ultra-left lurch within the USSR – abolishing the market system and installing a command economy in agriculture and industry – onto the drawing board of Comintern strategists. The abrupt change in direction was also distinguished by extremely sectarian polemics. The catchwords 'class against class' and 'social fascism' precluded differentiation: the social democratic and Labour leaders were now depicted as the Comintern's main enemies, their organisations as pillars of the hated 'bourgeois-fascist' state.[30]

The execution of the new 'line' went hand-in-hand with the prophylactic removal of its potential opponents. The method used was a new Party 'purge' (*chistka*), one of the periodic attempts to 'cleanse the Party of unworthy elements'. The perceived enemy in

1929–30 were the purported followers of Nikolai Bukharin, who had been at odds with Stalin on the brutal methods being employed to collectivise agriculture. Those Communist leaders suspected of supporting Bukharin were dubbed 'conciliators'; Moscow initiated political, internal Party intrigues against them and they were expelled or demoted.

The purge of autumn 1929 affected the students in the ILS on two grounds. Since they held candidate-member status in the VKP(b) and were organised in the Moscow city branch where the school was located, they were due for scrutiny like all Soviet Party cadres; and if they had been delegated to the school by Party leaders now in disgrace, they were expected to attest their loyalty to the new Muscovite canon of undifferentiated hostility to all non-communist strains of the Left. The purging of the students proceeded from the 'verification' of their credentials and then centred on their behaviour at the school. A joint commission, which met in October 1929, directed the 'cleansing' process. The *chistka* suspended teaching for weeks, subjecting the students to intense cross-examination. The Examination Commission scrutinised the students' biographies in private sessions and also decided whether or not appeals against its decisions should be granted. The Land Group hearings or general meetings of the *chistka* dealt mainly with the conduct of the cadre at the school. Each student had to submit, in a sealed envelope, a written biography with the following data: country of origin, date and place of birth, social origin and social position, general and political education, year of entry to communist youth movement and/or communist party, details of work in the movement and date of arrival in the USSR.[31]

Years later, Jim Larkin Jnr recalled how students from Poland were given a protracted grilling.[32] German students argued among themselves before the *chistka* commission about the leadership claims of the opposing KPD (Communist Party of Germany) factions led by Thälmann and Brandler. The Czechs and Slovaks, like the Poles, had to suffer for their Party's record of recalcitrance to Moscow edicts. Harry Wicks, the youngest British student, recounts how one Yugoslav colleague was denounced and arrested, which was to become the commonplace and ultimate sanction at the ILS ten years later.[33] Wicks, a railwayman from Battersea, was censured (endorsement of his Party card) because he thought learning how to drive trains should not be part of the curriculum. As *partorg*, he had to see to it that his colleagues attended the boring and unpopular 'driver and fireman' exercises and he voiced the view that the whole endeavour was a waste of time. During a *chistka* session, one Bulgarian student repeated the heresy of young Harry Wicks, but far more disconcerting for the Londoner was the fact that no one in his class spoke up in his defence.

The Irish student contingent underwent the same interrogatory procedures. The 'criticism and self-criticism' (*kritika i samokritika*) demanded at the purge sessions was very much a one-way street since the scope of the permitted 'criticism', which had to be 'positive', was determined by the Party cell leadership. The boundaries of 'self-criticism', on the other hand, were indefinite. Contrary to the Catholic practice, such confessions were made in public; the 'occasion of sin' (breaking school or Party regulations) was duly punished but never absolved: it could be exhumed at will, often in the form of new accusations that judged the infringement not under the pertinent circumstances of yesteryear but solely on the criteria set down by the contemporary and short-lived 'Party line'.[34]

Three Irish students encountered various degrees of criticism. Young Larkin and Charlie Ashmore were upbraided for having fallen behind in 'socialist competition'. The latter phrase, also known in industry under the term 'shock-work' (*udarnichestvo*), described the efforts of workers loyal to the regime to fulfil obligations over and above their normal work quotas. In the case of the two students, the term had a much narrower, specific meaning – subscribing to one of the National Loans launched to finance the gigantic industrialisation programme. 'Good Party elements' subscribed 200–300 per cent, that is, two or three monthly salaries, a sum which was deducted at source ten times a year. Larkin justified his subscription of one month's allowance (100 per cent) by the fact that he had to repay a holiday loan to the school administration. He subsequently donated two months' pocket money to the National Loan subscription. Ashmore stated that his 'minimum subscription of 50 roubles' was the result of debts to the school's Mutual Aid Fund and the costs incurred by the purchase of a new set of false teeth.[35] Despite these minor criticisms, both received excellent final marks. Larkin was recommended for 'leading Party work in his national Party', and, on the strength of his paper dealing with 'The German Revolution 1918–1919' was seen as a future assistant teacher for short courses.[36] Ashmore had 'made remarkable progress considering his ideological and political background', was 'ideologically reliable' and had 'complied with Party discipline'. He also represented a correct position on questions regarding the VKP(b), the Comintern, the CPGB, Ireland and internal school matters.[37]

By contrast, Breslin's encounter with the *chistka* commission was more abrasive and had far-reaching consequences. His situation in the Land Group was anomalous on several counts. First, in not coming from a republican or working-class background, he was an odd-man-out. Although Breslin, having joined the CPI in 1922, had the longest political biography of all Irish students, he was not a typical Communist. Second, his social origin was middle-class, or even distressed lower middle-class by 1928, and his interests were intellectual. That made him suspect in the eyes of Communist neophytes who transported the 'hard man' self-image from their IRA days to the semi-clandestine world of extreme left politics. Since Pat Breslin had met his future wife, Katya Kreitser, relatively early in his school career, married her in May 1929 and moved to her apartment in Leontevskii Lane near Gorky Street, he was spending less and less time with his Irish and British colleagues outside school hours.

The 'practical' summer work (*praktika*) in 1928 meant getting to know Soviet factories from the inside, staying with Russian worker families and analysing working-class family budgets. A post-mortem held in the school at the start of the new academic year came to the conclusion that the experiment had failed: the Russian workers remained reserved and saw the foreign students as being connected with the government. In the following year, the composition of the groups was on a voluntary basis and they could choose their destinations. We do not know where Pat Breslin spent the summers of 1928 and 1929. It is unlikely that he spent a longer period away from Moscow after his wedding. Wicks, Murray, Larkin Jnr and three other English-speakers spent the summer 1929 *praktika* in Daghestan on the Caspian Sea, and their actual holiday entitlement in Leningrad and the Ukraine. They noticed the shortage of food everywhere, a sign that the collectivisation of agriculture was running into difficulties. Wicks, who was Jim Larkin Jnr's best friend at the school, explained the reasons for Breslin's fateful clash with the *chistka* commission:

> Whenever a student insisted on introducing a subject, it got a discuss-
> ion. An instance concerns one of the Irish students whom Big Jim

Larkin had picked for the school. This lad was no recluse. He seemed to get on all right with a crowd of women schoolteachers; used to circulate in some girls' college and seemed rather successful in that way! But intellectually he seemed a loner, even among the other Irish students. One day, in a Rudas seminar on dialectical materialism, this chap suddenly became very vocal. He introduced the topic of spiritualism: he was convinced that 'materialisations' did take place and that spiritualism was therefore materialistic and thus all right. An extraordinary discussion ensued. At its end, Rudas took him to his office. At that time, the new edition of Marx and Engels' Collected Works were being published; so Rudas promised this lad an English translation of a piece by Engels on spiritualism.[38]

When this altercation took place is unknown, probably towards the end of 1929. Up to that time, Breslin (Brennan), as we have seen, had earned good grades. Rudas, in recommending him in February for candidate status in the VKP(b), wrote that he was convinced that 'Brennan will become a useful Party member'.[39] In the second such recommendation, another teacher held Breslin to be 'a developed and reliable Communist'. The third letter in this connection was effusive: the 21-year-old was described as 'Bolshevik-disciplined, with initiative and great capability for working on his own in the Leninist manner in a whole range of difficult questions [...] and could become a good propagandist'.

In mid-September 1929, Breslin's application for full membership of the Soviet Party was endorsed by the Croatian Vladimir Sen'ko, the secretary of the Party cell at the school. Sen'ko attained fame eight years later under his real name (Čopič) by commanding the 15th (English-speaking) International Brigade during the Spanish Civil War.

When Breslin was called to speak at the purge session of the VKP(b) school collective assembly on 12 January 1930, he began in the conventional manner by outlining in some detail his social origin and Party career. He was dismissive of Roddy Connolly's first CPI, calling it a 'mixture of groupings and some adventurers'. After his transfer to Larkin's IWL, Breslin went on, he had seen his *métier* in propaganda work and agitation among the unemployed. Referring to his academic record at the ILS, he said that while his marks were satisfactory, sickness had held him back. Changing to a self-critical vein, Breslin said that he had had an exaggerated opinion about his theoretical level and had made 'errors' in regard to the Easter Rising of 1916 and in trade union matters. The former probably referred to any disagreement voiced against Lenin's doctrinaire assessment of the Irish insurrection: 'The misfortune of the Irish is that they have risen prematurely, when the European revolt of the proletariat has not yet matured.'[40] An allegedly incorrect attitude in Irish trade union affairs may have centred on a defence of WUI tactics, a charge that was also levelled at Larkin Jnr.

The first question from the floor also hinged on what was, in all probability, collective opposition from the Irish group, namely anger at the removal of Larkin Jnr as *partorg* of the English-speakers. Breslin admitted that he had erred because his information on the case was scanty, but he put on record that he still believed that Larkin had done his job well. Turning to the main point in the indictment, his philosophical interests, Breslin recounted that he had studied astrology in Dublin and, in some unspecified cases, had the capability to predict the future. That was the reason for his conviction that things exist that cannot be explained by rational thinking. Asked by a student whether or not he had 'overcome' his religion, Breslin stated that he had rejected his Catholic upbringing at fourteen years of age and, in reply to a similar query about his attachment to Indian mysticism, he answered that his reading on the subject led him to the belief that, despite some valuable insights, its tenets could not be proven.

Faced with the interjection that the communist *Weltanschauung* rejected idealistic philosophy, Pat Breslin countered that he was not an idealist and, while fighting against the Catholic Church in Ireland, he had realised that the communist movement should recognise that not all phenomena could be explained by references to Marxist materialism.

The debate then proceeded to a new charge, that Brennan (Breslin) had 'links to a bourgeois journalist'. His response was that he had brought this man to the school (a breach of secrecy), but knew that the foreigner in question did not write for bourgeois newspapers. In this at least he found qualified support from a fellow-student. Andrew Auld (Bergson), who had joined the CPGB after the May 1926 General Strike,[41] admitted that he, too, knew this journalist. However, Auld was of the opinion that Breslin, although a good student, would never make a good communist. An American classmate voiced similar misgivings, as did Pro-Rector Rudas in his statement:

Brennan is at the school because there is no Communist Party in Ireland. Our task at the time was to educate some non-Party people from Ireland to be Communists, and we accepted them for the course. Brennan is an example of the failure of this policy, but despite that we succeeded in making good Communists out of the others.

Charlie Ashmore alleged that Breslin had consorted with the Dublin intelligentsia and, not having 'overcome' his mystical musings at the ILS, could not grasp the fundamentals of Marxist materialist philosophy. Larkin Jnr repeated Auld's and Ashmore's criticism and, speaking in the first-person plural, expressed grave doubts that Breslin could evolve into a good communist cadre.

Breslin had the final word. He began by mentioning that his wife, who came from the intelligentsia and worked in the Secret Department of the Soviet Foreign Ministry, did not share all his opinions. Referring to his activities in the IWL, he stressed that he had contacts with the working class but did not disseminate his esoteric philosophical views in such circles. Furthermore, he did not consider himself to be a spiritualist; he was interested in such questions because of the literature he had read in Ireland. Breslin's closing remarks suggest that the procedure of the *chistka* had not impinged on his independence of thought:

> Comrade Lawlor [Larkin Jnr] stated that I am a bad Party member, but that claim has no basis in reality. You may expel me from the Party, but don't force me to go over to the other side of the barricades. I believe that I can still remain a member of the Communist International. If you are of the opinion that what I have explained here is idealism, then I can't do anything about it.

The assembly decided to strike 'Brennan' from the list of candidates for membership of the VKP(b). His relegation from the ILS followed shortly afterwards. One month after his dismissal from the ILS course, Breslin applied to the school's Party Bureau for permission to stay in the USSR. He reasoned that, because his wife was an employee of the Foreign Ministry, she could not accompany him to Ireland and, since she was pregnant, she needed his emotional and financial support. He stated further that he needed to deepen his theoretical understanding of Marxism and referred to the 'divergences' in this respect which had led to his expulsion from the VKP(b). If he could not find work in a factory, he would teach the English language. Presumably since the causes for his expulsion from the course were so unusual and not political in the sense of showing sympathy for Trotsky or Bukharin, Breslin was offered a position by the ILS translation department in the autumn of 1930. He acquired two excellent letters of recommendation from his teachers, which attested that he was a good worker and 'loyal to Soviet power'.

NOTES

1. The Communist University for Western National Minorities (KUNMZ), which existed between 1921 and 1936, originally set out to educate 'Western' national minorities of Soviet Russia (Volga Germans, Karelian Finns, Belarussians and Poles) beyond primary school level. It later admitted Communist militants from the Balkans, Italy, Central Europe and Scandinavia. The Communist University for Eastern Workers (KUTV), also founded in 1921, had a Russian and a foreign section; it gave preference to candidates from the Middle East and the Eastern Mediterranean. Graduates of KUTV who afterwards became famous included Ho Chi Minh and Jomo Kenyatta. In 1925 followed the establishment of the Communist University for Chinese Workers (KUTK), where in the initial phase European and Chinese anti-imperialists were taught side by side. See Leonid G. Babitchenko, 'Die Kaderschulung der Komintern', in Herman Weber et al. (eds), *Jahrbuch für historische Kommunismusforschung 1993* (Berlin 1993), pp. 37–59.
2. RGASPI, f. 495, o. 164, d. 500, ll. 50–54.
3. J.T. Murphy, 'The First Year of the Lenin School', *Communist International*, 30 September 1927, pp. 267–69.
4. RGASPI, f. 531, o. 1, d. 15, ll. 179–88.
5. RGASPI, f. 495, o. 3, d. 46, l. 2.
6. RGASPI, f. 495, o. 3, d. 46, ll. 74–75.
7. RGASPI, f. 495, o. 7, d. 3, l. 4.
8. RGASPI, f. 495, o. 4, d. 24, l. 107.
9. RGASPI, f. 495, o. 3, d. 19, ll. 40–44.
10. RGASPI, f. 17, o. 98, d. 702, l. 7.
11. RGASPI, f. 495, o. 3, d. 46. l. 74.
12. RGASPI, f. 531, o. 1, d. 12, ll. 3–4.
13. RGASPI, f. 531, o. 1, d. 8, ll. 56–67.
14. Barry McLoughlin, 'Proletarian Academics or Party Functionaries? Irish Communists at the International Lenin School, Moscow, 1927–37', *Saothar*, 22 (1997), pp. 63–79; idem, 'Delegated to the "New World". Irish Communists at Moscow's International Lenin School, 1927–1937', *History Ireland*, Winter 1999, pp. 37–39.
15. RGASPI, f. 495, o. 218, d. 4, ll. 3–7.
16. RGASPI, f. 495, o. 218, d. 1, ll. 57–63; f. 17, o. 98, d. 681, ll. 3–4; Stephen Bowler, 'Seán Murray, 1898–1961, and the Pursuit of Stalinism in One Country', *Saothar*, 18 (1993), pp. 41–53.

17. RGASPI, f. 17, o. 98, d. 702, 744, 796.
18. The account of daily life at the school is taken from the autobiography of one of the British participants of the 1928–30 course, Harry Wicks (Tanner). See Harry Wicks, *Keeping My Head. The Memoirs of a British Bolshevik* (London 1992), pp. 72–125.
19. RGASPI, f. 531, o. 2, d. 3, l. 63.
20. Larry E. Holmes, *Stalin's School. Moscow's Model School No. 25, 1931–1937* (Pittsburgh 1999), pp. 8–9.
21. RGASPI, f. 495, o. 164, d. 500, ll. 56–58.
22. At the beginning of the 1929–30 school year, 42 teachers were members of the VKP(b) – RGASPI, f. 531, o. 1, d. 17. ll. 2–3.
23. Murphy, *Communist International*, p. 269.
24. RGASPI, f. 495, o. 218, d. 1, l. 72.
25. RGASPI, f. 495, o. 218, d. 17, l. 16.
26. RGASPI, f. 495, o. 218, d. 7, l. 13.
27. Wicks, *Keeping My Head*, p. 122.
28. 'Letters from Moscow. Correspondence of Bill Denn', *Labour History News*, no. 3, Spring 1987, p.10.
29. RGASPI, f. 495, o. 218, d. 7, l. 3.
30. Kevin McDermott and Jeremy Agnew, *The Comintern. A History of International Communism from Lenin to Stalin* (London 1996), Ch. 3.
31. RGASPI, f. 531, o. 1, d. 14, l. 166.
32. Information from Donal Nevin, Dublin.
33. According to a student list for the years 1926–31, three Yugoslavs were arrested in the years 1930 and 1931 – RGASPI, f. 531, o. 1, d. 32, l. 34.
34. Berthold Unfried, 'Rituale von Konfession und Selbstkritik: Bilder von stalinischem Kader', Hermann Weber *et al.* (eds), *Jahrbuch für Historische Kommunismusforschung 1994*, Berlin 1994, pp. 148–64.
35. RGASPI, f. 495, o. 218, d. 4, ll. 12, 19; f. 495, o. 218, d. 17, l. 10.
36. RGASPI, f. 495, o. 218, d. 4, ll. 1,18.
37. RGASPI, f. 495, o. 218, d. 17, l. 9.
38. Wicks, *Keeping My Head*, p. 88.
39. The account of the purging process is based on Breslin's Communist Party of Ireland file: RGASPI, f. 495, o. 218, d. 7.
40. A. Raftery, *Lenin on Ireland* (New Books, Dublin 1974), p. 34. Lenin's essay was written in July 1916 and included in vol. 22 of his Collected Works.
41. RGASPI, f. 17, o. 98, d. 679, ll. 2–5.

Life with Katya, 1929–36

Ekaterina (Katya) Genrikhovna Kreitser, Pat Breslin's wife, was born in St Petersburg in 1904. Her family was Jewish, and her grandfather is said to have corresponded with Jenny, the daughter of Karl Marx, and with Friedrich Engels. Genrikh Kreitser, Breslin's father-in-law, had been Professor of Chemistry at St Petersburg University and an agent for the Swedish explosives firm, Nobel. Katya, her brothers Boris and Andrei, and their parents Genrikh and Olga, belonged to the old Russian middle class, a population sector the Soviet authorities termed 'former people' (*byvshie liudi*). In a country where a proletarian background was a prerequisite for social advancement, 'former people' were permanently discrimina-ted against – losing the right to vote (1926–36), subject to expulsion from major urban centres in the mid-1930s and arrested *en masse* during the Great Terror of 1937–38. Boris was twice incarcerated in the Gulag (1937–44, 1948–54) and Katya served a prison sentence in the period 1938–44, but the family does not seem to have suffered unduly in the first decade after the October Revolution.

Katya was allowed to study Japanese at Moscow University and subsequently took up a translator's post in the People's Commissariat of Foreign Affairs. Her interest in the Far East began as a teenager, after she had a semi-mystical experience when visiting the Buddhist temple in St Petersburg.

She set up home with Breslin in 1929 at Leontevskii Lane No. 33, a side street off the shopping precinct Gorky Street. The Kremlin, Moscow University, Red Square, the Comintern headquarters and the Lenin Library were all within walking distance of the apartment. 'Flat No. 1 (ring five times)', the note beside the bell, signified that the Breslin couple, like most Muscovites, had but a room in a communal apartment (*kommunalka*), usually a former bourgeois residence which had been split up into its constituent rooms. Life in the *kommunalka* was a constant war of nerves, even in those rare cases where all the families in the apartment were considerate. All inhabitants shared the bathroom, toilet and kitchen. They had to agree whose turn it was to cook and for how long, and whose duty it was to clean up the communal areas. In that pre-refrigerator era, groceries were kept in padlocked kitchen cupboards. These were a breeding ground for cockroaches (*tarakany*), and in the badly ventilated rooms (keeping warm in the arctic temperatures was the main consideration) other crawling creatures sought human contact. Apart from the cramped and unhygienic living conditions, the inhabitants of the *kommunalka* had to hunt for scarce foodstuffs, as the vicious war of collectivisation against the peasants had led to food shortages.

Lack of living space and disruption in the supply of food were results of the gigantic and chaotically organised social 'experiments' undertaken at the end of the 1920s, namely industrialisation and the collectivisation of land. Over 3 million prosperous and middling peasants (*kulaks*) were expropriated and half of this figure exiled. The remainder, together with other rural inhabitants, were recruited for work in urban and mining areas. Between 1928 and 1932 (First Five-Year Plan) the population of towns and cities rose by 12 million, with the number of salary and wage earners doubling, from 11.4 to 24.2 million.[1] Since investment was channelled primarily to the building of industrial plants and not accommodation, the overcrowding in Moscow increased: in 1928 the average space (usually in a *kommunalka* room) per inhabitant was 5.9 square metres; by 1932 it had sunk to 4.6 square metres.[2]

Pat and Katya Breslin were privileged because they were attached to 'closed' food-supply circles, either at the Foreign Commissariat or at the Lenin School, where canteen meals were served. Such institutions also offered their employees food packages or set up cooperative grocery stores within the office building. These privileges, graded according to rank, confronted Breslin with the rigid class system of the Stalinist *nomenklatura*. Once more outside his place of employment, he would have seen the reality of the underprivileged – the human driftwood cast up by the war in the countryside, such as begging children and peasants in rags, in search of work and lodgings in the Russian capital.

Such intolerable living conditions, then as now, explain the Muscovites' urge to get out of the city as often as possible – to their wooden house in the woods (*dacha*) and its vegetable allotment. After his expulsion from the Lenin School, Breslin gave English-language 'grinds' to private pupils, and to civil servants in the Agricultural Commissariat. He and Katya spent July to November 1930 in Leningrad in the flat and *dacha* of the Kreitser family. Back again in wintry Moscow, Breslin met a French-born typist employed in the ILS, who advised him to contact the head of the school's translation department for a job. For unknown reasons, he was not kept on the permanent staff and had to leave after three months, though the ILS authorities continued to give him the odd translation commission. Although his salary of 180 roubles corresponded to what a skilled worker earned in a Moscow factory, Breslin applied for permission to send some money home to Ireland. It is not clear from his Party file if approval was granted, but that he wished to help his family in Dublin suggests that funds were scarce at 150 North Strand in January 1931. Being able to speak Russian fluently and in such a short time because of his wife's tutoring, Breslin was not dependent on his monthly salary since he could take on translations on a freelance basis. That was to be the pattern of his future career.

In March 1931, after his short stint at the ILS as an employee of the ECCI, Breslin joined the English translation department of the literary journal *International Literature*. His appointment as stylistic editor lasted until November 1932, but he remained in close contact with the magazine afterwards, translating six pieces, short stories and literary studies, between 1933 and 1937. His first commission, Isaac Babel's short story 'The Road', is a gripping chronicle of the brutality of the Russian Civil War. Babel was already a recognised talent in modern Soviet literature, fêted in the West since the publication in 1929 of his collection *Red Cavalry* in London and New York. This personal and starkly realistic account of the Civil War – a Jew from Odessa serving on horseback alongside anti-Semitic Cossacks in the Red Army – did not endear him to the top military men around Stalin. 'The Road' was in the same vein: the odyssey of a reluctant revolutionary from the Ukraine to Petrograd before taking up a translator's post with the *Cheka*, the popular acronym for the Soviet secret police. Here Babel's style reminds one of Hemingway's pithy prose, but more lyrical and pungent than the American's, sentences like flails of the knout or cracks of the Mauser, a masterful unity of style and content.

Three further short stories, on the revolutionary movement in Germany, Japan and Colombia, are by comparison pallid efforts with one-dimensional heroes. It is perhaps not coincidental that Breslin's final contributions to *International Literature*, in 1937, consisted of rendering scholarly articles on Russia's greatest poet, Alexander Pushkin, into readable English. By that date the ideological shift away from global class brotherhood towards chauvinist sentiment was long underway, not least in expectation of an armed conflict in Europe.[3]

This paradigmatic about-turn is also reflected in Breslin's journalistic, as distinct from literary, output. His longest term of employment in the Soviet Union (November 1932 to May 1938) was with the *Moscow Daily News* (*MDN*), by Soviet standards a lively newspaper, established in October 1930. The initiative to launch the paper, which in its best years appeared five times a week, came from Anna Louise Strong, a tough-minded American socialist from a Congregationalist background, who had settled in Russia in 1921. In touch with many bourgeois American engineers working on giant building projects in the USSR during the Great Depression, Strong pushed the idea of a crisp newspaper for such a readership. She engaged the assistance of Mikhail Borodin, an acquaintance from socialist circles in the United States before 1917 and now the Assistant Commissar of Labour. Another prominent sponsor was Valery Mezhlauk, Vice-Chairman of the Supreme Economic Council and candidate-member of the Central Committee of the VKP(b). Since Strong was a foreigner, she could not front the paper, so Mezhlauk sent one of his administrators, V. Vasiutin, to occupy the managing editor's chair. However, Strong virtually ran the paper and was allowed a free hand in selecting staff.

Anna Louise Strong soon ran into difficulties not of her making. The forceful 'workerist' current in literary and journalistic affairs, replicated by the Chinese Red Guards nearly forty years later in their condemnation of 'fascist bourgeois' such as Beethoven and Shakespeare, attacked the broad range of *MDN* reporting and contrived to set up a 'proletarian' counter-model, *Workers' News*, in early 1931. Simultaneously, Strong was faced with a new editor-in-chief, Viktor Vaksov, a former opponent of Leninism, who showed his loyalty to the ruling Party by removing a summary written by Strong of a Stalin speech and replacing it with the full, deadening text.

Miss Strong went right to the top, complaining about these practices in a letter to the 'boss' (*khoziain*), as Stalin was known among the top bureaucracy. Her directness paid off. At a conference some days later in the Kremlin, which Strong, Vaksov, Stalin, Kaganovich and Voroshilov attended, the headstrong American pleaded her case. She could convince the almighty circle that two papers for Americans was one too many (*Workers' News* was curtailed in April 1932) and that Borodin should take over from Vaksov. More staff were taken on and the *MDN* became a daily from 1 May 1932.[4]

The editorial office in central Moscow provided a port of call and employment for many communists and left-wingers from America and Britain. The American Harvey O'Connor organised the daily according to US standards, with a copy desk in the middle of a big room, where copyreaders sat together with a layout expert. Rose Cohen, from London's East End, was put in charge of the Foreign News department in 1931. Cohen was the wife of David Lipets-Petrovsky, the Comintern emissary for Ireland and Britain, where he was known by a variety of names and soubriquets – Bennett, Max or Humboldt. Anna Louise Strong portrayed the jocular atmosphere in the midnight newsroom:

> What are you going to do about 'Party' and 'Fascist'?
> I think, volunteers Bertrand, that Italian fascists are capitals and Polish fascists are small!
> Well, 'social fascists' are certainly 'small', comes an answer.
> As I understand, says Allen, we don't use 'social fascist' anyway in this paper. I'm cutting them out, and putting in simpler words [...].
> In the discussion on style, one new word was created – the contribution of the MOSCOW DAILY NEWS to the English language. In the argument whether whiteguard [opponents of the Bolsheviks in the Civil War] should be spelt with capitals, with a hyphen or just how, the two young men established their 'workers' control' over grammar and style sheets. 'They are neither 'white' nor do they 'guard' anything was their argument. Why not just 'whiteguard', the same as you write 'blackguard', all in one word? After all, they're just another form of blackguard.[5]

The paper was not totally fetlocked by the censor in 1932 and the quotidian fare for *MDN* readers was a mixture of the factual and classic reportage. Jennie Lee, the Scottish firebrand ILP Member of Parliament, was interviewed on her way to the Caucasus (23 May), and the arrival in Moscow of Berthold Brecht, famous for *The Threepenny Opera*, was announced with photograph (14 June).

More space was given to Sidney and Beatrice Webb, the ageing Fabian socialists who were so uncritical of what they saw in the 'First Workers' State' (29 June, 8 July, 6 October).

Two short notices that appeared in the paper before Breslin became one of its staffers concerned persons who were to play an important role in his subsequent life. The edition of 15 July announced a Moscow engagement of the noted 'workers' violinist' and Estonian revolutionary Eduard Soermus, who played a selection of classical pieces and Irish and English folk melodies in Gorky Amusement Park. Two months earlier (27 May) *MDN* reported on a teachers' delegation to the USSR which included the Irishwoman Margaret McMackin, who was said to have been 'particularly impressed by the close connection of the early polytechnical school with the factory, the state and collective farms'.

Judging by the comparatively few articles under his name, Pat Breslin was used first and foremost as a sub-editor at the new offices of *MDN* at Petrovsky Lane, a five-minute walk from the communal flat. His first signed article (20 January 1933) was a factual piece about the collectivised peasantry in the North Ossetian Autonomous District (Northern Caucasus). He wrote other articles in a lighter vein ('Spring Comes to Moscow', 'Tsarist Police Attempts to Arrest Marx'), reviewed plays, interviewed poets and writers, and translated well-known poems. His opinion of Konstantin Finn's farce *Vzdor* (Nonsense), which Breslin translated as 'bunk' for his predominantly American readers, was openly critical since he felt that the 'philistine traits' of the petty-bourgeois and indolent white-collar employees were 'accentuated to the point of the grotesque'. He was more impressed by Isaac Babel's play *Maria* (21 March 1934), a depiction of the violent world of the black-marketeering bagmen (*meshochniki*) during the Civil War:

> The dialogue, succinct and forceful, shows that Babel's mastery of the language has lost nothing over the years. Listening to him, I was reminded of Synge's dictum that every word in a play should resemble a well-seasoned nut.

Two other lifelong concerns of Breslin surface in his columns: education and the proper use of English. His 'Why Petya Fell From Grace' (15 March 1935) built on a report in *Pravda* about Petya Malek, a teenage cinema addict and school truant. Breslin took up the official line that neither the school authorities nor the Pioneers, the Party organisation for children, evinced much interest in the home circumstances of the pupils, for Petya lived practically unsupervised, sharing a flat with his aged grandfather. Breslin quoted successful examples of study circles in the afternoons as a remedy. He referred to A.V. Kosarev, secretary of the CP Youth section, Komsomol, who had deplored 'the shabby appearance and slangy conversation which are common among some of the Young Pioneer leaders'.

Breslin's true *métier*, however, was literature, especially poetry, and not political sermonising. In his early years at *Moscow Daily News* he was commissioned to translate works by interesting poets, in particular representatives of the pre-1914 Symbolist school who had shown loyalty to the new regime. One example is 'The Islands' by Alexander Blok, thoughts on a lovers' rendezvous in the frosty night air of imperial St Petersburg. Breslin's translation, while lively, is antiquated:

> [...] Ah me! It yields a dismal pleasure
> The thought that love must pass like snow.
> Then shall I promise love undying
> As knights were wont to, long ago?
>
> [...] There is a rite: the lap-robe deftly
> To arrange, embrace the slender form
> And whisper artful, honeyed phrases
> The while we speed athwart the storm.

Breslin's rendering of 'The Hammer and Sickle', a late work by Valery Bryusov, who had been an admirer of Baudelaire and the French 'decadents' before entering the ranks of the Bolsheviks in 1920, is punchy and, save for the awkward first line of the last verse, has the marching rhythm of a battle hymn:

> What if we suffered from the lash
> Of black defeat and cold and hunger?
> Above the world new symbols flash
> The sickle and the workers' hammer
> [...]
>
> But fair outmirrored to the view,
> The soul of man is young and happy.

The sickle whet for harvests new,
For coming battles keep the hammer.

In contrast to his literary and journalistic output, Breslin's inner life, not least his relationship with Katya, is largely uncharted. His letters home to the North Strand have not survived. Irina and Genrikh, his children by Katya, know little of their father, or indeed of their mother. Katya was permanently traumatised by her prison experiences, by the beatings and privations, and, as she continued to serve as a major in the secret police after her release (1944), she had to adhere to the fiction that she had been 'on secret work' and not a prisoner. So she was psychologically and vocationally bound by a vow of secrecy. According to her best friend, Mary Tsin, Katya was devoted to her Irish husband and heartbroken when he left her in 1936. In the preceding period, however, their life together seems to have been harmonious. At some time in the early 1930s Katya was recruited by the secret police and worked in the Japanese section of the foreign espionage service. Irina was born in June 1934, and Pat was a devoted father. Breslin's heavy drinking and consorting with the English-speaking Moscow foreign correspondents' community became a pattern only towards the end of the decade, at a time of deep mental depression. As long as he was with Katya, he moved more in Russian-speaking circles, among her friends. Mary Tsin remembers him as 'a very openhearted man, very amusing but sometimes sad because he was in an alien environment'. Her family took to him, considered him 'a brother' and he was a frequent guest, with Irina and Katya, at Mary's mother's *dacha*.[6]

His friendship with the painter Harry Kernoff developed after they met in Russia in August 1930. Kernoff was a member of the Irish delegation (Friends of the Soviet Union) to Moscow and Leningrad, and he brought Breslin a parcel from the North Strand. The Irish Special Branch took great interest in the voyage. Noting that Kernoff's Russian father had a furniture factory in Dublin's Little Denmark Street and that Harry, a past pupil of Synge Street Christian Brothers School, was not politically prominent, the report to the Irish Prime Minister William T. Cosgrave stated that Harry was a 'futurist' painter 'of some merit' and closely connected with stage design in the Gate Theatre.[7]

Other friends and acquaintances in Breslin's first decade in Moscow were drawn from his old Comintern contacts and the world of the literati. He was relaxed in the company of Tom Bell, Jimmy Shields and John Evans. Breslin had met Bell at the ILS, and again in the period 1934–36, when the Scotsman worked as a sector leader in the school. Bell knew Larkin Snr and James Connolly from mass meetings in Glasgow to support the Dublin Lock-Out of 1913.[8] Jimmy Shields was another 'old Moscow hand', a Scottish shipyard worker, who became a member of the Politburo of the CPGB and editor of the London *Daily Worker*. He had represented his Party at the ECCI in 1932–33 and, probably because of incipient tuberculosis, had spent part of the previous decade in South Africa, where he served as General-Secretary of the Communist Party of South Africa (CPSA) between 1925 and 1928.[9]

The arrival and departure of such functionaries were welcome distractions for Breslin, occasions to swap stories and news, to exchange gifts and parcels, and to wet the shamrock or the thistle. John Evans, whom Tom Bell introduced to Pat Breslin in 1935, held no Party posts but was a musician and man of the theatre. He learned Russian in Manchester, and after sending a Russian–English translation to the Foreign Language Publishing House in the Russian capital, was invited to take up employment there. Evans helped to bring out a three-volume edition of Shakespeare in English and translated huge chunks of Lenin and Stalin. He later changed jobs, becoming the Moscow correspondent of the British pro-Labour *Daily Herald* during World War II. Later, in London, during the 1950s, he began to compose music from Russian motifs.[10]

There were also surprise visitors from Ireland, like T.R. Fforde, a retired sea captain who lived in Donegal and came to Moscow with his wife in August 1932. Uncle John, Pat Breslin's first political mentor, asked his nephew to help Fforde find employment in the USSR. Fforde had taught himself cabinet making and hoped, on the basis of a recommendation from Jim Larkin Jnr and others of the Revolutionary Workers' Groups (the forerunner of the second CPI, which was founded in June 1933) to find a job in his field in the Soviet Union. The Anglo-American Secretariat of the ECCI recommended Fforde to Borodin of the Commissariat of Labour.[11]

Katya could have little active part in the Irish dimension of Patrick's existence, despite the fact that her command of English was by now perfect.

Whatever disposition she showed to outsiders, her top-secret post precluded meeting with, or taking a great interest in, foreigners. Her first loyalty was to the State and to her superiors in the Main Administration of State Security (GUGB) within the People's Commissariat of Internal Affairs (NKVD). The potential tensions at the heart of all cross-cultural marriages, then, were compounded in the case of the Breslin-Kreitser couple by persistent external interference: the secret police had never approved of the liaison and let Katya know that it was her duty to make her foreign spouse a Soviet citizen. In 1936 this pressure became intense. Breslin succumbed to his wife's entreaties and applied for a Soviet passport in February 1936. He was granted citizenship of the USSR on 1 November and an internal passport was issued in his name on 15 December.[12] The change in citizenship was Breslin's first step towards disaster since it deprived him of the only dependable source of support against the arbitrary terror of Stalin's minions: the intervention of the British Embassy acting in the name of the Irish government. He was fully aware of what he had done, and probably felt that he had no choice. In retrospect, his decision demonstrates his inherent decency, even if he tried to reverse it later under totally different circumstances. For the moment, at least, he decided that his place was with Katya and Irina, and by doing so had removed the most obvious threat to his family.

The policy of forcing foreigners to abandon their native citizenship for the scarlet passport of the USSR became general practice by 1937, especially in respect of political refugees from fascist regimes (Germans, Poles, Italians, Austrians, Bulgarians, Hungarians), of whom not a few were arrested precisely for rejecting this Greek gift. As regards Breslin's application, however, an unresolved dilemma in the internal security strategy of the NKVD came to the fore: while foreigners should become Soviet citizens and thus defenceless subjects of the totalitarian state, they were, on the other hand, unreliable, carriers of the bacilli of Western ideas and individualism. In the course of processing Breslin's citizenship file, the Secret-Political Department of the GUGB-NKVD reported on 1 June 1936:

> We inform you that Breslin P.F. has links to an element repressed by us. According to informers' reports, Breslin P.F. has made utterances of a religious-mystical nature. We are of the opinion that accepting him into Soviet citizenship is not desirable.[13]

One explanation for this apparent contradiction between Muscovite bureaucracies is the thesis that Stalin, and his subservient Politburo or the *Cheka* acting in their name, had not yet decided to enlarge the hostile spectrum of putative 'Trotskyists' by targeting foreigners as well. After all, 1936 saw the passing of the new Soviet Constitution, a model for democracy, at least on paper, and the dawning of wide coalitions abroad in support of the Soviet Union. Under the slogan of the anti-fascist 'Popular Front' movement, governments friendly to the USSR had been elected in France and Spain.

That is a retrospective insight based on studies published since the collapse of the system in 1991. In 1936, for Breslin and other intelligent observers who read between the lines of official communiqués and *Pravda* editorials, there were few grounds for comfort. Friends had been arrested, and the reverberations from the shots that killed Leningrad Party secretary Kirov on 1 December 1934 had not died away. The assassination led to draconian summary executions, the expulsion of 'oppositionists' (alleged supporters of Trotsky and Zinoviev, the former chairman of the Comintern) and *byvshie liudi* from the larger cities,[14] and to a new Party purge. The 1935 'cleansing' of the VKP(b) cohorts, unlike the preceding rake-outs (1920, 1929, 1933), had no time-limit and was to last until 1938. Arrests for 'counter-revolutionary crime', dropping from the high levels of the early 1930s, still reached a yearly average of 100,000 in 1934, 1935 and 1936.[15]

The considerable misgivings Breslin must have felt when he surrendered his Irish passport could only have deepened as the months of 1936 passed. His newspaper was losing ground to the exigencies of Stalinist propaganda, a situation taken to heart by Anna Louise Strong, who resigned from the board of *MDN* in October 1936. The occasion for her capitulation before *force majeure* was the first of the three great show trials of Stalin's former comrades-in-arms. The proceedings against the sixteen defendants, including ex-Trade Minister Kamenev and the former Comintern Chairman Zinoviev, opened on 19 August and ended, with sixteen capital sentences (death by shooting), five days later. Miss Strong was of the opinion, commonly held in the West, that it beggared belief when heroes of the Bolshevik cause confessed to the most heinous crimes in an open court. While aficionados of Kremlinology were aware of the various divergences from the Party 'line' committed by the prominent defendants in the past, the indictment was an implausible and primitive concoction: that Zinoviev and his consorts were acting on Trotsky's orders to seize power in the USSR and to assassinate the Stalinist leadership.

Under the heading 'The Terrorist Band Condemned', the *MDN* editorial of 2 September stated that the trial was just:

> There was the deepest feeling of indignation, the earnest and sober realization that the people guilty of such crimes should pay the full penalty of the law. And in this country, the law and the people are not at variance – they are one and the same.

In this atmosphere, during the trial, Breslin was to meet the woman he later married and hoped to follow to Ireland – Daisy McMackin.

NOTES

1. Sheila Fitzpatrick, 'The Great Departure. Rural–Urban Migration in the Soviet Union, 1929–33', in William G. Rosenberg and Lewis H. Siegelbaum (eds), *Social Dimensions of Soviet Industrialisation* (Bloomington and Indianapolis 1993), pp. 15–40, here pp. 22,24.
2. Hans-Henning Schröder, *Industrialisierung und Parteibürokratie in der Sowjetunion. Ein sozialgeschichtlicher Versuch über die Anfangsphase des Stalinismus (1928–34)* (Berlin 1988), p. 104.
3. See David Brandenberger, 'Soviet Social Mentalité and Russocentrism on the Eve of War, 1936–1941', *Jahrbücher für die Geschichte Osteuropas*, vol. 48, 3, 2000, pp. 388–406.
4. Paula Garb, 'The Forgotten Pages of Moscow News', *Moscow News Weekly*, no. 23, 1989, p. 16.
5. Anna Louise Strong, 'How Your Newspaper is Put Together', *Moscow Daily News*, 14 May 1932, p. 1.
6. I am grateful to Mairead Breslin Kelly for a copy of the tape she made of an interview with Mary Tsin in October 1993, and to Martin Grünberg (Vienna) who helped me with the transcription of the Russian dialogue.
7. National Archives of Ireland (NAI), S 50474B, Department of Justice to the Secretary, Department of the President, 29 October 1930.
8. Tom Bell, *Pioneering Days* (London 1940), pp. 47–53.
9. RGASPI, f. 495, o.18, d. 1085, l. 114.
10. For a humorous pen-portrait of Evans, see Alexander Werth, 'The Other Stratford', *New Statesman and Nation*, 10 April 1954, pp. 464–66.
11. RGASPI, f. 495, o. 218, d. 26, ll. 1–3.
12. National Archives of Ireland (NAI), DFA 202/458, note by Phyllis Ryan, M.Sc., n.d. [January 1938].
13. GARF, f. 10035, o. 2, d. 2988, l. 230.
14. Lesley A. Rimmel, 'A Microcosm of Terror, or Class Warfare in Leningrad:

The March 1935 Exile of "Alien Elements", *Jahrbücher für die Geschichte Osteuropas*, vol. 48, 4, 2000, pp. 528–51.

15. J. Arch Getty and Oleg V. Naumov, *The Road to Terror. Stalin and the Self-destruction of the Bolsheviks, 1932–1939* (New Haven and London 1999), p. 588 (Secret Police Arrests and Sentences, 1921–1939).

Life with Daisy

Pat Breslin's meeting with Margaret (Daisy) McMackin was not a chance encounter but took place at his request, through the offices of 'Santos' (not identified), a Lenin School graduate who brought the pair together in his room in Hotel Soiuznaia on Gorky Street on an August evening in 1936. Breslin had heard that an Irishwoman was working as a translator at ITIR, the Russian acronym for Co-operative Publishers for Foreign Workers in the USSR, the most important producer of foreign-language books in the Soviet Union.

They probably joked about not having bumped into one another much earlier, for Daisy had worked as a translator in Moscow four years before, from April to October 1932. Her love for the Russian language had grown over the years, at first a side interest that subsequently became her profession: she was the first woman in Ireland to teach Russian at university level and co-founded the Russian Department of Trinity College Dublin, where she worked as a lecturer from 1944 to 1969. This achievement was all the more remarkable considering the unpropitious circumstances of her upbringing. Born in Dungloe, Co. Donegal, on 12 March 1899 as the third of nine children, Daisy received her elementary and secondary schooling in Belfast. Her father, John McMackin, was a small landholder's son from Beragh, Co. Tyrone. Forced to work as a hired boy for prosperous farmers at the age of nine, McMackin later joined the Royal Irish Constabulary (RIC). The elder children were born in Dungloe or Ballymena, the younger ones in Belfast, after John had left the police for personal reasons. Money was scarce in the large household. His earnings as a bookie's runner were meagre; his wife, a trained dressmaker, also contributed to the family income.

Daisy supplemented the McMackin budget in Hawthorne Street from the age of thirteen, from her low wage as a 'mill girl' in a blouse factory. Since her eldest brother, Bernie, was very gifted and had received a scholarship to attend St Malachy's College, the nuns of the Dominican Convent on the Falls Road heard of the talented McMackin children and offered Daisy a free place at their school. She was an exemplary pupil, regularly winning monetary prizes from the Irish Educational Board and, at the age of seventeen, a three-year scholarship to attend Queen's University. Graduating in 1919 with a First Class Honours BA degree in Modern Languages (French and Irish), she was awarded a one-year studentship at the Sorbonne to study French and Celtic philology.

As a 21-year-old, Miss McMackin had already imbibed foreign culture and travelled abroad, embarking on a freelance intellectual career that was fraught with economic insecurity. Having to fend for herself from an early age, she had a strong sense of independence and very definite political views. Her interest in politics and social justice originated not so much in the world of books as in personal experience of the Irish struggle for independence. Her parents were nationalists, and at least three siblings were supporters of armed separatism. The death of her brother Bernie at the age of 20 in 1917, and that of the second brother, Charlie, during the great influenza epidemic a year later, were losses from which she never recovered. Bernie had written a 'seditious' newspaper article on the Easter Rising. During imprisonment in Frongoch Camp, Wales, with the participants of the rebellion, his health broke down and he died of tuberculosis shortly after his release. Annual visits to Rannafast in the Donegal Gaeltacht (Irish-speaking area), at first to learn Irish, became a source of emotional support for Daisy, who formed strong links with local families and writers like Séamus Ó Grianna.

It was not until 1925, however, that she found a circle of like-minded friends in the Irish capital. Teaching posts in Britain (Wolverhampton and Manchester), while the War of Independence and the Civil War were raging in her homeland, had not led to any strong emotional or personal attachments. Following a year of part-time teaching in Belfast in 1923, Margaret McMackin moved to Dublin, on the strength of a six-month teaching job. She never liked secondary school teaching; perhaps because she, for all her independence, was basically shy and had problems imposing discipline. She also found the religious orders haughty and snobbish, as she later recalled of her teaching at the Convent of the Sacred Heart at Mount Anville in the Dublin suburb of Goatstown.

McMackin shared a large flat at 21 Dawson Street, the address of the Radical Club, founded by Fred Higgins that very year. Her flatmates were as unconventional and politically radical as she was: Mary McCarthy, Kid Bulfin, Kathleen McLoughlin and Roisin O'Doherty, all of whom were to marry IRA leaders at the end of the decade. C.S. (Todd) Andrews, a future leader of Irish state enterprises but at that time a gauche Civil War veteran of 20, learned about culture, especially modern English and foreign literature, from the Dawson Street female intellectuals. He thus helped to free himself from the narrow puritanical code of his male comrades-in-arms embittered by the savagery of the Civil War:

> We held strongly to the social ethos of Republicanism in that, with one exception, we were puritanical in outlook and behaviour. We didn't drink [...] we disapproved of wearing formal clothes [...] we disapproved of horse racing and everything and anything associated with it. We disapproved of any form of gambling [...] we disapproved of anyone who took an interest in food. We ate our meals in the same spirit of detachment with which we dressed or shaved every day.[1]

Andrews, like most of the IRA men visiting the flat, had no income. He was treated to an evening meal two or three times a week, and to invigorating exchanges about politics, religion, theatre and literature. Kathleen McLoughlin, a Donegal woman with a degree in German, introduced him to the work of Thomas Mann and that writer's first great success, the novel *Buddenbrooks*, while Daisy McMackin recommended that he read Mauriac and the poetry of Hugo and Ronsard.[2] Andrews was greatly impressed by the slightly built Belfast linguist:

> Daisy MacMackin was a woman of exceptional intelligence. She was petite, with striking red hair and a beautiful speaking voice. [...] Her intelligence and scholarship were entirely subordinated to an immense compassion for all who were poor or lonely or sick or in any way underprivileged. All the energy which might have produced a great academic career was spent in helping the lame, the halt and the blind, and working to create a society which would willingly accept its obligations to the disadvantaged and to those constitutionally unable to cope with day-to-day living. Her heart was bigger than her great intelligence.[3]

The ménage of learned young women gradually broke up. In 1929, Daisy McMackin returned to Belfast and to part-time teaching, completing an MA course in Celtic languages. Back in Dublin in the early 1930s, she found the flat she was to occupy until her death in 1983, a second-floor apartment at 59 Grafton Street. She was now over 30, an age at which most of her friends had married, and without a steady income – the private lessons she now gave were hardly remunerative or intellectually satisfying. It was also the time of the Great Depression, a period which seemed, to some, to mark the final collapse of the capitalist system. Most of the communist militants in Ireland were ex-IRA members and she knew many of them, including Seán Murray and Peadar O'Donnell. The early 1930s also saw an upsurge in radical activities in independent Ireland, and the sitting Cumann na nGaedheal government, in collusion with the Catholic hierarchy, whipped up a 'Red scare' in the autumn of 1931. Despite the hysterical propaganda, the government was well informed of the minuscule extent of rock hard communist support. What generated more concern, if not outright panic, in the Cosgrave administration was the growing consolidation of the republican constituency, now represented in the Dáil by Fianna Fáil, and the drift of the more social-minded IRA members towards radical socialist policies.

Daisy McMackin was delighted when the February 1932 general election carried de Valera, with the support of the Labour Party, into office. She was probably present at the giant rally on St Stephen's Green on 13 March to 'welcome home' the IRA prisoners released from Arbour Hill military prison.[4] The political transformation did not improve her material situation in the short term, however, and she wanted to give her life a new direction, a novel challenge. She was keen to intensify her study of the Russian language, which she had commenced in Paris in 1920, so she arranged to live in Moscow for a few months. Peadar O'Donnell, who had started the agitation among small farmers against the payment of land annuities to the British Crown some years before in his native Donegal, was highly thought of in Moscow. He attended two conferences of the Comintern's peasants' organisation, Krestintern, in Germany in 1930 and was considered a gifted agrarian agitator and writer by the Soviet institution that offered McMackin a contract on the strength of his recommendation – the International Agrarian Institute, founded in 1925 as the think-tank of Krestintern.

Travelling on a British passport, Margaret McMackin left Ireland in late April 1932 with the delegation of Irish Revolutionary Workers' Groups invited to the First of May festivities in Moscow. English and Scottish delegates, some of whom, like Daisy, were involved in education joined them in London.[5] Her letters to Kathleen McLoughlin in Dublin (by now the wife of IRA leader Moss Twomey and soon to be the mother of a baby boy) suggest that she was, predictably, disorientated by her new surroundings, missed her friends and Irish newspapers (*The Irish Press, An Phoblacht, Irish Workers' Voice*) and remained a critical observer of what she saw and was told. She first wrote to Kathleen on 28 April from the Grand Hotel in Moscow, shortly before embarking on the delegation's tour of the country. She mentioned membership figures disclosed to her by the German staff at the Agrarian Institute in respect of O'Donnell's anti-annuities activities, adding, with some irony: 'People here think that P[eadar] is the future of Ireland.' The 'tentative programme' of the educationalists' tour included visits to Leningrad and Kharkov, with nine specific institutes to visit and three lectures to attend in the capital.[6]

Back in Moscow on 21 May, Daisy McMackin wrote to Kathleen McLoughlin that she had skipped the Leningrad leg of the tour and settled down to work. She dubbed herself 'prematurely aged', somewhat listless, and tired of being asked about her impressions of the vast country.

Her correspondence to Dublin is peppered with initials and vague references, partly as a ruse to circumvent the censorship authorities, who had let her know that writing in Irish was forbidden. Soon her thoughts ineluctably circled around the basic necessities of life – coping with the exasperations of living in a shortages economy. While her wage of 225 roubles monthly (roughly £3 a week) for a six-hour working day sufficed and there was always the possibility of earning supplementary income by teaching a foreign language, writing articles or translating into English, acquiring suitable accommodation and food, or battling with the vastly overcrowded transport system (the Metro did not go into operation until 1935) were constant sources of frustration.

Because Stalin had abolished the small private businesses allowed by Lenin after the privations of the Russian Civil War, it was well nigh impossible to get anything repaired, and Miss McMackin's fashionable shoes gradually disintegrated. Being a foreigner and the holder of the much sought after INSNAB booklet which entitled her

to shop in special stores at reduced prices, it seemed initially that the
grocery problem was solved. But she often gave up in frustration,
dreading the prospect of the rough-mannered buffeting in the queues
after she had stood in line often for an hour or more.

Finding a decent place to live was itself a saga. Knowing that she
would have to leave the hotel after the delegation had returned to
Britain and Ireland, Daisy applied for and was given a room in the
Agrarian Institute, an old building in Ulitsa Vozdvizhenka, a busy
street between the Lenin Library and the Arbat quarter in downtown
Moscow. However, there were no proper cooking or washing
facilities, and she had to traipse from one end of the building to the
other to fetch cold water. Her living conditions became even more
trying with what, at first glance, seemed to be an improvement: the
Institute was moving to a new building in the north-west of the city.
During the transit, the table and chairs of Comrade McMackin went
'missing', only to turn up, just as mysteriously, weeks later.
Nowadays near the metrostation Sokol, Ulitsa Peschanii was then a
string of new buildings out in the countryside, a 40-minute tram ride
from the centre. Since seats were invariably occupied, Daisy had to
stand and be jostled for about 80 minutes every day:

> The tram ride is disgusting, you cannot conceive how crowded the
> trams are and the people are abominable about seats – no such thing
> as manners, or even consideration for old people.

She sensibly stayed in town as late as possible in order to avoid a
further daily ordeal in the tram. She therefore had to find a place to
eat and to wash – a daunting prospect because of the insalubrious
hygienic and sanitary conditions. One of her favourite places to kill
time between appointments, or just to relax, was the lounge of the
Hotel National, the famous establishment at the end of Gorky
Street. While still at the institute, McMackin hoped that a job at the
MDN would pay more and provide accommodation. Seán Murray
accompanied her twice to talk to Anna Louise Strong. Daisy was
offered a one month's trial contract that entailed dictating at least
five pages daily on politics for a monthly salary of 250 roubles;
anything she wrote above that would be paid extra, up to a
maximum of 400 roubles. She did not feel ready for this right away
and feared losing her full-time job, and room, at the institute. The
editor acknowledged that this might be a distinct possibility, and

that the paper had no more apartment accommodation for its staff. Consequently, save for a handful of translations, Daisy's links with the paper remained tenuous. Had she agreed terms with Miss Strong, there was a fair chance that her stay in Moscow, which she deliberately left open-ended, might have lasted much longer and led to meeting Breslin in 1932.

For the 33-year-old Irishwoman the greatest problem in making friends was married couples' self-satisfaction: what she called, using her German, *die eiserne Front* (iron front). There were exceptions, like the German Rosa or May from Wales. The available men were, in her eyes, either physically or emotionally unattractive and usually married. Being told time after time that one was 'politically under-developed' was not a boost to a self-esteem growing ragged at the edges in a strange environment, even if what one translated was generally praised. Daisy seems to have had two crushes on German comrades, experienced revolutionaries whose stories reminded her of Todd Andrews' tales of the 'Munster Republic' in 1922/23. Erich flits in and out of the letters to Kathleen McLoughlin, but the Viennese professional revolutionary, Gerhard Eisler, turns up in each missive. Daisy fell in love with him, and he was interested in her conversation. Eisler valued her knowledge of Ireland and closeness to the communists there who were preparing to refound the CPI. Using her good knowledge of written German, she helped him to pen the article 'The Irish Free State and British Capitalism' (*The Communist International*, May 1932).[7]

The year 1932 featured one of the few occasions when the Comintern took an active interest in Ireland, believing in the 'objectively revolutionary' situation – the chance to exploit the new departure in the Irish separatist struggle in order to weaken British imperialism. However, there remained the task of 'unmasking' de Valera and his 'social reactionary character'. Eisler's article was nonetheless differentiated in that it recognised that de Valera had abolished the Oath of Allegiance, laid down in the 1921 Treaty, and had curtailed the remittance of land annuity revenues to London. These achievements, Eisler concluded, had been misread by the British *Daily Worker* newspaper, which attacked the Irish premier when the pro-imperialist press of Fleet Street was damning him from a right-wing standpoint.

Seán Murray, who sojourned in Moscow between mid-June and mid-August 1932 and kept in close contact with Daisy McMackin, saw to it that this Comintern line was maintained. In the letter to the CPGB drafted by him and Gerhard Eisler and adopted by the Comintern on 9 August, the following excerpt from the *Daily Worker* of 25 June was termed a 'vulgar distortion of the position, which entirely denies the national struggle, [...] indicative of the deep-rooted misunderstanding among class-conscious workers in Britain of the national question in general and particularly in regard to Ireland':

> The squabbles of Irish capitalism and British imperialism are not important in the form they take, or the acrobatics which are performed, for the British and Irish workers the enemy is the same, be it represented by de Valera, J.H. Thomas or Tutti-Quanti – capitalism. It is against capitalism that the workers must realise a United Front.[8]

Letters were also issued to the Comintern sections in Britain and the USA calling for the collection of funds for their Dublin comrades.[9] Murray made a good case for increased subvention and was granted $1,088 for the last quarter of 1932 in order to clear election and printing debts, and to pay the weekly wage bill of £5.[10]

Daisy liked Murray, a diffident Glens of Antrim man, and was not in awe of his position as Ireland's leading communist. Indeed, she laughed in his face when he suggested she take notes, for an official deposition to the Comintern hierarchy, from the economic history of Ireland written by the University College Dublin (UCD) academic George O'Brien: 'I said Dublin was the place to do that and extolled the Kildare Street Library.'

In fact, Daisy McMackin was still attached to the socialist republicanism of Frank Ryan or Tod Andrews, being sceptical of Muscovite directives on the 'Irish Question'. She was in two minds concerning her judgement of Liam O'Flaherty's *I Went to Russia* (1931), a humorous account of the writer's travels to the USSR in 1930, but all the same an unequivocally valedictory statement on the attachment to revolutionary Russia he had harboured in the early 1920s. O'Flaherty liked the Russians but disliked the functionaries and fanatics. She knew too much about the difficulties of coping with everyday life in Moscow to discount fully the Aran man's strictures. She refers to him in a letter to Kathleen McLoughlin, lines that show her ambivalence towards the Bolshevik experiment:

Now I find myself between two worlds and belonging to neither (I hope L.O'F. didn't say this but I believe he did). And I have decided that it is a great comfort to believe in Dia [God] .... After all, when you see nothing in front, what can you do but invoke some help! I think K.B. [Kid Bulfin?] is right in one thing she said about it – 'unspiritual' or to that effect.

She summed up her dilemma in the last letter to Kathleen in October, written on the eve of boarding the Berlin train:

> In the tram I felt myself 'mouthing' a phrase about 'the narrow sectarianism of C[ommunism]'and then I realised more definitely that that is what is wrong. On the one side I find myself turned wistfully towards Críostuigeacht [Christianity] and the Sermon on the Mount and with the R.C. [Church] and all its trimmings and mortal sins and marriage laws. Then 'the suffering exploited humanity' pulls you to the other side and you find yourself confronted with the new dogmas: 'only under the leadership of the C.P. etc.' with the C.P. insisting on destroying your Críost before recognising you as a developed adult. The path is straight and narrow the grave.

Little is known about Daisy McMackin's life after her return to Ireland and her second departure for the Soviet Union in April 1936. Finding a permanent job in the Ireland of the hungry 1930s was a fairly hopeless venture; her capital was her knowledge of several languages, her library and her dictionaries. Contacts to An Gúm, the government publishing house for books in the Irish language, led to contracts, mainly translations of Turgenev and Chekhov.

Despite her ambivalence about life in Moscow, Daisy stayed close to the communists, writing articles on the political situation in Belfast for *Irish Workers' Voice* and offering 'the comrades', as she always called them, her flat for meetings. Their headquarters at Great Strand Street had been destroyed in a two-day siege in late March 1933. The perpetrators, a vociferous mob fired by Catholic propaganda, went on to attack the Workers' College and Larkin's Unity Hall, meeting police intervention only after they had begun looting shops in O'Connell Street.[11]

The stifling atmosphere engendered by Catholic hegemony may well have prompted McMackin's second journey to the USSR. Her political world, the broad coalition of left republicans and communists, was falling apart: the IRA purged its ranks of communists in

1933 and leaders like Peadar O'Donnell and Frank Ryan resigned one year later. What was left of Marxist-inclined republicanism could not agree on political tactics, neither among themselves nor with the communists, thus destroying the Republican Congress movement of 1934 before it had a chance to get off the ground. The most passionate political confrontations since her return from the USSR were between republicans and blueshirts, the defeated and victors, respectively, of the Irish Civil War. This regeneration of the 1922–23 hatreds strengthened de Valera's electoral basis rather than the fragmented Left. The 'revolution', which in Ireland was primarily seen as a republican and not a social agenda, was now institutionalised.

Under these circumstances, the Soviet Union arguably became more attractive for intellectuals in Ireland. The worst sectarianism of Comintern politics was being replaced by broad alliances of the Popular Front, a policy approved by the 7th Congress of the Communist International in Moscow in 1935, which Seán Murray attended. The Soviet Union's entry into the League of Nations and the signing of a military assistance pact with France indicated that the vast country was tentatively moving away from hermetical isolation to a policy of peaceful coexistence with the Western democracies. Murray, now General Secretary of the relaunched Irish Communist Party, provided Margaret McMackin with the necessary letter for obtaining a job in Moscow. Further recommendations were required on arrival and later, especially to have the one-month tourist visa issued in London renewed and registered by the local police. Robin Page Arnot, the representative of the British Party in the Comintern, wrote the requisite documentation and named Jimmy Shields as a guarantor.[12] Shields was now working in the Cadres Department of the Comintern and probably first met Daisy when he attended the inaugural conference of the CPI in June 1933, and the Republican Congress meeting in Rathmines the following year.[13]

McMackin's employer, the Co-operative Publishing Society (ITIR), was situated in the centre of Moscow, behind Red Square in a beautiful Jugendstil building at Nikolskii Lane No. 7, a street with all the charm of Old Moscow. Founded in 1931, ITIR was a large enterprise, publishing on average 150 titles a year in a total print run of one million. Since the initiative to set up the enterprise had come from skilled German workers in Moscow, most of the titles issued between 1931 and closure in 1938 were in the German language. In early 1936 ITIR was divided into seven large language departments, an editorial group for educational books and thirty language sections. Its main purpose, of course, was to disseminate Marxist writings (Marx, Engels, Lenin and Stalin), programmatic speeches of Soviet leaders or booklets issued by the Comintern, followed by memoirs and novels.[14]

Comrade McMackin was allotted to the English Section, at a salary of 700 roubles a month. According to the questionnaire she completed for her employer, she could type two or three pages of translation hourly into her mother tongue, English (Irish was the second), from French or Russian. She did not mention her knowledge of German and was cautiously modest in not including Russian in the languages that she spoke freely. Her own reading of Russian at the time consisted mostly of Pushkin's dramas. She translated books and articles about contemporary social conditions and politics, specifically Pavel Kerzhentsev's *Life of Lenin* and accounts of expeditions to the Arctic.[15]

She remained true to form in that she rescued one 'lame duck' shortly after arrival. Jacob (Jack) Miller, a young man from a large Jewish family and a graduate of Sheffield University, struck up a friendship with Daisy on the steamer from Tilbury Docks to Leningrad.[16] He was the first English student to study the Soviet planning system at first hand, mainly on the strength of letters of recommendation from Beatrice and Stanley Webb, the 'Friends of the Soviet Union' and the Sheffield District Committee of the CPGB, all of which were confirmed by the British representative at the Comintern, as Soviet bureaucracy demanded.[17]

Miss McMackin had not taken up her position as yet, nor did she have a permanent address after one month in the Novo-Moskovskii Hotel. Like all newcomers to the capital, Miller and McMackin had to be 'written in' (registered) by the police in order to receive an official place of residence. The crux was a typical inanity of Soviet officialdom: arrivals in Moscow could be 'written in' only when they could confirm that they had employment. Neither the 23-year-old Briton nor the Belfast woman could do this straightaway because of bureaucratic delays. While Miller had to sleep where he could for three months, McMackin was fortunate to have temporary lodgings in Dom Pravitel'stvo (Government House), the 'House on the Embankment', immortalised in Yuri Trifonov's novel of the same name. This is where the Soviet elite lived in comparative luxury, and Daisy was given a room in a huge apartment. Her host was a woman eager to improve her English, the unmarried daughter of a prominent Bolshevik. Miss Solts was in charge of the procurement and allocation of railway sleepers for the entire railway system of the USSR, a prominent position within the Transport Commissariat. It was as yet a very 'safe' address, for her father, Aron Solts, who knew Stalin from the Petrograd underground before World War I and still addressed him in the familiar *ty* form, worked in the State Prosecutor's Office and was Chairman of the Party's Central Control Commission. He was generally known as 'the conscience of the Party' because of his integrity. He survived the Terror, but in a psychiatric hospital on account of his criticism of the widespread arrests in 1937.[18]

Miller slept on the floor in Daisy's room when he had nowhere to stay, slipping out at dawn to escape being discovered by the early-rising maid. He spent unduly long periods sitting on the lavatory bowl scrutinising the toilet paper, which consisted of the torn minutes of apparently high-level Party meetings.

For three long months he tried unsuccessfully to gain admittance to classes at the academy of Gosplan (state planning agency). His requests were rejected on security grounds, but he was offered a part-time paid post in August to teach the trainee planners English, and was given a bed in their hostel. In the intervening period, perhaps with Daisy's assistance, he was taken on by ITIR as a proof-reader. During his three months there, he noticed the growing condemnation of things foreign, and that the atmosphere towards Westerners had become yet more paranoid in the run-up to the August 1936 show trial. Until then, he remembers, 'bourgeois' British newspapers arrived freely at ITIR, but soon the incoming *Manchester Guardian* was in tatters, large gaps having been cut out by the censor. Shortly afterwards the only British newspaper in the translators' office was the *Daily Worker*.

During the hot Moscow summer of 1936, the city was in the grip of an epidemic of bloody dysentery. Jacob Miller, now in the student hostel, fell sick with high fever, but his colleagues were satisfied by the diagnosis of the local doctor that the Englishman was not suffering from anything serious. Fortunately, Daisy McMackin called on an unannounced visit and, seeing that her young friend was seriously ill, whisked him off to hospital. In a letter he was to write

60 years later to Mairead, Daisy's daughter, Miller acknowledged that this resolute action had saved his life. Their friendship deepened subsequently and Daisy told him of the searing loss she had suffered when her brother Bernie died in 1917. But there was good news as well, especially about her new love, Patrick Breslin. Miller's recollection of him is one of the rare testimonies of the short time the young couple spent together:

> I don't remember when I met Paddy Breslin. He and Margaret were obviously very much in love. I remember him as of medium height, beginning to bald, mid-thirties. I recollect the impression that he would have little time to waste on anyone other than Margaret.

It was a whirlwind romance – the first meeting in August and a registry-office marriage on 5 October. They lived in Room 8 at Hotel Soiuznaia (since demolished) on Gorky Street, just across the road from Hotel Lux, where Comintern staff and foreign communists were lodged.

Breslin still visited the flat of his ex-wife, Katya, at Ulitsa Ogareva 9, a short distance away, sometimes taking his daughter Irina to his Irish lessons in Daisy's hotel room. His interest in Irish and things Irish was naturally rekindled: he was – as Daisy confided to Miller – 'sick for Ireland'. His longing for the land of his youth was something he did not hide from Katya and her friends. Mary Tsin remembers him saying: 'I don't want to live in a country like this. I made a mistake coming here.' On another occasion, when Mary was shocked to see him intoxicated, Breslin shunned conversation, but finally pleaded, 'Let me go!' Irina still needed her father, and another child was on the way. Genrikh, called after the grandfather, was born six months after his parents had divorced. We can assume that this situation preyed on Breslin's mind and affected his new marriage. Both he and his Irish wife knew that it would be difficult for him to leave the country, seeing that he had two children who were Soviet citizens. The requisite exit visa might not be issued, even if he was still in possession of his Irish passport, which he was not.

Daisy and Pat shared a circle of friends – Jacob Miller, and his wife Sylvia, who started employment in a Moscow travel agency in 1937, Jimmy Shields and his wife Violet, Tom Bell, John Evans, other translators, Comintern functionaries like Max Raylock and English-speaking journalists. In February 1937, after four months of marriage, Daisy McMackin applied, through Robin Page Arnot, the British CP representative in Comintern headquarters, for an exit and re-entry visa.[19] The reason he gave was that she had to complete the Irish translation of the *Communist Manifesto*, something Murray had been badgering her about for years. Another version was that she had signed a contract for An Gúm to translate a book into Irish about the Young Ireland movement of the 1840s and was behind schedule in getting it completed.

We may speculate that there were other reasons for her interlude in Dublin, which was intended to last from April to June but which she had extended to August 1937. There is circumstantial evidence that the marriage was not going well. Husband and wife may have thought that a break in Ireland for Daisy, with the guarantee of re-entry to the USSR, would give them both time to think about their future. Breslin had visited the Institute of Neuropsychiatric Prophylaxis in 1928 'because of excessive irritability', and another psychiatrist five years later for the same reason. In 1936, alcoholic abuse on his part had led to 'night fears'. One way to combat the inner demons was to get out of Moscow, as in January 1937, when Daisy was still in the capital. On the advice of Tom Bell, Breslin travelled to Magnitogorsk, the steel centre in the Urals, to visit their mutual friend John Scott, an American engineer. The planned series of articles on this city of iron was never written, for Breslin fell ill and had problems finding accommodation. He adopted a similar strategy during Daisy's absence in Ireland, spending months in the warm climate of Abkhazia, the Georgian coastal strip around the port of Sukhumi. His articles about his travels for *MDN* (12 and 24 April, 18 July 1937) are well written but, considering the spirit of the times, uncritical of the collectivised farms he visited, especially the prosperous villages of German tobacco-growers and fruit-farmers.

In this wonderful climate the growing terror against foreigners was nevertheless an inescapable fact of life. Since the March 1937 plenum of the Central Committee, the newspapers were full of calls for vigilance against 'enemies of the people', catalogued by Stalin in his speech of 3 March. He revealed his murderous venom against foreigners, a potential Fifth Column as in Spain, alleging that 'the comrades had forgotten' that the USSR was surrounded by capitalist countries, states that were also combating one another by sending spies, murderers and saboteurs to cause havoc in other bourgeois countries. In typical catechetical fashion, Stalin posed the rhetorical question:

> Is it not clear that as long as the capitalist encirclement [of the USSR] exists there will continue to be present among us wreckers, spies, saboteurs and murderers, sent into our hinterland by the agents of foreign states?[20]

Breslin, while travelling through Georgia, learned that an ex-colleague, George Fles, had been arrested the previous August. Fles had worked with Breslin at the *MDN* in 1932–33 and settled in Georgia with his English wife, Pearl Rimmel. He had left his job at the newspaper, and other posts, because he had problems establishing the accuracy of his Party record in Germany, France and Britain. From a rich Jewish family in Amsterdam, Fles was sentenced to five years in the Gulag because of possession of 'Trotskyist' literature, magazines and pamphlets sent to him by his father and his English sister-in-law Anita, a member of the Independent Labour Party (ILP) in London.[21]

George Fles, it may be surmised, turned up in conversation between Pat and Daisy, and most definitely between her and Jack Miller, whose wife Sylvia was the sister of Pearl Rimmel. Miller involved himself in the case, by unwittingly providing Fles with 'counter-revolutionary' literature, and by sending parcels of food and clothing to Fles once he was in detention. By queuing for hours in long lines formed by distraught wives and mothers at the NKVD information office in Moscow, Jacob Miller saw the fallout of the mounting terror at first hand. Pearl Rimmel had returned to Britain to have her baby there shortly before her husband was arrested. As long as George Fles was sending letters from the Gulag, she played the loyal party member. She gave up pretending when her letters were returned with the stamp 'address unknown'.[22]

Daisy McMackin arrived in Moscow for the third time in August 1937. She could not have picked a worse time to live there. The campaign of mass arrests was beginning: 1.34 million persons were seized and 700,000 shot during 1937–38.[23] At the *MDN*, meetings were called to denounce 'saboteurs' on the staff, after Abram Lazarev, the head of the editorial office, had been arrested on 3 September.[24] For Anna Louise Strong, this was the last straw. She left for Spain, a revolution about which she could write with enthusiasm, and confided to an American friend:

> I would not go to the meetings of the Moscow News trade union which 'gave thanks' to the Soviet Power for removing the 'wreckers' from the staff, when I knew that these same 'wreckers' had been until yesterday considered our hardest working, most devoted people, and that nobody would tell us WHY they were 'wreckers' now [...] It was impossible for a person of American background to think that it was right that no civil liberties organization to investigate and defend such persons should exist.[25]

Among Breslin's friends arrested around that time were the Polish writer Bruno Jasensky, Mary Tsin and her husband Roman Kim. The couple, Katya's closest friends, survived the Gulag regime. Jack Miller, because of his British passport, felt reasonably safe. We cannot say whether Daisy, also the holder of travel documents issued by the British Foreign Office, felt personally threatened at first. At her publishing house fewer and fewer people were reporting for work; most, if not every single member, of the German section were hauled out of their beds in the dead hours by arrest squads of the NKVD.[26] Apart from the Germans, even in this early phase – arrests peaked in Moscow between November 1937 and March 1938 – Japanese, Korean and Bulgarian colleagues of Daisy were arrested on 'espionage' grounds.

Jack Miller had seen enough. At the trade-union meetings he was compelled to attend in the Institute of Planning Research within Gosplan, reference to the 'danger of imperialism' from Stalin's speech of 3 March was an obligatory part of the staged proceedings. Boris Troitskii, head of the Financial Planning Department of Gosplan and director of the institute where Miller taught, was hounded out of office and arrested in June 1937. Further meetings were called on 'the lessons' to be drawn from the arrest of this 'wrecker', but his successor, despite denunciatory speeches, soon disappeared as well. That was a typical characteristic of Stalinist terror: in contrast to the Nazi regime, there were frequently no sharp lines dividing perpetrators from victims. Far more disturbing for Miller than the bear-baiting atmosphere of the purge meetings was the pressure he was undergoing from NKVD agents to inform on other foreigners. Although he had still six months of his scholarship to complete, he left for Britain in November 1937. By then, in his own words, he had 'nowhere to stay and no heart for the place'.

Daisy McMackin embarked on the long journey home the same month. Perhaps she, too, had seen enough and hoped that her husband would escape before things got worse. Their future life together hinged on whether or not the letter he had penned in October 1936 renouncing Soviet citizenship would be accepted, thus leaving him free to return to Ireland. When talking to her confidantes at home, Daisy adhered exclusively to the obvious reason for coming back, namely that she was pregnant and wanted to have the baby in Belfast where she knew and trusted a doctor on the Falls Road. A Moscow doctor had voiced concern that she might have difficulties giving birth because of her slight build and suggested that she should have the baby among her own people in Ireland.

NOTES

1. C.S. Andrews, *Man of No Property* (Dublin, second edition 2001), p. 23.
2. Ibid., pp. 29–30.
3. Ibid, p. 28.
4. Conor Foley, *Legion of the Rearguard. The IRA and the Modern Irish State* (London 1992), pp. 105–6.
5. GARF, f. 5451, o. 13a, d. 442, microfilm 5.
6. GARF, f. 5283, o. 3, d. 195, l. 17.
7. Reprinted in the series issued by *The Cork Workers Club* in 1976.
8. RGASPI, f. 495, o. 4, d. 207, ll. 168–69.
9. Ibid, ll. 168–71, 207–10.
10. RGASPI, f. 495, o. 4, d. 205, ll. 6, 12–23.
11. *Communist Party of Ireland Outline History* (Dublin n.d.), pp. 19–20. For an official record of Communist activities, see *Notes on Communism in Saorstat Eireann*, November 1936, UCD Archives, McEntee Papers, P 67/523 (8).
12. RGASPI, f. 495, o. 14, d. 220, l. 65.
13. RGASPI, f. 495, o. 89, d. 90, ll. 39–40. See also his accounts of these conferences in *International Press Correspondence*, 18 August 1933, pp. 781–2; 12 October 1934. p.1,396.
14. Günther Schick, *Bibliographie deutschsprachiger Veröffentlichungen der 'Verlagsgenossenschaft ausländischer Arbeiter in der UdSSR'*, Moskau, Leningrad (Berlin 1992), pp. 1–6.
15. RGASPI, f. 495, o. 198, d. 557, ll. 3–4.
16. All information on Jacob Miller is taken from the biographical notes that he placed at the disposal of Mairead Breslin Kelly.
17. RGASPI, f. 495, o. 14, d. 220, l. 70.
18. Roy Medvedev, *Let History Judge. The Origins and Consequences of Stalinism* (Oxford 1989), pp. 429–30 (revised and expanded edition).
19. RGASPI, f. 495, o. 198, d.557, l. 6.
20. *Voprosy Istorii*, 3, 1995, pp. 5–6.
21. National Museum of Labour History, Manchester, file George Fles (translation of his NKVD file). I am grateful to Andy Flinn for copies and

information on George Fles. For more details on the Fles case, see Francis Beckett, *Stalin's British Victims* (Stroud 2004).

22. Alison McLeod, *The Death of Uncle Joe* (London 1997), p. 266.
23. J. Arch Getty and Oleg V. Naumov, *The Road to Terror. Stalin and the Self-Destruction of the Bolsheviks, 1932–1939* (New Haven and London 1999), p. 588.
24. Lazarev was accused of being a 'Japanese spy' and executed in Butovo, near Moscow, on 3 November 1937. See Lidia Golovkova (ed.), *Butovskii poligon 1937–1938. Kniga pamiati zhertv politcheskikh repressii, vypsuk chetvertyi* (Moscow 2000), p. 123.
25. Garb, 'the Forgotten Pages'.
26. Schick, *Bibliographie deutschsprachiger Veröffentlichungen*, p. 4.

Patrick Alone

Before Margaret McMackin returned to Ireland, she told Pat Breslin she felt she was 'leaving him to the wolves'. Her premonition proved true in several senses. The Stalinist terror she had seen at second hand did not abate. Her husband sent her press reports and brochures on the third major show trial (March 1938), which condemned to death Nikolai Bukharin and twenty other prominent Bolsheviks on the invented charges of spying for foreign regimes. The court body, the Military Collegium of the Supreme Court, in other sittings, also separately sentenced at least two of Breslin's colleagues.

Jakov Shvartsstein, the executive secretary at the *MDN*, was arrested on 1 December and shot dead two months later.[1] Rose Cohen was arrested in August and executed in November, as a 'resident-agent of British Intelligence'.[2] Her husband, David Lipets-Petrovsky, the ex-Comintern emissary to Britain and Ireland, was also shot. A NKVD arrest squad had seized him in March, and Rose, alone with her son Alyosha, had few visitors afterwards. One exception was Ivy Litvinov, the English wife of the Soviet Foreign Minister. Since Litvinov, too, was jeopardised because of his anti-German foreign policy and was soon replaced by Molotov, he tried to dissuade his wife from visiting Rose, who now was officially 'the wife of an enemy of the people'.[3] Following Katya's arrest in April 1938, the net seemed to be closing around Pat Breslin.

The fear of arrest, then, though rarely explicitly stated, overshadowed the Breslin–McMackin correspondence between January 1938 and late 1940. Both were well aware of the stringent Soviet censorship: neither correspondent wished to give the Russian authorities *prima facie* evidence of 'disloyalty' since that would undermine the husband's chance of leaving the country legally. This consideration prompted Daisy not to attract publicity to the case but to choose a strategy of using Irish and British diplomats, proceeding through official channels. Husband and wife frequently chose postcards to communicate with one another since letters were often confiscated. Daisy's communications to Moscow are not extant: they were destroyed by the Soviet secret police in 1941. The British Embassy file on Breslin's repatriation efforts fell victim to the bureaucratic whim of a Whitehall mandarin, who ordered its destruction when sifting through Foreign Office material in the 1960s.[4]

Breslin's correspondence to Daisy, and some letters from mutual friends to 59 Grafton Street, provide a chequered account of hoping against hope, of reassuring oneself and the loved one, of coping with day-to-day concerns in an atomised society. Poignant admissions of resignation and depression feature alongside humorous and tender expressions of affection.

Breslin's first letter, written just before Christmas 1937, announced a change of abode owing to a huge rent increase, and a recommendation that all post be sent to him *poste restante*. His main occupation in late 1937 and early 1938 was the translation of Stalinist drivel, solemn paeans written by 'national poets' in praise of the Soviet dictator. One verse from a Daghestan bard which Breslin translated reads:

> But I shall sing this in my lay
> Of him who every night and day
> Has lit our path with flaming ray
> Who ever guides us all – our Stalin![5]

The Irishman also had to translate the following chorus of a Ukrainian song:

> We are mounting ever higher,
> Striking in the foe dismay.
> Soaring like the sunlight eagle
> Stalin shows to us the way![6]

A welcome respite from such hagiographic dross was Breslin's preoccupation with the Georgian language, and with the Georgian national poet-hero, Shota Rustavelli. Extracts in English from his thirteenth-century epic 'The Knight in the Tiger Skin' appeared under Breslin's name in the *MDN* issue of 26 December 1937.

Breslin, lonely in the half-room he now occupied, a 30-minute tram ride from the city centre, found comfort in company. One of his closest friends was Max Raylock, who returned to Britain in

March 1938. Raylock, a Londoner and an expert on Ireland within the Comintern section responsible for the English-speaking countries, came to cheer Pat up with good food and drink. Raylock had his own kind of predicament, a state of suspension that demonstrates how difficult it was for even a trusted Comintern functionary to obtain an exit visa. Although his contract with the Communist International (CI) ended in June 1937, he was still waiting six months later and in danger of losing his living allowance.[7] The delay in processing visa applications was the result of the continuing terror. The Department of International Communications in the Comintern (OMS), which had done the necessary paperwork up to that time, was paralysed by arrests among its staff, and all requests to travel abroad were now in the domain of the NKVD.

Patrick Breslin, who had made formal requests to relinquish Soviet citizenship in October 1936 and December 1937, visited the British Consulate in early January 1938. Knowing that visitors to the Embassy were watched, he afterwards preferred to contact the British diplomats by telephone. Mr Macrae from the Embassy asked the Foreign Office on 10 January if Breslin, as he had requested in person, would be issued with a British travel document on being released from Soviet citizenship.[8] Downing Street sent a copy of the report to the Irish Department of External Affairs, with the request for an official Irish answer to the British Embassy in Moscow. In the meantime, Breslin had written about his latest repatriation attempt in a coded passage to his wife in Dublin:

> The Irish book I gave to the library cannot be returned. I shall have to get a new one. Some people here said they would see if it can be arranged. They have written to London but inquiries may have to be sent on to the people who published the book in Merrion Square in Dublin. I think O'Kelly is the name of the publisher.

The Irish Foreign Ministry was then situated in Government Buildings in Merrion Street, and O'Kelly was a reference to the Minister for Local Government and Tánaiste (Vice-Premier), Seán T. O'Kelly, whose wife, Phyllis Ryan, was a good friend of Daisy McMackin. Phyllis prepared a summary of the case for her husband, who, in turn, wrote to Seán Murphy of the Department of External Affairs. O'Kelly posed the vital question: 'Would Breslin be allowed to land here if he returns? That is the problem I want you to consider.' The reply from the Department of Justice (4 February 1938) was unequivocally negative:

> I am directed by the Minister for Justice to state that it is understood that Mr. Breslin became naturalised as a citizen of Soviet Russia during the year 1936, i.e. after the passing of the Irish Nationality and Citizenship Act, 1935, and, accordingly, under Section 21 of the Act, he is no longer a citizen of Ireland. He would not regain such citizenship on obtaining his release from Soviet citizenship, and in the event of his being so released, he would, it is thought, become a Stateless person. Applications by Stateless persons for travel documents are in the ordinary way made to the Government of the country in which such persons happen to be, and it would seem that the British Consulate at Moscow is not in a position to assist.

While the last sentence above did not subsequently prove to be true, the quoted section of the 1935 Act only stated the obvious, namely that any Irish citizen over the age of 21 who became 'a citizen of another country shall thereupon cease to be a citizen of Saorstát Eireann'. Furthermore, according to Section 15, marriage to an Irish citizen (Margaret McMackin) did not confer Irish citizenship on the 'party to the said marriage' who was not an Irish citizen (Patrick Breslin). Nor did the Act include any provisions for stateless persons or the reinstatement of former holders of an Irish passport to Irish citizenship. This was the crux of the matter, for, as Breslin wrote in a postcard to Daisy on 10 March: 'The emergency cert is an authorisation to go back without a passport. I need a formal statement that would be issued and that the old status [Irish citizenship] would be granted before I can make the withdrawal [from Soviet citizenship].'

On 19 March, British Dominions Secretary, Malcolm MacDonald, at the time embroiled in the long negotiations with de Valera on the Economic War and the Treaty Ports, found time to remind Dublin of his original, and as yet unanswered, letter on the Breslin case. The same day Daisy McMackin saw Seán Murphy at Government Buildings, on the initiative of Phyllis Ryan, who urged her to make the strongest possible case for her husband's repatriation. De Valera, in his second capacity as Minister for External Affairs, answered MacDonald on 28 March 1938, repeating the arguments of his civil servants, namely that Breslin would not regain Irish citizenship on giving up his Soviet passport, and that it was not clear what kind of travel document could be issued to the stateless Irishman by British diplomats in Moscow. His closing paragraph, stating more than the Merrion Street officials had previously advised, was presumably the result of interventions by the O'Kellys for Daisy:

> The Irish Government are, however, prepared to allow Mr. Breslin to enter this country if he can be provided with a document enabling him to travel to Ireland.

The summary of this answer was sent in the diplomatic bag from London to Moscow in early April. There the matter rested, at least in terms of diplomatic correspondence, until the outbreak of World War II. Daisy apprised Pat of the gist of de Valera's reaction, and Breslin felt Dublin was hedging, as his postcard of 7 April to Grafton Street makes clear:

> I don't understand how the question of Dublin issuing a travel certificate could have arisen. The whole point is to authorise the Sassenachs here. Until I get a promise of being restored to my original status I cannot make the withdrawal application.

Did the Irish do enough? What Breslin needed was a certificate from Dublin that he would be reinstated to Irish citizenship. Since there was no such provision in the 1935 Act, the Irish authorities did not countenance making such a promise, at least not in the official correspondence with Whitehall. Whether or not a letter on Saorstát notepaper signifying Breslin's readmittance to Irish nationality would have induced the Soviets to grant him freedom of passage is a moot point. The rule of law counted for nothing in Stalin's empire because the Party (and the police acting in its name) interpreted the law as it thought fit. For instance, regulations governing arrest, including the Politburo resolution of 5 January 1936 giving the Soviet Foreign Ministry the right to intervene in order to protect the rights of foreign citizens under suspicion,[9] were ignored during Ezhov's rule as head of the secret police (September 1936–November 1938).

The reinstatement document was a Soviet precondition before deciding on Breslin's application to renounce his Russian passport. However, it was no more than a ploy in a cruel cat-and-mouse game, for further conditions could be imposed at will: for example, that

Breslin had to stay in the USSR because his children were Russians, or that he was 'needed' as a presumptive 'accessory to the fact' because Katya Kreitser, his first wife, had been arrested as a 'Japanese spy'. Breslin's constant concern was for his Irish wife, her state of health and how she was faring emotionally and financially.

Another problem for Breslin and Daisy McMackin was that of coordination, with letters never arriving, or taking weeks to arrive, or that their coded content would be understood by the recipient. What does not surface in their correspondence, or indeed in the dispatches emanating from British or Irish departments of state, is Daisy's possession of a British passport or Breslin's place of birth, London. Could the repatriation case have been facilitated by the fact that both, born before the Irish Free State came into being, were entitled to British citizenship? Probably not, for Breslin could not have changed his Soviet citizenship for a British one, seeing that he had chosen an Irish passport when travelling to Moscow in 1928 and had given it up, albeit reluctantly, when he applied for Soviet papers in 1936. He could not change horses in mid-stream, even if he had two reserve mounts.

A more general problem was that of mentality, of comprehension. Very few people in the West had the information or the lurid imagination to understand what daily life meant for a practically stateless foreigner in the Moscow of 1937–38. Some government ministers in Dublin were sympathetic to Miss McMackin because of her good republican credentials, and there may have been residual sympathy within de Valera's Old Guard for the Russian Revolution. Indeed, the man responsible for questions of citizenship, Justice Minister Gerry Boland, had led an IRA delegation to the USSR in 1925.[10] Officially, Ireland had no diplomatic relations with the Soviet Union, and no intention of establishing such links in the face of the strong anti-communist opinion fostered by the Church triumphant. Interventions for Breslin, then, were always at one remove – via Britain.

The British consular staff in Moscow, for all their elitist views – 'public school prospectuses in the waiting room proclaimed the old world' (Jacob Miller) – knew what was afoot. Some of their Russian-born staff, drivers, laundrywomen and typists, stopped coming to work in 1937–38. Nina Bengson from Odessa, for example, who worked as a translator in the consular department, was arrested in September 1937, and executed on 'espionage grounds' two months later.[11] The British Consulate staff therefore knew the dangerous world outside their aristocratic palace on Vorovsky Street and, appreciating Breslin's vulnerability, issued him with a statement of information on 9 May to the effect that he would be issued an emergency travel certificate by the British Crown as soon as the Soviet authorities granted his withdrawal from Soviet citizenship. An obstacle, it seems, had been removed, but the waiting game continued.

In February 1938 *MDN* ceased daily production and was henceforth issued as a weekly and renamed *Moscow News*. That meant the end of night shifts for Breslin, but also fewer commissions. One of his first pieces for the Saturday tabloid-format was the translation of a dramatic poem (20 April 1938) on the founder of the *cheka*, 'Iron Feliks' Dzerzhinskii, who, unlike most fellow-members of the Bolshevik elite, died from natural causes, in 1926. That this sinister figure was accorded a whole page in *Moscow News*, as had also been the case in respect of Ezhov the previous November on the twentieth anniversary of the founding of the *cheka*, was in keeping with the times – eulogising the executors and executioners of the Terror. Other foreign-language papers (*Deutsche Zentral-Zeitung* and *Journal de Moscou*) were restructured in content and form to win foreign subscribers and to function as unofficial propaganda sheets of the Soviet Foreign Ministry. Since foreigners resident in the Soviet Union were prospective Fifth Columnists, the need for newspapers to cater for their interests belonged to the past.

Breslin was enjoying a paid holiday at a writers' rest home in Kuntsevo just outside Moscow, especially enjoying the excellent food and the absence of the usually obligatory morning physical training at Soviet holiday homes, when he was called back to the capital. An NKVD arrest squad had called to the house at Ulitsa Ogareva 9 on 20 April 1938, pounding on the door of apartment No. 52, the home of Katya and her children. Irina, not yet four, was playing outside in the snow when the nanny called her in. The men, she was told, were taking her mother to the police station for a short talk. According to Genrikh Kreitser, who saw his mother's prosecution file, Katya, and roughly thirty other Japanese experts, were denounced by an over-vigilant female colleague. Using an agreed code, Breslin informed Daisy of the disaster, and of the dangers he was facing:

> Shura's girl has been unwell. She was taken to hospital the day before yesterday. If it should happen that I stop writing you must continue to get everything settled, at least in principle, for the future.

He now moved back into the old flat to look after the children, assisted by Mrs Kreitser, who had hurried down from Leningrad. To escape the noise of the playing children, Breslin spent part of the day in the tearoom of the Hotel National, translating poems. Now, however, there was very little work at *Moscow News* and not even enough money to send Daisy the books she needed. On some evenings he met John Evans, Jimmy Shields or John Gibbons for a beer. Gibbons, another ex-shipyard worker from Scotland, had studied at the Lenin School in 1930–31 and later found work in the English-language section of Radio Moscow.[12] Breslin undertook daily translating stints at the radio station, but was never taken on the permanent staff. In late May 1938 he lodged a new passport withdrawal application, which this time included the British note promising an emergency travel certificate. It was an existence in a Kafkaesque antechamber – waiting for Katya to return home, waiting for his release from the bondage of Soviet citizenship, waiting for job contracts and, most importantly, in early summer, waiting for news from Belfast, where Daisy was staying with her sister Edith and expecting her baby.

Mairead was born there on 8 June. A telegram, a copy of the birth certificate (for the Soviet authorities) and snapshots of the baby girl delighted Pat. The good news increased his longing and concern, for Daisy had had a difficult birth, was confined to bed for two weeks and suffered one of her recurrent glandular upsets during the summer. Work at the radio station (translating play dialogues and poetry) was intermittent, and he thought fondly of old times when a recital of Irish songs was transmitted, including John McCormack singing 'Annie Laurie'. Translation work came in dribbles, mainly of poetry, for the English-language propaganda magazine *Soviet Land* and for anthologies. His occasional pieces for *Moscow News* reflected the spirit of the times, fostering war-preparedness:

> We'll shoulder our rifles and sharpen our lances
> And march in the shade of the banners of red –
> Uzbeks and Kazakhs and Tajiks and Turkmenians
> And the threescore of tribes who arose from the dead![13]

Fortunately, he found some respite from propaganda, grappling with Mayakovsky's verses and those of the Ukrainian national poet Taras Shevchenko, or, for the first time, trying his own hand at versification. For a year or more, it seems, the children stayed with their grandparents in Leningrad. Breslin's desperation and loneliness grew with the onset of the long Russian winter. Newspapers from Dublin were no longer arriving and he began to explore another line of escape, a last resort – appeals from his mother and Daisy to President Kalinin. For the time being, however, he clung to the official solution in missives to Grafton Street:

> If the answer [from the Russians] is unfavourable, which I hope I can let you know, or if I stop writing for a long time, perhaps you could get Seán [T.O'Kelly]'s people to induce the Sassenachs to issue a travel certificate on the strength of the fact that re-instatement would follow a period of residence. I don't think it's likely but if John [Breslin] does go to Bridewell [prison] to join Bob [Boris Kreitser] and his sister, you must not worry.

There was still no response from the Soviet Interior Ministry regarding his application to renounce his Soviet passport. He was informed in January 1939 by a Russian bureaucrat that the emergency travel certificate must be issued before he could be officially released from Soviet citizenship. The British and the Irish, as remarked earlier, had made it clear that the order of things was the exact opposite. And, of course, one other condition was not likely of fulfilment then or later – that he be given back his Irish citizenship. His position was further complicated by the arrest of Katya, from whom he had heard nothing in months.

Then, in February 1939, the correspondence from Breslin to Dublin tapered off, with a break of half a year. He had given up hope and once more started to drink heavily as Daisy learned in April 1940 from his friend Virginia Soermus:

> When you told him you thought you were 'leaving him to the wolves' you had no idea how hellishly true it was. Twelve months ago, when we first knew Pat, he was terrible – a real disreputable, down and out drunkard – my God! You have no idea what he looked like: ragged, unshaven, shaky and staccato-like movements.

His 'vodka bout' lasted for three months in 1939, and was followed by a year of abstinence from hard spirits. Gordon Cashin, an American news correspondent and a recent friend of Breslin's, sent Daisy welcome news of her husband via Helsinki in June 1939: Pat was in good health and getting by on what he earned; the attitude to foreigners was improving; Katya's case was still under review by the state prosecutor, and she might be released, as were many others in the wake of the 1937–38 Great Terror; the stateless Irishman now advised his wife to have the British Embassy make an official inquiry to the Soviets as to the status of his case, which might expedite the decision about his release from citizenship, and to have his mother Christina make a similar request via London somewhat later. Shortly afterwards, Breslin wrote to Grafton Street, stating that he was well and promising to explain his long silence, because of bad health, in greater detail at their first meeting. For her part, Daisy McMackin initiated a flurry of correspondence in August between Dublin and the Irish High Commissioner in London, who pressed the Foreign Office for news on the Breslin repatriation case. On 4 September 1939, the day after Britain's declaration of war on Germany, Pat sent Daisy a postcard to inform her that the British Embassy had contacted him, and that Katya was still in a Moscow prison. He was in good health, he added in a humorous postscript, even though the ceiling of the bathroom in the flat had fallen on his head.

The British reply of 3 October, which took a month to reach Dublin, stated that Breslin had neither contacted the Embassy for eighteen months nor reacted to the letters it had sent him. His reply to their September 1939 letter had been intercepted by the secret police. Mr Trant of the Embassy saw three possible reasons for Breslin's silence: he had changed his mind about relinquishing his Soviet passport, he was being forcibly prevented from doing so, or he was being stopped from contacting the British diplomats at all. Trant surmised that Breslin had severed ties to home because he was not known to the chaplain of Moscow's only Catholic church, but he deduced that the Irishman was still in Moscow since a translation of his had appeared in the *Moscow News* of 25 September. The last verse of the enclosed translation (a Belarussian folk song) could have applied to his own longed-for homecoming:

> The way to your cottage
> We know very well,
> So now we will often
> Be ringing your bell.
>
> Each time there's a baby
> We'll come with a present,
> We'll sing and make merry
> And all will be pleasant

Mr Trant suggested that Daisy be asked if she was still receiving communications from her husband:

> If such a disposition is manifest it might be considered worthwhile to help him further; but if he has ceased communicating with his wife it would seem that any further intervention on our part would be pointless and unavailing.

Frederick Boland of the Department of External Affairs sent a précis of the British note to Daisy, and to Seán T. O'Kelly. She waited for news from Pat before visiting Boland. The postcards from Moscow, taking a month or more to arrive at Grafton Street, contained bad news, despite the tender packaging:

> I was told yesterday [21 October 1939] that my application has been rejected. Don't take it too much to heart as I shall keep on until I succeed, as I am sure I will in time. I have already written to Kal[inin], asking for the case to be reconsidered, and for a personal interview. I'm sure, anyway, that when the war is over, you will do your best to stay here for a while, if I don't succeed by then. Naturally I am disappointed, but I am keeping my heart up. I am longing to see you and our baby and I often dream of you and Dublin. I have plenty of work and that will help to keep my mind occupied.

Since Patrick Breslin's naturalisation file has not been found in the State Archive of the Russian Federation (Moscow), the official reason for the rejection is unknown. Perhaps there was none, and he was certainly not told why. Each subsequent postcard sent by him in the early winter of 1939/40 contained reminders that Daisy, too, should make an appeal to the aged Soviet President. When she met Frederick Boland on 8 December, Daisy said it was 'undesirable for the British Embassy to pursue their enquiries on behalf of her husband, having regard to present Soviet feelings against Great Britain'. That was a reference to the Hitler–Stalin Pact of 22 August and the *volte-face* in Soviet diplomacy. Now Britain was, like France, a 'plutocracy', engaged in an 'imperialist' war against Germany. She thanked the Department of External Affairs for the action it had taken on her behalf and requested that no further steps be taken until her next visit. Knowing that many of her letters had never reached Breslin's *poste restante* pigeon-hole in Moscow's General Post Office, she mentioned to Boland that she was sending her husband a letter via Maisky, the Soviet Ambassador to Britain.

Nothing further of note happened in the case for a whole year. Breslin hoped that Kalinin would accede to his request if and when the grandparents were granted adoption of Irina and Genrikh and had them registered in their own passports. But the children, too, were hostages, following their mother's sentencing in December 1939. They subsequently experienced traumatic years in one of the orphanages for children of 'enemies of the people', before being fetched by Mary Tsin in 1944. Their mother, Katya, was no ordinary Gulag *zek* (prisoner), but a *sharashka* (scientific work) inmate, forced to carry out her translations behind barbed wire or prison walls. On New Year's Eve 1938, while she was still denying the 'espionage for Japan' indictment, Katya wrote a poem in a communal cell of Butyrka prison. Since it later turned up in Breslin's NKVD file, she probably wrote it for him:

> Our horizon smells of Lysol fluid
> Hemmed by the cluster around the WC bucket
> Prison. Only in our songs are sun, air and fresh ozone.
>
> Walks around the lawn of stone,
> Carrot tea in the celebratory cup,
> For dinner cheap porridge of pearl barley,
> And leaden sleep in the airless night
>
> Not forever, our disaster, I am sure
> Or the slanders loaded with guilt like baggage.
> Sweep them away like noisome rubbish!
> I'll take any sentence passed
> And I fault you not, Comrade Homeland,
> In my musings.

The three verses are an expression of 'Soviet patriotism': the system was worth fighting for, her imprisonment was a 'mistake', the result of malicious denunciations. This was not an avowal which Breslin could have shared, even at the best of times together with Katya, and certainly not during the Great Terror.

In the second year of war, Breslin's circle of friends was beginning to thin out. Shields was back in Britain and many other English-speakers had returned to isolationist America or the Britain of the 'Phoney War'. John Evans remained a true friend, inviting Pat to his summer *dacha* or to long literary discussions over afternoon tea in a Moscow hotel. Breslin, not wanting to burden his friend any further with his personal problems, called Evans less frequently in 1940. The children had returned to Moscow, but Breslin sometimes stayed with the musicians Virginia and Eduard Soermus in order to write in peace. They had more or less adopted him despite his occasionally wayward and self-destructive behaviour.

The winter of 1939/40 was the harshest in Moscow for a hundred years, adding to Breslin's gloom. Ireland was never far from his thoughts, especially on Christmas Day, when he listened to the King's Speech and Ulster folk-singers on the BBC. The Kreitser flat was up for subletting after Katya's sentencing. Pat Breslin hoped that it could be exchanged for one in Leningrad once Mrs Kreitser had officially adopted the children, who left for the Northern capital with their grandmother. Their father wrote often and sent them each a pair of *valenki*, the wonderfully warm and expensive felt-boots for the snow and slush. However, the guardianship application on behalf on the children was getting nowhere, and no answer had arrived from Kalinin's secretariat. Breslin had to concede one room in the Ogareva apartment to a new tenant, a female lawyer. He was now resigned to the prospect of not seeing Daisy until after the war, if ever.

Following several bouts of influenza, Pat Breslin had a nervous breakdown in the late spring of 1940. He was probably under-nourished, not looking after himself and was drinking excessively again. By July 1940, as he wrote in a long-promised letter to Daisy, he was back in harness, 'hardly drinking at all' and working at Radio Moscow. He enclosed a children's book he had translated, *The Telephone* by Korneus Chukovsky. Another translation he fashioned at this time was included in Herbert Marshall's anthology of Mayakovsky's poetry published by The Pilot Press in London: the poem for children 'What is "good" and what is "bad"', a whimsical piece:

Tiny toddler told his Dad:
'I am puzzled so!
What is good and what is bad?
Answer if you know!
Secrets I will always shun –
Nothing could be worse!'
All the Papa told his son
I have put in verse . . .

'If the boy is black as pitch,
If his face has dirt on,

Then his skin is bound to itch –
And that is bad for certain.
If the boy likes soap and water,
Toothpaste, brush and comb,
Then he's very good and ought to
Be a pet at home...

All must grow from small to big –
Nothing ought to baulk us.
Boys are bound to grow up pigs
If the boys are porkers.'
Tiny toddler understood.
Tiny told his dad:
'I will always do what's good
Never what is bad.'

Breslin now spent much time at the flat of the Soermus couple on Leningrad Chausee, moving in their circle of musicians and intellectuals. There he met a certain Ivan R., who, knowing of Breslin's plight, said that he could arrange his escape to Afghanistan through the offices of a district party secretary he knew in Tajikistan. The smuggling fee was 1,000 roubles. Breslin did not pursue the matter, probably sensing that the man was an *agent provocateur* of the NKVD. Communicating his thoughts to Dublin in coded or open form became more difficult in the wake of the Nazi victories of May–June 1940 in France and the Low Countries, with post and travel to Britain being rerouted via America.

Virginia Soermus, a concert pianist, departed from Moscow just before the Western Blitzkrieg, to nurse her ailing mother in Welwyn Garden City, Hertfordshire. In her letters to 59 Grafton Street, Virginia urged Daisy to ask the British Embassy in Moscow to take up Pat's case again, a tactic the Irishwoman was reluctant to pursue in view of the strong anti-British trend of Soviet foreign policy. Following this advice and a cable from her husband in August ('Keep up heart. All my love. Pat.'), Daisy McMackin visited Frederick Boland on 20 September 1940, requesting him to send her letter to President Kalinin through diplomatic channels. On this occasion, however, British assistance was not requested, the letter being handed to the London Embassy of the USSR by the Irish High Commissioner. The Department of External Affairs sent two enquiries to the High Commissioner in October before learning that the letter had been accepted, with the promise from Soviet consular staff that it would send on confirmation that the appeal of Miss McMackin had been delivered to the Kremlin.

Patrick Breslin was unwittingly in close contact with British diplomats in the late summer of 1940, for the new British Ambassador, the Labour politician and noted lawyer Sir Stafford Cripps, and Lady Cripps, were friends of the Soermus couple. Eduard Soermus fell seriously ill, and died in a Moscow hospital on 17 August. Since Pat was a close friend and looked after the couple's flat, he reported to Virginia by cable on the course of the illness, and of Eduard's death. Stafford Cripps spoke personally to Breslin shortly before Eduard's demise, sending his personal limousine to bring the Irishman to the Embassy to discuss the possibility of Virginia Soermus coming to Moscow to be with her dying husband. The arrival of the Embassy car at 120 Leningrad Chaussee was duly noted by the secret police, and the identity of its passenger. Police touts also informed the Lubianka about one of Breslin's raucous nights out during the following month – in the Cocktail Hall on Pushkin Square he had sung 'God Save the King'. We may assume that his friends were shocked, as was he himself when he realised the provocation of singing the national anthem of a country hostile to the USSR. By November he had decided he must change his ways, signing himself into the psychiatric hospital on 11 Radio Street to 'dry out'. John Scott, his engineer friend who had left Magnitogorsk to become *News Chronicle* correspondent in Moscow, lent Pat money and presented him with a fashionable suit to cut a good figure with the hospital staff. At this juncture Scott was as disillusioned as Breslin, shocked by the mass arrests of 1937–38 and remained in Russia until 1941 only because of his Russian wife and child. In Scott's masterful study of Soviet industrialisation, published in 1942, the author's résumé was bitter:

> Westerners have no place in Russia [...] Men and women from Western Europe and America may occasionally succeed in under-standing it, but it is almost impossible for them to fit into it.[14]

In one of her replies (postcard of 4 December) to Pat's telegram of 28 October ('Please send some message Love Patrick Breslin'), Daisy mentioned Mairead's great vocabulary, some of their mutual friends and that there was still no news of Frank Ryan, the Irish Republican taken prisoner by fascist troops in Spain in March 1938. Writing on

20 January 1941, Daisy voiced her anxiety that she had not heard from Pat since his cable. Informing him of Mairead's progress ('very intelligent, but not annoyingly precocious'), of the Christmas celebrations at Kathleen Twomey's and of a meeting with Harry Kernoff, she reminded her husband of their good times together in Moscow. Putting a brave face on their intractable separation, Daisy ended on an encouraging note:

> This waiting is so long that one gets discouraged, but after all we'll have good days yet. I am always regretting that you can't see your 'marvellous child', as some of the habitués jokingly call her. Best love from us both – & keep your head on! Margaret

Her postcard was returned in April, her January letter in July, both stamped *retour non réclamé*.

NOTES

1. Eremina and Roginskii, *Rasstrel'nye spiski*, p. 443.
2. RGASPI, f. 495, o. 198, d. 733, l. 3. For an account of the Cohen case, see Barry McLoughlin, 'Visitors and Victims. British Communists in Russia between the Wars', in John McIlroy, Kevin Morgan and Alan Campbell (eds), *Party People, Communist Lives. Explorations in Biography* (London 2001), pp. 222-23.
3. J. Carswell, *The Exile. A Life of Ivy Litvinov* (London 1983), pp. 207–8.
4. Records Branch, Foreign and Commonwealth Office, to British Embassy, Vienna, 1 February 1994.
5. *Moscow Daily News*, 24 November 1937, p. 3.
6. *Moscow Daily News*, 7 November 1937, p. 19.
7. RGASPI, f. 495, o. 14, d. 243, l. 179.
8. NAI, DFA 202/458. All references to Anglo-Irish cooperation in the Breslin repatriation case are taken from this file.
9. RGASPI, f. 17, o. 162, d. 19, l. 24.
10. Michael McInerney, 'Fianna Fail Grows to Full Power' (Part Four of the Gerry Boland Story), *Irish Times*, 11 October 1968.
11. Eremina and Roginskii, *Rasstrel'nye spiksi*, p. 43.
12. RGASPI, f. 17, o. 98, d. 780, l. 1.
13. *Moscow News*, 1 May 1938, p. 11.
14. John Scott, *Behind the Urals. An American Worker in Russia's City of Steel* (Bloomington and Indianapolis 1989), pp. 248–49 (enlarged edition prepared by Stephen Kotkin).

Interrogation

R adio Street, still the site of the psychiatric hospital, is situated in an idyllic part of Old Moscow. The district, away from the frenzied traffic of the multi-laned Garden Ring, grew around the estate of Francis Lefort, the Geneva-born soldier, sailor and diplomat who was the closest friend of Peter the Great in the early eighteenth century. Radio Street stops at the bridge over the Iauza, a winding tributary of the Moskva which skirts Lefortovo Park. After the bridge, Red Barracks Street climbs to the east before turning right to meet an arterial road. In a side street near the Aerodynamics Institute is Lefortovo gaol, originally Lefort's palace, later a military and today a high-security prison.

Patrick Breslin probably walked this area in the short daylight hours of the early winter of 1940–41, during the intervals between tests and medical consultations, visiting Lefortovo Park and its three ponds. From his apartment he had taken a slim volume of Russian fairy tales he had been commissioned to translate, his address book, some notebooks and a photograph. During Christmas Week 1940 the 'organs' of State Security in the city of Moscow (UGB) decided to arrest the Irishman. It was a relatively quiet time for the secret police after the bloodbaths of 1937–38. The NKVD had been purged of Ezhov's paladins, and those remaining had received a huge hike in pay, part of the 'professionalisation' of the service after Lavrenti Beria's promotion to landlord of the Lubianka headquarters in late 1938. The total of 'political' arrests had fallen from 640,000 in 1938 to 70,000 in 1940.

The 3rd UGB Department, responsible for 'counter-espionage' in the capital, sifted through the informers' reports on Patrik Frantsevich Breslin. In typing up the 'resolution to arrest' on 19 December, Second Lieutenant Gandraburov of the 4th Section of the 3rd UGB drew on a plethora of sources to justify the issue of an arrest warrant: Breslin's expulsion from the Lenin School, his denial of a 'materialist outlook', the arrest of his first wife for 'spying for

Japan', his links to the British Embassy and, finally, remarks and passages in letters of an incriminatory nature. Breslin's statement that 'it is better to be an interned British citizen than a free Soviet one' was interpreted as strongly anti-Soviet. 'Suspicious' was also a sentence in a letter from his wife signifying an intervention strategy based on Dublin rather than London sources: 'I think we are both working for the nation.' Gandraburov also saw a sinister hidden meaning in a letter sent by the British Embassy to Breslin's room at Ulitsa Ogareva 9, in which it was suggested handing over some of the musical instruments from the estate of the 'Red Violinist' Soermus to Soviet musicians.

The warrant, issued the next day and containing the correct spelling of Breslin's patronymic (Frantsisovich), directed Comrade Shinin to arrest and search the suspect Irishman. Shinin and Gandraburov arrived at the clinic in Radio Street at 2 a.m. on 21 December 1940. The procedure took an hour and was witnessed by a doctor and the hospital janitor. A list was made there and then of Breslin's personal effects, a document countersigned by him and the witnesses. These personal documents were sealed in a separate package and sent to the 7th UGB, the unit for analysing coded material.

The arrest party and their prisoner left in one of the NKVD's American sedans or, if the night was busy, in a *chernyi voron* ('Black Raven'), the Soviet 'Black Maria', a truck with six inner cells and camouflaged as a food delivery van. The journey did not take long in the dead of the Moscow night. Stopping at the back gate of the Lubianka (Inner Prison No. 1), the vehicle passed through two further gates and halted in a courtyard. Breslin was led into the reception area, where his fingerprints and photographs (front and side view) were taken before he was conducted to the shower room and the medical inspection. He looked remarkably well for somebody suffering from alcoholism and an interrupted night's sleep: a handsome, sensitive face, a steady gaze from strikingly blue eyes, the receding hairline of a man in his mid-30s dressed in an elegant white suit over an open-necked shirt. He was then searched and given a receipt for his meagre belongings: 10 roubles and 25 kopeks, a shirt and a belt.

The Polish poet Aleksander Wat, transferred to the Lubianka from Kiev in late 1940, was amazed by the comparably correct behaviour of the staff in this main prison: polite, reassuring ('Your case will be cleared up and you'll be released'). Wat's one-man cell was narrow but clean, the food well-cooked, but the portions were inadequate. At the beginning, five cigarettes were even issued to him daily. After three days Wat was transferred to a communal cell (No. 34), a room of twelve square metres for four prisoners, with an iron bedstead and night-locker for each, and a samovar (for making tea) on the table by the window.[1] For most prisoners, however, the sojourn in the Lubianka was short because they were transferred to a general prison for investigative custody inmates (Taganka, Butyrka) after the first interrogation. In all Soviet prisons, the prisoner's file accompanied the transit detainee since the investigating officer's rooms were in the same building, generally on the upper floors. The Lubianka prison, at the core of NKVD headquarters, was demolished after Stalin's death. It had space for 570 prisoners in 1940, a relatively modest total compared with the capacity of 3,500 for the Butyrka.[2] Breslin was first lodged in cell No. 4 in the Lubianka, presumably on the ground floor. Toilets were in the corridor; exercise took place (twenty minutes daily, usually at night) on the roof atop the six stories, within a concrete box surrounded by six metre high walls.[3] On arrival, Breslin had completed the prisoner's questionnaire in which he gave biographical details of himself, his Irish family, his wives and his three children. Either from a warder or from the copy of the prison regulations hanging on the cell wall, he would have learned that prisoners under pre-trial investigation were allowed to sleep only between 10 p.m. and 6 a.m. The bright light in the cell was never turned off; the prisoner, if seated, was expected to face the door; the peephole was opened regularly, mainly to check that the inmate was not trying to sleep on the stool.

The interrogating officers, called investigators (*sledovatelia*), were dressed in smart uniforms, including a Sam Browne belt and highly polished riding boots. Their blue collar flashes and blue cap band made them instantly recognisable as the elite of the secret police. State Security (GB–Gosudarstvennaia bezopasnost') officers had a special ranking system, starting from sergeant and ending at major, being two steps below the corresponding Red Army ranks. The majority of interrogators were sergeants or lieutenants and earned between 1,500 and 2,000 roubles per month in 1940, which was four to six times the average monthly wage.[4] They had their own food and clothing supply systems and, similar to Gestapo staff in respect of the Jews, demanded first call on the apartments and other property stolen or confiscated from prisoners.

The composition of GB staff had changed greatly since the establishment of the NKVD as a separate ministry for the entire USSR in 1934, mainly because of the purges initiated by the Commissar for State Security (Ezhov 1936–38, Beria 1938–40): the veterans had disappeared and the majority of the 30,000 'operative staff' countrywide in 1940 had less than five years' service and were in their 20s. Under 10 per cent had attended a third-level institution and approximately two-thirds had not finished secondary school. Such interrogators had never been abroad, did not speak a foreign language and knew next to nothing (apart from propaganda images) about life in a Western democracy.

A warder fetched Breslin from his cell shortly after nine in the evening, eighteen hours after his arrival in the Lubianka. Walking along the carpeted corridors (hands behind his back), the prisoner on his way to interrogation often heard the metallic clang as the warder tapped the bundle of keys on the buckle of his belt and ordered 'Face to the wall!' Another prisoner and escort marched past unseen: the prisoner was not to be recognised, nor should he recognise others. Any Soviet citizen trudging along the carpeted corridors to his first interrogation felt a vague sense of guilt, in the knowledge that persons were arrested not for what they had done, but for what they believed or what they had said. Their arrest was a kind of 'social prophylaxis', a preventative measure to stifle and punish dissent before the delinquent could begin 'serious plotting':

> The punishment of potential crime was as justifiable as the punishment of actual crime. Indeed, it was better, because, as in the case of disease, prevention was better than cure.[5]

In justifying its existence and manifold privileges within the totalitarian state, the NKVD inflated the significance of opposition to the regime. They drew on the vast reservoir of 'objective enemies', who were considered *ipso facto* to be inveterately hostile to Soviet power (priests, ex-bourgeois, rich peasants, criminals). The other great victim constituency consisted of those 'enemies' invented in a given political context. In the pre-war situation of 1937/38, the latter segment consisted of non-Russian ethnics whose historical homelands bordered on the Soviet Union or who were politically hostile to Bolshevism (Poland, Germany, the Baltic states). Pat Breslin, being of British extraction and in close contact with the British Embassy, belonged to the 'invented' category of potential subversives since his arrest had taken place in the period August 1939 to June 1941, during Stalin's alignment with Hitler and before Britain and the USSR became official allies following the German invasion of the Soviet Union.

Breslin's questioning by Second Lieutenant Gandraburov on the night of 21–22 December 1940 was the first of sixty gruelling interrogations spread over seven months (390 hours). Why did the NKVD officers go to such extraordinary lengths to obtain a confession? Since he had committed no crime in the accepted sense of the term and the secret police did not 'arrest the innocent' (and rarely released detainees without a charge), the confession was a retrospective legal pretext: Breslin had to provide the 'legend' for the indictment, the content of which varied according to the tactics of the interrogators. Nonetheless, the rule of law had to be seen to apply, and 'the organs' could not openly admit that their arrest policy was prophylactic and not reactive, as in a democracy.

Unlike the Gestapo methods of torture to extract real information from real adversaries, the NKVD strategy in the investigative stage of invented political offences was perforce more subtle. Since no material evidence of a serious nature existed, the victim of 'prophylactic' repression had to incriminate himself. In many cases that took time. The merciless beatings employed in Soviet prisons in 1937–38 were probably no longer in general use by 1940. The uniformed interrogators instead relied on psychological pressure: an initial persuasive phase, then shouting and threats of physical violence, of a harsh sentence or of the arrest of family members; forcing the prisoner to stand or to sit during uninterrupted questioning sessions lasting for up to a week or more; or transferring the prisoner to another cell, often one grossly over-crowded, thus increasing his disorientation and curtailing the bonds of friendship and support he had forged with fellow-inmates with more experience of the interrogators' tactics.

The main weapon of the NKVD investigators, however, was not the rubber truncheon or verbal abuse but the systematic use of sleep deprivation. Two prisoners in the Ukraine, who afterwards fled to the West, described the effects of not being allowed to sleep over a long period:

Continued lack of sleep has a severe toxic effect. The need for sleep ultimately displaces every other sensation, even hunger and thirst; it overcomes all resistance and displaces all powers of concentration [...] Hallucinations frequently occur; one sees flies buzzing about, one is surrounded by beetles or mice, smoke seems to rise before one's eyes and, as one is usually forced to stand during the concluding stage of the process, one's feet swell into shapeless lumps. It was scarcely credible for how long some prisoners endured it [...] Toward the end, of course, one collapsed unconscious almost every twenty minutes, and had to be brought around with cold water or slapping.[6]

This is what faced Patrick Breslin, in an uneven battle of wits with the five interrogators, who often worked in teams, thus subjecting their prisoner to the *konveier*, round-the-clock interrogation, over three to seven days. In the eleven remaining days of December 1940, Breslin was interrogated for eighty hours in fourteen sessions, eight of which were during daylight hours. The intensive period was up to Christmas Day; afterwards the *chekists* reverted to daytime questionings. He spent little time in his cell during the sleeping time of 10 p.m. to 6 a.m. on the following nights:

21–22 December, 1½ hours;
22–23 December, 2 hours;
23–24 December, nil;
24–25 December, 4 hours;
25–26 December, 3 hours.

'Production-line' interrogation was employed again from 14 to 16 January. The next month was the worst, 107 hours in fifteen sessions, with no sleep, and daytime interrogation as well, from 8 to 20 February. March, April and May were relatively quiet, for reasons that shall be explained later. The final phase, in June, was a regular offensive on the psyche of the prisoner, with two phases of complete sleep deprivation on nine nights.

The interrogation protocols, written by the NKVD officer who posed the questions, are not a verbatim record of the dialogue. Breslin had to sign the interrogator's written version of each answer, and again at the end of the protocol, stating that the statements so written corresponded to what he had actually said. Some protocols are quite short, supposedly reflecting what was said over six to ten hours, which suggest a contest of wills, intimidation and non-cooperation. Breslin had the protocol corrected frequently on minor points, but on the way back to the cell he must often have thought that the interrogator had twisted his words, that he himself had not protested enough about distorted passages. The *chekists* were not interested in differentiation, measured arguments or acts open to interpretation. They wanted a confession and a conviction, at all costs.

Judging by the first few interrogation protocols, the team of investigators, headed by Gandraburov, approached their adversary from different angles: in order to size him up, they first had to know who he was. They may have employed, alternately, the 'nice guy–bad guy' strategy, when persuasion gave way to intimidation and *vice versa*. Of course, we know nothing about the *mise en scène* in the interrogator's office: whether Breslin could stand or sit (the prisoner's seat was screwed to the table so that it could not be used to attack the interrogator), or if the NKVD man, ignoring his presence, ate and drank or smoked in order to degrade his victim, who was missing prison meals and liquids because of round-the-clock questioning.

The first bouts centred on Breslin's autobiography: why he had come to the USSR, the reasons for his expulsion from the VKP(b), his political life and employment in Ireland, and his interest in theosophy. On his second day in the Lubianka, Breslin realised that he was fighting for his life since he acknowledged, by his signature, that he was suspected of crimes against §6 of Article 58 ('counterrevolutionary crime') of the Soviet Criminal Code. That was the indictment 'espionage for a foreign power'. He knew that, if found guilty, he would be killed.

A standard demand made at the early stage of such investigations was to name names – acquaintances in the USSR and abroad, and, somewhat later, of those already arrested. Then followed detailed probing about Breslin's links to foreign embassies in Moscow. He had visited the British Consular Department twice in the early 1930s to extend his Irish passport and, as noted earlier, renewed such contacts later in the decade, and in 1940, in respect of his withdrawal application and the estate of Eduard Soermus. Gandraburov, in the early hours of Christmas Eve 1940, accused Breslin outright of spying in the USSR and 'taking tasks straight from foreign intelligence'. Breslin vigorously denied the charge, and his opposite, changing tack, enquired whether Breslin knew members of the Irish parliament and Irish civil servants. The grilling then moved to the friendship with Cyril Fagan and their last meeting in Dublin in March 1928. Breslin mentioned a joke that Fagan had made at their parting, that Pat could make a lot of money spying for the British, or the Soviets, when living in Russia. Breslin added immediately that he 'couldn't be a spy, as it was against my nature'.

A second, if short-lived, attempt to entangle Breslin in an espionage indictment centred on his acquaintances who were British or American ex-servicemen. That line of enquiry drew a blank. Captain Jack White DSO, who had drilled the Irish Citizen Army (ICA), had no contact with Breslin after 1925, and George Hannah was vouched for since he had been employed as a radio operator in the Comintern before moving to Radio Moscow.[7] During a fifteen-hour bout (26–27 December) of wringing Breslin through the mangle, Gandraburov and his assistant attempted to trap their prisoner by distorting his answers.

The first altercation arose because of the background to Breslin's departure from Ireland. In the knowledge that Breslin would not be granted a passport for travel to the USSR, Jack Carney had advised the twenty-year-old to write 'student travel in western Europe' on the application form for his Irish passport. Gandraburov interpreted this as an 'illegal' exitus and alleged that Breslin had broken 'rules of conspiracy' from the very start by telling his family of his destination. The circumstances of Breslin's first renewal of his Irish passport (valid for five years) at the British Consulate in 1933 led to the second clash with the NKVD officer. Breslin stated that the consular official had noted his address, his place of work and his marriage to a Russian citizen before commenting that the Irish journalist would have problems 'getting his Russian wife out'. That 'exposed Breslin before the investigation': he had voluntarily given the ideological enemy information about his private life.

The colleague replacing Gandraburov on the shift gained a bridgehead with the third psychological assault. Starting from Breslin's open avowal of ideological deviancy at the Lenin School, the interrogator homed in on other expressions of anti-Soviet sentiment by the prisoner – in 1930–31 against the Soviet suppression of free thought or a free press, the collectivisation of agriculture and, more recently, the telling of 'anti-Soviet' jokes.

The nocturnal interrogation of 27–28 December, Breslin's eighth night of complete or partial sleep deprivation, shifted to a scrutiny of intimacies, in particular Pat's relationship with Margaret McMackin and his attempts to follow her home. He recounted his three unsuccessful attempts to renounce Soviet citizenship through normal channels (October 1936, January 1938, May 1938), a fourth application handed in personally at President Kalinin's office in the summer of 1939, its rejection in October 1939 and the appeal, which had gone unanswered. His more forthright disclosures have the ring of truth – that he wanted to join Daisy because a child growing up without a father in Ireland would be stigmatised, in contrast to the USSR, where his children by Katya would be looked after by the State; or that, sometime in 1940, he had resigned himself to the fact of living in Russia and had voluntarily undergone treatment 'to pull myself out of the dirt into which I was sinking as the result of acute alcoholism. I wanted to become a real man again.'

The interrogation over the following two days centred once more on Breslin's contacts with British diplomats, his friendship with John Evans, and the incident at the Cocktail Hall on Pushkin Square three months earlier. Breslin admitted that his rendering of the British national anthem had a 'provocative meaning', but denied ulterior motives because he was drunk at the time. On 29 December, the probing seems to have been haphazard, although the interrogator did reveal that he had informers' reports to hand, including the contents of a conversation, which Breslin could not remember, at a bus stop between the Irishman and a newsreader from Radio Moscow.

After the brief questioning session ended at noon, Breslin was transferred to the 'home' prison of the Moscow UGB, the Taganka, a four-storied block dating back to Tsarist days, which was closed in the 1960s. This transfer is open to several interpretations. If Breslin was still considered to be a dangerous 'enemy of the State' or a 'spy', he would have been held in isolation in the Lubianka. Lodging him in an over-crowded, general type of prison with thousands of custodial inmates is an indication that his tormentors either believed they had not yet 'unmasked' him or felt that the investigation was not progressing beyond the phase of a run-of-the-mill prosecution – wrapping up the case against an *antisovetchik*. The move most probably brought Breslin immediate disadvantages, since the food was far worse than the Lubianka fare and, for the first time, he was confronted with *urki*, the criminal class who lived by their own code and terrorised the 'politicals' if they got the chance. According to his Taganka index-card, Breslin arrived in sports trousers, a jumper and the cheap sailcloth shoes with rubber soles that most Russians wore. The card also mentions that he had a scald mark on his right leg, but that may have been an old injury.

The interrogations that followed went over old ground, in particular his attempts to renounce Soviet citizenship by asking the Comintern functionaries Shields and Raylock, and the *Daily Worker* correspondent Ben Francis, for advice, or the approaches made by Virginia Soermus on his behalf to the British Labour Party politician Ernest Bevin. Gandraburov signed an application on 2 January, which Breslin acknowledged by signature the following day, to continue with the §6 (espionage) indictment. A frequent ruse in achieving that goal was to link the prisoner to one or more victims already convicted, preferably foreigners. In answering the question about those acquaintances 'repressed by the NKVD', Breslin mentioned first and foremost his Lenin School classmate Vladimir Čopič, the commander of the 15th International Brigade in Spain. Breslin stated that the Croat 'was arrested at the end of 1938, a few days after his return'. Čopič, who was recalled from Spain in August 1938,[8] was arrested in Hotel Lux on 3 November and shot, with ten other leaders of the Yugoslav Communist Party, in April 1939.[9] Breslin also spoke about George Fles and a certain Tevil, who had worked in Stalin's Chancellery.[10] Such 'leads' were pursued desultorily, if at all.

The pendulum then swung back to Breslin's very rare dealings in the currency black market, the purchase of pounds or dollars at four times the official rate, an offence which Breslin admitted. Gandraburov depicted the money exchange as 'a crime of political nature [...] undermining the economy of the USSR'. His assistant Sursky took over the last leg of an interrogation marathon and questioned Breslin for thirteen hours from midnight on 14 January. Reviewing the prisoner's political career in Ireland, the NKVD man tried to portray Breslin as an incorrigible anti-communist from his teenage years. But that was not enough: he wanted a confession about espionage, starting an absurd dialogue with Breslin. The starting point was Fagan's silly joke about making money in that field in Moscow:

> S: When did he make a proposal to you to become an agent and work for English and Soviet intelligence?

> B: During the first and second meeting [in March 1928] he made no proposals to me to become an agent.

S: You are contradicting yourself. You stated earlier that in the conversation about your trip to the USSR he said that if you wanted to make big money, you could become an agent and work for English and Soviet intelligence. Now you are saying that he made no proposals. Why are you changing your statement?

B: I don't consider it a proposal. It was expressed as a thought.

S: But the expressed thought is a proposal. You know that. Why are you now saying otherwise?

B: He simply expressed a thought that there would be such a possibility. He did not try to persuade me, and proposed nothing definite.

S: If he did not make a proposal, why did he talk about it?

B: He expressed that thought without any purpose.

S: If he expressed that thought without purpose, why then did he not talk about it earlier, but mentioned it at the moment when you already had everything prepared to go to the USSR?

B: I don't know why he did not talk about it earlier, but mentioned it when I had to go to the USSR. [Refuses to sign the answer]

S: Why did you refuse to sign the answer to the question?

B: I refused to sign because I answered the question with 'I don't know.' What is written in the full answer are not my words.

S: Did you agree to become an agent?

B: He did not propose that I become an agent. My answer to the thought expressed by Fagan was that I could not be a spy because it was contrary to my nature.

S: Why did you reply like that?

B: I replied like that because I felt I could never be a spy.

S: That means that he did not just propose but demanded of you to become a spy. That is the only way you can answer.

B: He did not propose and he did not demand of me to become an agent.

Second Lieutenant Sursky then turned to another prospective agent, the pensioner sea-captain Fforde from County Donegal. An interesting aside by Breslin throws light on his home life in 1932 – that he could not invite Mr and Mrs Fforde back to his flat because

Katya feared complications if she entertained foreigners. Now, in the last dialogue of the seemingly endless inquisition, Fforde surfaced in Moscow as a messenger of British intelligence, which Breslin denied.

After a respite of eight days, the cruel carousel restarted in the second week of February, when Skudatin, Gandraburov's immediate superior, felt obliged to enter the fray. He tried to link Breslin to 'Trotskyism', a lethal catch-all phrase for all those seen to disagree with Stalin's catechetical and primitive Marxism. Tom Bell had told Breslin that Carney was a Trotskyist by 1936. Carney had fully supported Larkin Senior's break with the Comintern in 1929, but he cut all links to the labour leader in 1936 because Larkin, fearing attacks from fanatical Catholic elements, had forbidden him, as a WUI employee, from appearing on platforms in defence of the Spanish Republic. Carney later emigrated to London.[11] Skudatin alleged that Larkin, a practising Catholic, and Carney, a Trotskyist 'enemy', had sent Breslin to the ILS for sinister ends. Breslin insisted that the only purpose behind his 'commandeering' to the Lenin School was study. Requests made by the NKVD to the Comintern archive produced little 'evidence' on the WUI leaders: not a word about Carney's politics, merely that he had been sent by Larkin to the ECCI in 1925 to represent the IWL; and that Larkin Senior, now in the Irish Labour Party, was a 'renegade'.

Informed on 12 February that the espionage indictment was still being pursued, Breslin confessed in the ensuing week of round-the-clock grilling that he had 'misled the investigation' in not giving a full catalogue of his 'anti-Soviet' views. His 'slanders' against the Soviet government included the expressions of dissent mentioned earlier (rejection of collectivisation and of the abolition of private trade), his equation of the USSR with fascist countries, the farce of elections to the Supreme Soviet which ignored the candidature of more than one party as laid down in the 1936 Constitution, the huge bureaucratic state apparatus 'living off the workers', and the Russo-German Pact of August 1939:

> I was against the above-mentioned treaty and stated that the Soviet Union was moving away from its Communist principles and in fact was helping Fascism because the Government did not want war with Germany as it was not sure of the support of the nation in view of the big dissatisfaction among the working people [....] Regarding the decrees of the Presidium of the Supreme Soviet of the USSR of 26 June

and 10 July 1940, I stated that those decrees were enslaving the workers, were considerably worsening the position of working people and totally contradicted Communist principles.

The labour decrees constituted the last step in abolishing contractual relations between employee and employer. Just as peasants were tied to the land because they were refused internal passports from the early 1930s, legislation in December 1938 had introduced the issue of work-books to curtail worker mobility and tighten up discipline, especially 'loafing' on the factory floor and not arriving on time. Such misdemeanours went under the collective phrase *progulka* ('going for a walk'). Arriving late for work or knocking off work early at lunchtime or at the end of the shift without a valid reason could, after warnings and reprimands (three in one month or four within two consecutive months), lead to instant dismissal. That also meant eviction, since most accommodation was provided by the employer. 'Case law' was so interpreted that being more than twenty minutes late for work constituted unjustified absence and was therefore a ground for dismissal without notice. Managers who failed to apply the full battery of punishments were liable to imprisonment of up to one year. The legislation of 1940 introduced a seven-day working week (the eighth day was free) and an eight-hour day. The punishments for *progulka* were drastically increased, to forced labour at the place of employment or even prison sentences. From 1942, military tribunals tried such cases.[12] Breslin was now admitting to expressing what fellow Soviet citizens were feeling in 1940: blue- or white-collar employees terrified of arriving late at their workplace and afraid to visit the doctor or report sick.

One of the last attempts to link Breslin with espionage – his anti-Soviet feelings were already catalogued and sufficed for a Gulag verdict – was Gandraburov's insistence that Breslin's reason for visiting the British Embassy in 1935 was not the second renewal of his Irish passport, but that the consular officials had instructed him to apply for Soviet citizenship, which could have given his 'espionage activities a good cover'. Breslin categorically denied this claim, and with some passion since he demanded from the NKVD officer that he show him his Irish passport and the renewal stamp inserted in 1935.

In mid-March, Gandraburov's team gave up, handing the case over to the Investigations Department (*sledchasti*), and to lower-ranking

officials, the sergeants Chernov and Vislov. Chernov hoped that the
spying indictment might yet be proven. He intended, in effect, to
begin from scratch: checking all fifty persons mentioned by the
Irishman to date, and examining the files of his arrested acquaintances and friends. Looking through the previous interrogation
minutes and noticing that Breslin had complained of failing memory
(most probably owing more to sleep deprivation than simulation),
Chernov ordered his examination by psychiatrists with the following
argument (20 March):

> During the interrogations Breslin claims to have had mental disorders,
> says that he was hospitalised in the Kuibyshev District hospital (Radio
> Street 11, Moscow), complains of absentmindedness and bad
> memory, using it as an excuse not to give answers to the questions put
> to him by the investigation.

The relatively few interrogations carried out in March and early
April must have been a relief for Breslin. Not only had he time to
recover from the bouts of conveyor-belt grilling, but now Chernov
was merely going over trampled paths, learning the Irishman's
potted biography and the history of Irish left-wing politics in the
1920s. The sergeant could not desist from sneering at Breslin's
revolutionary credentials, describing his role as propagandist and
seller of CPI literature as the tasks of a 'newspaper boy', and setting
the word revolutionary in inverted commas.

Patrick Breslin was brought under guard to the out-patients
department of the Central Institute of Criminal Psychology on 3
April. The experts found him communicative and devoid of
'pathological reflexes'. The core of their diagnosis convinced
Chernov that Breslin was simulating illness:

> All statements of the patient are concrete, real and in line with the
> views expressed in literature on these matters ['mystic sciences']....
> All the failures of the recent period and also his arrest he attributes to
> his alcoholism. He does not admit that he is guilty of the charges made
> and defends himself actively. There are no abnormalities in the
> emotional sense. The patient's judgements are correct and his critical
> attitudes are not distorted. There is a tendency to self-analysis and a
> correct understanding of painful experiences (during the periods of
> alcoholic abuse). There are no delirious ideas or hallucinations at
> present. On these grounds the commission has come to the conclusion

that P. Breslin is NOT suffering from any mental illness; he has a psychopathic personality with the signs of chronic alcoholism. As a person NOT suffering from any mental illness, BRESLIN should be considered SANE in regard to the offences with which he is charged.

The report was received on 8 April, the day Breslin was transferred to yet another prison, the notorious Lefortovo. In 1940 this prison of the central NKVD units had room for 625 prisoners, and a staff total of 315.[13] The rows of cells formed a 'K' at the core of the fortress, surrounded by higher buildings housing special cells and the interrogators' offices.[14] Lefortovo had a special wing for executions and punishment cells (*kartser*) for recalcitrant prisoners. It was known for its torture chambers, sadistic staff and the appalling noise from the wind-tunnels of the Central Aero- and Hydrodynamics Institute practically next door, which made conversation in the cells impossible. Almost everything was painted black, even the asphalt floor; the heating, controlled by a warder from the corridor, could be reduced or increased to 'soften up' the prisoners.[15]

Whether Breslin was stuck in the punishment cells, beaten or given 'special treatment' of one kind or another is unknown. The tone and paltry results gained from the interrogations in Lefortovo prove that he did not capitulate to the espionage accusations, but the long breaks between questioning (no further sessions in April and only two in May) may indicate that he was given a 'cooling-off' period in isolation. Another interpretation is that Chernov was overworked or combing through the evidence gained hitherto. His research included the perusal of informers' reports on Breslin, on his ILS classmate Maggie Jordan, or on Daisy, and summaries of visits to her in Moscow hotels during 1932 and 1936. Chernov also applied for prosecution data on Breslin's contacts in Sukhumi (1937) and Moscow, including Rose Cohen. He found no mention of the Irishman in Cohen's file. Intensive interrogation was resumed on 9 June. During the 9–10 June (9 p.m. to 5 a.m.) bout Breslin was confronted with the spying charge once again. He was 'advised' by Chernov 'to stop being stubborn and to make truthful and detailed statements about your counterrevolutionary espionage work on the territory of the USSR'. The record of this eight-hour interrogation fits on one page of foolscap and the answers are comparably terse. At the end, and, as it transpired, for the last time, Breslin protested his innocence on this point:

I repeat once again that I was not involved in any espionage work and I have nothing to say.

Eight further all-night interrogations followed, with no disclosures of note. Then the German *Wehrmacht* invaded the USSR, at dawn on 22 June 1941. The *chekists* had now more pressing cases, such as rounding up the putative Fifth Column of those Germans who had escaped the 1937–38 arrests, or interrogating Red Army officers brought from the front for trial in Moscow because they had retreated in the face of the Nazi onslaught.

Chernov and Breslin met for the last time six days later. On the table for signature were three documents. The first stated that the espionage charges were being dropped ('not proven'), the second that the prisoner would be sent for trial on a §10 political indictment ('anti-Soviet agitation'). The 34-year-old translator probably forgot his miserable state of health for an instant, relieved that he would not be executed. The third sheet was a list of the documentation seized during the house search in Ulitsa Ogareva 9 on Christmas Eve 1940: 183 photographs, 266 letters, six notebooks, nine folders, and the pension book and residence permit of Eduard Soermus. Now, Breslin had to comply with their destruction in the prison furnace, save for the Soermus documents and some letters he selected for forwarding to old Mrs Kreitser in Leningrad. The formalities completed, Chernov demanded that Breslin expand once more on his anti-Stalinist views. The Irishman, knowing that the case was watertight, replied:

> I gave the facts of my anti-Soviet agitation at previous interrogations. I confirm them and can add nothing new.

Breslin had been taken from the Lefortovo hell-hole on 24 June and now awaited further developments in cell No. 422 of Taganka prison.

NOTES

1. Aleksander Wat, *Jenseits von Wahrheit und Lüge. Mein Jahrhundert. Gesprochene Erinnerungen 1926–1945* (Frankfurt am Main 2000), pp. 358ff. For the English-language edition, see *My Century: The Odyssey of a Polish Intellectual* (New York 1990).

2. Aleksandr Kokurin and Nikita Petrov, 'NKVD. Struktura, funktsii, kadry. Stat'ia vtoraia (1938–1941)', *Svobodnaia mysl'*, 7, 1997, pp. 115–16.
3. For a description of the Lubianka exercise cage, see Alexander Solzhenitsyn, *The Gulag Archipelago*, vol. 1 (Collins/Fontana Paperbacks 1974), p. 136.
4. Real wages stagnated between 1938 and 1941. While average yearly wages rose from 3,047 to 4,054 roubles (35 per cent), retail prices, especially those on the free market, increased at a faster rate, so that a fall in real wages of 10 per cent can be assumed for the years 1937–40. See Alec Nove, *An Economic History of the USSR*, p. 259.
5. F. Beck and W. Godin, *Russian Purge and the Extraction of Confession* (London 1952), pp. 196–97. For another study of Soviet 'prophylactic' repression, see Hannah Arendt, *The Origins of Totalitarianism,* New York 1958ff (new addition with added prefaces).
6. Beck and Godin, *Russian Purge*, pp. 52–54.
7. Hannah was arrested in 1949, following a denunciation from a colleague in the Foreign Publications Publishing House in Moscow. For some details of his case, see McLoughlin, 'Visitors and Victims', p. 225.
8. RGASPI, f. 545, o. 2, d. 363, l. 30, farewell letter from Čopič to 15th Brigade, *The Volunteer for Liberty*, 13 August 1938, p. 5.
9. V. Tikhanova (ed.), *Rasstrel'nye spiski. Vypusk 1. Donskoe Kladbishche 1934–1940* (Moscow 1993), pp. 89–92.
10. He was shot in March 1937. See ibid, p. 64.
11. Emmet Larkin, *James Larkin Irish Labour Leader 1876–1947* (London 1977, reprint), p. 298. See also Fearghal McGarry, *Irish Politics and the Spanish Civil War* (Cork 1999), pp. 101, 185.
12. Solomon M. Schwarz, *Labor in the Soviet Union* (New York 1952), pp. 100–20.
13. Kokurin and Petrov, *Svobodnaia mysl'*, 7, 1997, p. 116.
14. Jacques Rossi, *The Gulag Handbook* (New York 1989), pp. 199–200.
15. Solzhenitsyn, vol. 1, pp. 180–81.

Transit and Terminus

Following his last interrogation on 28 June, Patrick Breslin was given his thick file (225 pages) to read. He made no supplementary statements or complaints. In early July, Chernov summarised the case for the last time, recommending that the Irishman, because of his 'suspicious contacts and way of life', be considered a 'socially dangerous element' (*sotsialno-opasnyi element* – SOE). That was Stalinist shorthand for somebody the regime wanted removed from society but, as Chernov now stated, for whose crimes there was 'no material evidence'. The State Prosecutor's Office in Moscow adhered to this interpretation and, noting that Breslin had confessed to 'counterrevolutionary agitation', advised that the case should go before the Special Board of the NKVD 'because the evidence is based on operative materials which cannot be made public in court'. The Special Board, known by its Russian initials OSO (*osoboe soveshchanie*), met in secret. The defendant was not present and learned of the verdict, which he took cognisance of by signing the reverse of the sentence slip, just before being transported to a labour camp. Set up in 1924 to sentence persons to internal exile or forced labour, the OSO processed over 600,000 cases until its abolition in 1953.

The long train journey to the Gulag, in cattle wagons and under armed guard, was known by the simple word *etap* (from the French *étape*, i.e. stop, station). It signified an unknown destination, punctuated by stopovers in transit prisons along the route. Most long-term custodial prisoners, weakened by the bad food, crowded conditions and bad ventilation of the collective cells of a Moscow prison, were more often than not glad to hear the call 'Out with all your things!', which meant the transport was beginning to leave: the food could not be worse in the camps, and work in the fresh air might stabilise a weakened constitution. Everything is relative in the life of a prisoner, and it was all too human to hope that what was to come could only be better. However, the departure of Breslin and thousands of others was delayed because of the war, since the Soviet rail system, chronically overloaded at the best of times, now had to serve military priorities.

While languishing in the mass misery of the Taganka, Pat Breslin wrote two appeals. Both were ignored; they are still in his file. The first, dated 16 July 1941, was a request addressed to the State Prosecutor for permission to make an additional statement and to re-examine his own prosecution file, in particular the interrogation protocols. Chernov had played a trick on him during the last questioning on 28 June: he had the prisoner sign the self-incriminatory protocol concerning anti-Soviet statements before informing him that the espionage charges had been dropped. Naturally, Breslin wanted to put his confession of dissenting views in a proper perspective because he had exaggerated them to fend off the lethal spying indictment. The second letter (4 September 1941) was addressed to the director of the Taganka, the third version of a specific complaint hitherto ignored. Breslin wanted to use the money held in his name in the prison depository to buy groceries. He had just recovered from a bout of diarrhoea with a high fever, which had led to his transferral, as a sick inmate, to a single cell. While the diarrhoea had subsided, Breslin still felt very weak and needed additional food after eight months of prison fare. We may wonder who had sent him the accumulated sum of 1,000 roubles which he was never allowed to use. The donor was someone in the country, Evans or Scott.

In late August, Captain Fliagin drew up the draft of the indictment summary against Bresin, for sentencing behind the closed doors of the OSO. There were no mitigating circumstances:

> Breslin is charged with a hostile attitude to Soviet power and for many years he carried out within his circle extreme anti-Soviet propaganda by means of hostile and slanderous statements in a provocative way in order to discredit the politics of the VKP(b) and the Soviet Government. He has pleaded guilty to the charge of anti-Soviet agitation. Apart from his confession, there are operative materials which incriminate him.

The extra-judicial OSO passed the verdict on case 994 against Patrik Frantsisovich Breslin on 16 September 1941: eight years in a Gulag camp 'for counterrevolutionary agitation', back-dated to the day of arrest (21 December 1940). The verdict was confirmed not in

Moscow, but in Kuibyshev (Samara), where many ministries had been hurriedly evacuated during the German offensive on Moscow. Breslin's destination was Viatlag camp in the Kirov Region, 800 kilometres to the north-west of Moscow. The population of Viatlag, one of the many slave-labour lumber camps set up in 1938, grew by 70 per cent in the second half of 1941.[1] For unknown reasons, Breslin's place of penal servitude was changed to Omsk (Western Siberia) and later to Kazan, with a long period of detention in prison at Chistopol on the great Volga-Kama river convergence in Tatarstan.

While there is little documentation on Breslin's own odyssey, fellow-prisoners who took the same route (Taganka–Kazan–Chistopol–Kazan) have written gripping accounts of Soviet prison conditions in Tatarstan during the first years of World War II. Gennady Simonov, a student of metallurgy in Moscow, was among the 1,500 prisoners hurriedly entrained in Moscow on 10 October 1941 for transportation to the Tatar capital of Kazan. As the city had only a transit prison in the ancient Kremlin, the *etap* continued by barge to Chistopol. The prisoners were marched in columns to Chistopol Prison No. 4 on the morning of 18 October.[2] After delousing, a bath and a nominal medical examination ('no contagious diseases'), Breslin was passed by the Taganka doctor as fit for travel on 10 October. He arrived at Chistopol prison on 23 October.[3] Speed had been of the essence at both ends of the journey: in Moscow because the Germans were at the gates and bombing the city from the air; in Tatarstan because the Volga and Kama rivers were not navigable owing to thick ice between November and April.

A more detailed account is provided by Henry Ralph Löwenstein-Johnston, later a doctor and noted nature photographer in the Marii Republic of the Russian Federation.[4] He does not remember Breslin, but because he shared the same *via dolorosa* in 1941–42, his experiences were similar to those of the Irish journalist-translator. Löwenstein, born in Nikolaiev in 1918, where his Montana-born father worked as a submarine-engineer, had escaped the chaos of the Russian Civil War with his mother, finally reuniting with his father in the Dutch port of Vlissingen in 1920. The marriage broke up after a year, and Henry's mother moved to Berlin to work at the Soviet Trade Delegation. She soon married a Soviet diplomat posted to Copenhagen. Henry was put in the care of an aristocratic Berlin family, the widow and daughter Bettina and Katherina von Seydlitz-

Kurzbach. From Katherina he learned the better Prussian virtues – honesty, keeping one's word and respect for persons regardless of rank. Henry attended a good Berlin gymnasium and mixed with the sons of the old Wilhelmine upper class, in particular the godson of Field-Marshal von Ludendorff. When Henry rejoined his mother in Moscow in 1932 and attended the Karl-Liebknecht secondary school, he kept his Berlin bourgeois past to himself and proclaimed loyalty to the Soviet system. This avowal of anti-fascist solidarity with the USSR, which he shared with his fellow-pupils, the children of German and Austrian political refugees, was not shattered by the Great Terror. Although his stepfather and two uncles were arrested and shot in 1938 on account of their German nationality, Henry saw Stalin's Soviet Union as his homeland, chose to study medicine and married a Russian girl called Mila.

Löwenstein's arrest in September 1941 was not due to any act on his part. His German background was his undoing, for Stalin decided to clear Moscow of Germans, and 'to arrest the most suspicious elements' . The 'German' operation lasted from 10 to 15 September in the capital and led to the forced exile of over 8,000 ethnic German Muscovites to Siberia, the Far East and Kazakhstan. By the end of October some 873,000 Germans, half of whom were inhabitants of the German Volga Republic, had been forcibly uprooted throughout the USSR.[5] Henry hoped that the expulsion order for his family might be waived because he was about to sit his final medical examinations.

However, when he went to the office of the Dean of Medicine at Moscow University to state his case, he was shown into a room occupied by a stranger. The NKVD officer in mufti pushed the arrest warrant across the desk and accompanied Henry to the communal flat. Henry's mother arrived during the search and understood immediately what was happening. When Mila had packed his rucksack with warm clothing, Henry entreated her not to wait for him longer than three years. She replied that she would wait longer, until he returned.

Despite the humiliating body-search and unfriendly warders, Löwenstein soon settled down to prison life in the Taganka. Almost all his cell-mates were ethnic Germans, from all walks of life, and there were even a few who had known him from schooldays. The toilet bucket in the corner (*parasha*) served as a urinal, and the prisoners were taken twice daily to the outside sit-down toilets, that rumour exchange at the end of the corridor shared by other communal cells. The prison schedule could have been worse: there were several chess-sets and enough books on loan from the prison library. The food, of course, was inadequate: tea-water and sugar and 450 grams of bread in the morning, with 1.5 litres of thin watery soup (*balanda*) at noon and in the evening.

On the sixth day in prison, the interrogation bouts commenced for Löwenstein. Like Breslin, he was worn down by lack of sleep, and the NKVD expected him to provide the 'legend' for 'counter-revolutionary activities'. The questioning was interrupted by Löwenstein's transfer to a small prison near the Lubianka where conditions were better. His new fellow-prisoners advised him to admit to 'lesser sins' for the good of his health. Henry Löwenstein was confronted by a report of a conversation he had held the previous February with a fellow-student in a Metro station. The young German had questioned the wisdom of building the fantastic 420 metre-high Dom Sovetov, another glass palace for the Stalinist bureaucracy (which was never erected) in the city centre at a time when the living conditions for most Muscovites were 'not resolved'. The interrogator interpreted this as anti-Soviet, that Löwenstein 'was against the decision of the Party and the Government to build the Dom Sovetov'. Once Henry signed a statement confirming his preference for workers' flats, the NKVD officer seemed satisfied. He did not comment on Löwenstein's remark that accusing him of being at odds with government policy contradicted his right to hold a personal opinion.

With Hitler's army *ante portas*, the prisoners smelt the crisis: not the acrid stench from buildings wrecked by Luftwaffe incendiaries, but the pervasive smell of burning paper emanating from the stoves in the first-floor offices of the interrogators. After dark, when taken to exercise on the rooftop, the prisoners saw countless wisps of charred paper in the night sky.

The small prison was precipitately evacuated one evening in October. In the windowless interior of the 'Black Raven', Henry deduced from the changes of gear and direction at street junctions that he and his comrades were not bound for one of the prisons (Lefortovo, Taganka, Butyrka). And he was right. The destination was a goods yard in a remote part of Kazan railway station, a phantasmagoric siding lit up by another German air-raid, searchlights and anti-aircraft fire. Shouting guards and their lunging

Alsatians herded the one thousand or so prisoners to the cattle-wagons, where, before the open door, an officer, torch in hand, compared the name and visage of each prisoner by glancing at the photograph and data in their personal files.

The train journey to Kazan took three days. Owing to the complement of forty men to a freight car, the transitees slept on the wooden bunks in packed rows. Neither that nor the fact that many suffered dreadfully from the cold because they were still wearing the summer clothing they had been arrested in caused the greatest hardship at first. The initial torment was thirst, made worse on the first day because the prisoners had quickly consumed the early handout of their travel rations – a soggy square of bread and a heavily salted roach. Some military men in the wagon, now en route to the Gulag because they had retreated before the German jugger-naut in June, imposed a queuing schedule: the contents of the two buckets of water were distributed equally. As in prison, the tally of prisoners was taken at night, during a halt. Those prisoners who were slow to scurry to the side of the car lit by the guards' torches were driven there from the bunks under curses and blows from pickaxe-handles.

Kazan in early winter witnessed the sorry spectacle of the unwashed, half-starved and ragged columns trudging through the rain uphill to a disused church. After three days in the large, unheated building, the prisoners marched down to the river and the long-awaited *navigatsiia*, the river-crossing to Chistopol. The route was south down the widening Volga and then due east up the Kama. For the ferrying of small contingents pleasure-steamers were used, and the prisoners experienced the 200-kilometre journey in the locked and guarded saloon below deck. The mass transport of 700, with Löwenstein in its bedraggled midst, however, was herded into the dark hold of an old barge. The three-day crossing in semi-darkness was a nightmare: there was only room to sit and one lavatory barrel for all.

From the pier, the column marched uphill to Chistopol Prison No. 4, a penitentiary built in 1855 and consisting of a three-storied block flanked by a long bath-house (*bania*), where incoming prisoners had their hair shorn and clothing deloused before being hurried through the shower-room. After waiting an hour in the October drizzle before the wooden prison gates and dreaming of a warm bunk and hot soup, Löwenstein was allocated a place in a communal cell on the first floor. The oblong room measured 9 by 5 metres and was to house eighty-two prisoners. Gennady Simonov's cell, which held 104 inmates, was even smaller – 41 square metres. Since the bunks (without mattresses or bedding) along the walls were occupied in the first rush and the remainder of the prisoners did not have enough room to stretch out on the wooden floor, a democratic decision was reached – sleeping in shifts, one half by day, the other by night.

Henry soon realised that a normal prison schedule did not exist in other respects either, divergences which, unlike the sleeping by day or by night, had long-term and disastrous effects. First, for months on end the prisoners were not taken out for exercise or for ablutions. Second, there was no prison library. Löwenstein realised that he must occupy himself somehow. He fashioned for himself what most prisoners did – a sewing needle from a metal clasp in the waistband of his trousers, using a broken piece of glass as a scissors. Jacket padding provided the necessary thread for mending the increasingly tattered hiker's apparel into which Henry had wisely changed during the search of his flat. Most of the cell inmates took to tailoring – some darning, others making sewing needles, and a minority, the criminals, in sharpening knife blades from pieces of tin they had found in the bath-house.

Nine-tenths of Henry's companions in the muggy cell (the gross over-crowding compensated for the absence of heating pipes) were 'Germans': a small group of German or Austrian Communists, but mainly native Russians who had been in a German POW camp in the 1914–18 war, members of the Volga German minority and individuals who had relatives or pen-friends in Germany. They were all potential 'spies'; that is, political, as distinct from criminal, prisoners.

The preponderance of 'politicals' from a common culture ensured that the criminal *urki* did not get the upper hand. A just system of bread distribution (morning and evening) was overseen by eight group-leaders who personally handed out the bread slabs (*paika*). The tastier crusted ends of the loaf were given in rotation or the group-members drew lots for the crisp 'doorsteps'. An augmentation to the inadequate diet was provided, for some at least, by the inveterate smokers: their reserve of rough tobacco (*makhorka*) from the Moscow custodial prison was now exhausted and, since the authorities in Chistopol had not yet begun to distribute the loathsome shag, tobacco became the scarce commodity which could be exchanged for

1.   Pat Breslin, Lenin School, 1928.

2.   Pat Breslin, Moscow, 1930.

3.   Jack Carney, c. 1928.

4.   Jim Larkin at 5th Comintern
     Congress, Moscow, 1924.

5. Sean Murray, Moscow, 1935.

6. Peadar O'Donnell, Berlin, March 1930.

7. Pat Breslin and Irina on holidays, July 1936.

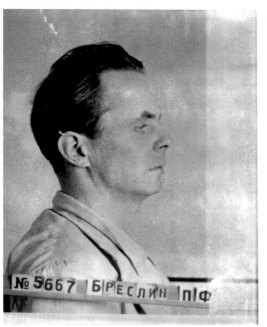

8.   Pat Breslin, Lubianka, December 1940.

9.   Prisoners beginning the journey to the Gulag, Moscow, October 1941.

10. Henry Löwenstein, Moscow 1935.

11. Henry Löwenstein, 1956, after release from the Gulag.

12. Genrikh Kreitser, Katya's father.

13. Olga, Katya's mother.

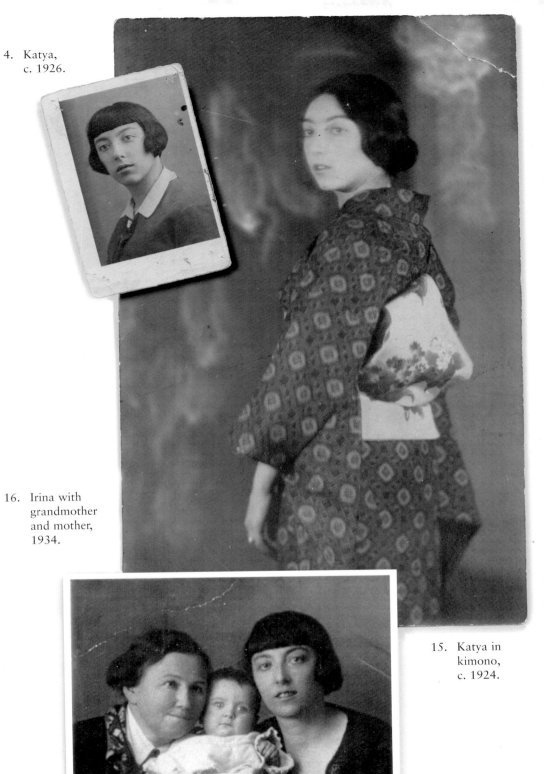

4. Katya, c. 1926.

16. Irina with grandmother and mother, 1934.

15. Katya in kimono, c. 1924.

17. Katya, Genrikh and Irina, ca. 1948.

18. Daisy McMackin as schoolgirl, c. 1915.

19. Daisy McMackin, Belfast BA graduation 1919.

20. Daisy McMackin and Jakob Miller and an unknown woman, Moscow 1936.

21. Mairead Breslin, 1955.

bread. Bread was also the basis for chess tournaments, which Henry initiated. The figures were kneaded from breadcrumbs, and although his first set was eaten during the night, the chess craze caught on, distracting them from the main misery – hunger.

Everyone knew that it was impossible to survive until the next *navigatsiia* on two squares of bread and three litres of salted soup per day. Löwenstein, a final-year medical student, was asked to give lectures. Seeing that the warders did not allow anybody to leave the cell save for interrogation, he could not give the usual tips – keeping oneself clean and exercising in the open air. Henry warned against over-straining the heart by drinking too much water, by consuming salt and by smoking. He concluded with the expression of hope that the fresh air and work in the camps after the river had thawed would improve their physical condition. Realising that he was hedging the issue of slow death by starvation, Baumann, a former university lecturer from Moscow, asked what were the minimal calory requirements in order to stay alive in the unhygienic conditions of the prison cell. Löwenstein explained that a man weighing 70 kilos and leading a peaceful life needed 1,600 calories a day, a woman roughly 1,400, but the prison diet supplied only 1,000 calories. That meant, Baumann concluded, that the prisoners, who had long shed any excess weight, were each losing three to four kilos a month. Henry countered by saying that the weight-loss varied from person to person and the type of under-nourishment (starvation diet as against fasting bouts), but yes, he had lost at least 22 kilos in the five months since his arrest.

The next query was logical. How much weight can you lose and still stay alive? That depended not only on calories but also on the protein intake, which in Chistopol prison was only a third or a quarter of the 70–100 gram. daily minimum. And the consequences? Dystrophy (muscle wastage) in the forms now visible among some prisoners – skeletal or with swollen bellies and legs, or scurvy or pellagra, when the skin cracks and insanity often ensues. Henry tried to end on an optimistic note by saying that if one avoided drinking too much water and eschewed salt, most of the little community would see it through until the river ice melted in April. But he expected the first cell mortalities in the coming weeks. The acute diarrhoea cases, who spent most of their day near or on the *parasha*, were taken to the sick-bay and never returned. A nurse appeared occasionally, but she rarely distributed medicine.

Early in the New Year the first cell death occurred, that of Stepanov, a simple Moscow working man. His demise was concealed from the authorities for 24 hours so that his rations could be distributed. Later, when most of the prisoners were sleeping, the *urki* fell on the corpse and extracted the gold teeth.

Hope was dwindling fast. Intellectuals, Henry felt, were more liable than sturdy peasants 'to let themselves go'. Storytelling was now a favourite pastime – tales of foreign lands or culinary delights. The criminals, counting for no more than five or six among the politicals, tried their antics again and again. One young thief 'appropriated' Baumann's bread ration and, when challenged, took up the typical enraged stance of the *urki,* who generally settled the manner by attacking the complainant immediately. However, he was no match for the gaunt huge frame of Baumann, who was known affectionately as 'elephant'. The older man grasped the *urka* by the neck and forced him to the floor. Two of the thief's confederates jumped down from the bunks to save their half-strangled comrade but their path was blocked by a pair of tough politicals. The wheezing youth returned Baumann's square of bread. The criminals kept very much to themselves after that, preferring their incessant card games to another physical confrontation.

The prisoners were without news of the front and few of them were summoned to interrogation. Questioning took place in the town, not within the prison itself. The first to be led out of Henry's cell, in February 1942, was Müller, brigadier on a state farm near Odessa. He was a devout Baptist and made no secret of the religious views for which he had been arrested. He came back a changed man and had only time to utter one word, 'vyshku' ('to the highest punishment'), to his expectant friends before being led away to the death cell. There he could linger for months on end, before word came through that his appeal for clemency had been rejected. Müller's sentence had a profound effect on the entire cell. Men felt that there might be a last chance, a final instance called God. Most took to praying; others had always prayed in secret. One hour daily was set aside for Bible studies. Löwenstein, with his Lutheran background, was an active participant.

Men dreamt of the approaching spring, of an end to the unbearable life in the cell, which was now thinning out because of the increasing mortality rate. In April the survivors were moved to a new domicile, a huge room that held two to three hundred.

Conditions there were rougher because of the numerous criminal element. Henry Löwenstein was taken to the sick-bay to cure his infectious rash and, when he returned, most of the inmates had left on the *navigatsiia* barge, to one of the local Gulag sub-camps.

There are few documents in Patrick Breslin's prison file pertaining to his sojourn in Chistopol Prison No. 4. He was not in good health when he arrived there, and the following months were a form of slow death by starvation. Examined by the medical section of the prison on 27 April 1942, presumably in connection with the forth-coming transfer to a work-camp, he was held to be basically healthy and fit for *etap*. Breslin was given two sets of injections, one against smallpox. Because of the huge workload in confirming sentences (most of the transit cases from Moscow, unlike Breslin, were sentenced after arriving in Chistopol), Breslin's verdict of eight years in the Gulag was not confirmed by the Tatarstan NKVD until June 1942.

On 9 June, in the presence of the prison secretary, Breslin confirmed, by signature, that he had been informed of the eight-year stretch. His destination was Volgolag, in the city of Kazan, a small camp with over 5,000 prisoners, of whom a fifth were political prisoners. The work-slaves were employed in building a railway line or on a local state farm.[6] On the questionnaire, with photograph, which was to accompany Breslin to his new place of incarceration, the doctor noted that the prisoner was healthy, and that no epidemics had broken out in the prison during the previous three weeks. According to an undated medical note, Breslin was suitable for physical labour, but he was 'psychologically weak'. Miachina, the female medical doctor who examined him on the day of his departure for Kazan (15 June), confirmed that the transitee was healthy and inoculated, and that there had been no contagious infections in his cell.

When he arrived in Kazan, the doctors gave a different diagnosis, stating that Breslin was very emaciated and suitable for 'only light physical labour'. It is probable that he was carried from the barge to a transit prison and sick-bay within the old Kazan Kremlin, which now houses a cancer hospital. On 21 June 1942, two days afterwards, he died there, allegedly of 'heart failure caused by TB'. Patrick Breslin's final place of rest is unknown, but local tradition has it that prisoners were buried in mass graves in a secluded part of the local graveyard.

It is ironic that Henry Löwenstein was to become the chief of the sick-bay in that same transit prison two years later. He was subsequently sent to a harsher camp. Gennadi Simonov, who was sent from Chistopol to a camp in the city of Kazan in July 1942, was the only one of the 1,500 detachment from Moscow of 10 October 1941 who survived Chistopol prison and the Gulag hell. He had to work twelve to fifteen hours daily, manufacturing shells for the Red Army. Simonov maintains that more of the detachment died in the Kazan Gulag than in Chistopol: they arrived in the provisional factory already in a severely debilitated condition and soon succumbed to one of the classic diseases brought on by near-starvation: pellagra, dysentery or scurvy.

NOTES

1.   N.G. Okhotin and A.B. Roginskii (eds), *Sistema ispravitel'no-trudovykh lagerei v SSSR 1923–1960. Spravochnik* (Moscow 1998), pp. 200–1.
2.   Pasternak Museum Chistopol, account of G. Simonov (Samara), 10.8.1993.
3.   The sparse information on Breslin's sojourn in Tatarstan is taken from his prison file (no. 5851), which is held in the Tatarstan Ministry of the Interior, Kazan.
4.   Henry Ralph Löwenstein (Johnston), *Za reshetkoi i koliuchei provolokoi* (Ioshkar-Ola 1998).
5.   Ibid., pp. 8–9 (text of the NKVD orders).
6.   Okhotin and Roginskii, *Sistema*, p. 189.

PART II
Brian Goold-Verschoyle

Youngest Son of the Manor House

Soviet espionage scored its greatest success in the inter-war period at the very heart of the British Empire. It recruited disaffected upper-class young men who, on account of their background and Oxbridge education, had been offered promising careers in the British government apparatus. Accounts of the treason committed by Philby, Burgess, Maclean, Blunt and Cairncross are legion and often sensationalist, underestimating the other bountiful sources of information provided by lowly Foreign Office clerks or members of the CPGB. As holders of a British passport, then held in high esteem internationally, either category could move freely across Europe without expecting awkward scenes at the frontiers.

Brian Goold-Verschoyle, at first glance, seems to belong to the former group: upper middle-class origin, public school education, a gift for languages, long terms of domicile in the United Kingdom, membership of the CPGB, and a British passport. However, he differed from the five master spies in that his entry into the service of the Soviet state came about mainly because of his persistence, rather than the initiative of his 'minders'. The dangerous career he chose lasted only four years and was that of a technician rather than an informant.

Goold-Verschoyle was of old Anglo-Irish stock, born on 5 June 1912 as the fifth child and youngest son of the family owners of the Manor House, Dunkineely, County Donegal. The village is on Inver Bay, five miles east of Killybegs. The family home, despite its grand title, was a Victorian house on the main street of the village. Hamilton Verschoyle, Bishop of Kilmore and paternal great-grandfather of Brian, married Catherine Hawkins, the daughter of the Rector of Killaghtee, which is on the outskirts of Dunkineely, in 1833. The new Manor House was to be the place of residence for the unmarried Hawkins ladies. The erection of the building, completed in 1884, was delayed because the lower storey was dismantled for rock-throwing during the first and only Orange march in the village, on 12 July 1881, the anniversary of King William's victory at the Boyne. When the last Miss Hawkins, Georgina, died, the newly wedded Goold-Verschoyles, Brian's parents, inherited the house.

Brian's father, Hamilton Frederick Stuart Goold-Verschoyle (1874–1942), was a barrister who gave up the profession because of his weak lungs. The family lived mainly on the receipts from extensive land holdings and foreign investments. The paternal line of the family tree begins with the Dutchman Hendrick Verschuyl, who died in Dublin in 1623, and a Stuart from the Western Isles who settled in County Tyrone in the reign of Elizabeth I. The Goold sub-branch, the forebears of Brian's paternal grandmother Frances Goold (1847–1942), contains the names of pro- and anti-Union members of Grattan's Parliament and of the man behind the main source of family wealth, Thomas Goold. He squandered his inheritance by high living in Dublin in the 1790s, made a fortune at the bar and purchased an estate of 15,000 acres around Athea in west County Limerick. By the nineteenth century, both the Goolds and the Verschoyles had sons in holy orders: Hamilton Stuart Verschoyle (1844–1932), Brian's paternal grandfather, was Vicar of Dunkineely and son of the Bishop of Kilmore, and on the Goold side Frederick, the other grandfather, was Archdeacon of Raphoe. Family tradition has it that a condition of the marriage between Hamilton Stuart and Frances in 1873 was that the couple and their offspring now adopt the double-barrelled name Goold-Verschoyle. At that time the father of Frances still possessed almost 11,000 acres in Limerick.

Her husband, Rev. Hamilton Stuart of Dunkineely, was also a landlord, who took his favourite grandchild, Brian's sister Sheila, with him at Christmas when delivering little bags of coal to his tenants. Family history details before 1914 also show that the political tensions in Irish society encroached on the Manor House. While the grandfather vicar was gun-running for the Orangemen, the Goold cousin Constance Goore-Booth, better known as Countess Markievicz, had co-founded Fianna Éireann, the Republican boy-scouts, and become a dedicated Larkinite.

Brian's mother was Sibyl Mary Le Mesurier (1873–1946), daughter of a Colonel of Engineers from a family long established on the Channel Islands. Among her Irish antecedents were the Burkes and Brownes of Mayo, including Colonel John Browne, the lawyer of Patrick Sarsfield, and Maud Burke of Westport, the great-great-granddaughter of Gráinne O'Malley. Sibyl's maternal forebears also included the family of William Ussher, who printed the first Irish translation of the New Testament, and Henry Ussher, the founder of Dunsink Observatory.

Brian's parents, Sibyl and Frederick, met in Dublin at the turn of the century. They found that they were kindred spirits, feeling ill-at-ease in the formal atmosphere of balls and receptions at Dublin Castle. Sibyl had previously often feigned weariness to escape the attentions of her father's subordinates, the young lieutenants eager to dance. She retired to bed to read Carlyle. Frederick, a kind and gentle man who took after his mother, Fanny Goold, and not his stern Loyalist father, had attended the glittering evenings in court dress only to please *paterfamilias*. The couple married in 1900 and settled down in Dublin. After the birth of Eileen (1902), Sheila (1903) and Neil (1904), the Goold-Verschoyles moved to the family home in County Donegal. Denis was born in Dunkineely in 1910 and Brian two years later.[1]

Largely thanks to the encouragement of the Irish writer Dermot Bolger, Sheila became the chronicler of the years before the children left the nest – impressions, with drawings, of an idyllic childhood on the Donegal coast.[2] The father, Hamilton Frederick Stuart, known as 'Tim' to his wife, was a freethinking and pacifist Home Ruler. Now rarely practising at the bar, he occasionally penned the 'An Irishman's Diary' column for the *Irish Times*, read voraciously and went to church on Sundays only to hear and take part in the Gregorian chants. Because he had been a sickly only child, his education had taken place at home, first with a nanny, then with a tutor, who taught him to sing in German, French and Italian. Music was his great passion, composing melodies, playing the piano in the evenings and singing old sentimental songs. With Sheila in tow, 'Tim' sometimes visited the local farmers with his fiddle, ever eager to learn new tunes. He was often taken abroad on holidays as a child, when his father acted as locum to the expatriate Church of England community. Despite the weary round of visits to art galleries and old churches, the young boy inherited his father's gift for languages. A love of literature was shared by all family members, with Sibyl choosing Browning, and 'Tim' Whitman, as their favourite poets. The mother of five had other hobbies. She was extremely interested in astrology and psychic phenomena, sometimes staging séances with her friends. The children, who were encouraged to think for themselves and keep an open mind, showed little curiosity for the esoteric.

Sheila does not remember being caressed or hugged as a child, but stresses the great interest the parents took in the daily activities and mental development of their children. It was a very unusual family, a kind of democratic federacy where each one had his or her own space – the mother's bed-sitting-room, the father's study, the studio under the roof for the girls (Eileen weaved, Sheila painted or drew) and the coach house for the boys, who turned it into a laboratory. The activities were recounted at meals or in the evenings, when the family gathered in the father's study to listen to his music, to read, sing or play word games. Sibyl suffered badly from arthritis and was often confined to bed. Eileen, at an early age, more or less took over the running of the house, giving instructions to the cook and the parlour maid. Mrs Goold-Verschoyle often absented herself to talk for hours to the gardener's wife about women's problems.

The family did not believe in ostentation. Their car for many years was an ancient second-hand Ford, its canvas roof secured by a piece of rope. At the beginning of the Civil War, the local republican column 'borrowed' the family car, but it was returned the next day after Eileen, who had just learned to drive, had gone to the rebel headquarters with Sheila and Neil to lodge a protest. During the episode they had locked their highly strung father in a room, deciding to resolve the matter themselves.

The beautiful natural surroundings – the caves of Maghera, the beaches of Inver Bay or the climbing challenge of Slieve League and the awesome beauty of Glencolumbkille in the extreme west of the county – inspired summer outings, often on a dray. Sheila was wont to go on solitary walks, sometimes before dawn. The summer was generally wet and in Donegal it was often an Indian one, with the best weather occurring in September and October. Picnics were organised by Sheila and Eileen, frequently with relatives or neighbouring Protestants such as the Fforde or Combe families. The boys were encouraged to bring home friends from their boarding school and all pitched in to 'save the hay' of the garden meadow, visited the Killybegs regatta or took part, in fancy dress, in the high point of the summer, Sheila's birthday on 28 August.

Other favourite pastimes were boating and mackerel-fishing with Neil and Brian. While Sheila emphasises that she was rather the dreamy sister given to solo excursions in the neighbourhood with her drawing equipment, and Eileen the practical one, her portrayal of her brothers, while affectionate, is considerably more vague. There is more mention of the older siblings than the younger ones since the children in most families pair off according to age: the first group of Neil, Eileen and Sheila, the second of the two younger boys, Denis and Brian. The boys were interested in science and 'gadgets', once cycling with their father to Donegal Town (twelve miles each way) after they had heard that somebody was demonstrating the wonders of the new-fangled 'wireless'. For sixpence one could listen, through headphones, to sounds over the ether. Neil was enthusiastic and built a radio for the sitting-room from various spare parts. This interest was shared by or passed on to Brian, who, in his formative years at least, looked up to Neil as a role model.

The atmosphere of the home was unusually liberal by the standards of the rural Anglo-Irish upper class – Irish and inter-national culture rather than the pursuits of hunting and shooting. The family kept neither horses nor dogs, preferring cats. The girls loved to sing local songs and dance Irish set-pieces such as 'The Waves of Tory' or 'The Walls of Limerick'. Family discussions frequently centred on religion, politics, birth-control or the poetry the children had learned by heart. The writers mentioned spanned the nineteenth and early twentieth centuries – Hardy, Samuel Butler, Shaw, Ibsen, Chekhov, Joyce, D.H. Lawrence and James Stephens. In some years the Goold-Verschoyle family shut up house for one month in winter and travelled to Dublin by train, via Strabane. In the capital there were visits to the Abbey and Gaiety theatres and to relations.

The remote location of the family home had disadvantages. The local doctor was good – he cured Sheila of a congenital back ailment after he had persuaded the parents to take her out of hospital and the traction-bed. The nearest decent dentist, however, was in Derry, three hours away by train, with a change at Strabane.

Living in Dunkineely also posed problems for the children's education, specifically the schooling of young Protestants. Eileen attended the French School in Bray before transferring, with her sister Sheila, to Londonderry High School. Neil received his secondary education at Cheltenham, a school he hated, while Denis attended Portora Royal School in Enniskillen, County Fermanagh. Brian went to school for the first time at the age of nine, having probably had a governess or home tutor before that. His stay at Aravon School in Bray lasted only for one year and he moved to Portora in 1923.[3] The school, founded in 1618 and located on a steep hill overlooking Enniskillen, was a popular learning academy for Protestants. According to Samuel Beckett's sojourn at the school between 1916 and 1923, as recounted by his biographer James Knowlson, the pupils were divided along two lines: Northerners against Southerners, boarders against lower-rank day boys ('day dogs'). The day pupils, usually the sons of local shopkeepers, policemen and small farmers, were taught separately from the boarders, whose fathers were often British Army officers, bank managers or Church of Ireland clergymen. Portora resembled similar institutions across the Irish Sea: strict discipline, compulsory religious service, military training in the Officer Training Corps (OTC), and an emphasis on sport (cricket and rugby). When Beckett attended the school, the food was appalling, either burnt (breakfast porridge or 'fry') or over-cooked (potatoes, cabbage and meat). The only relief were the 'grub boxes' sent from home. 'Honesty, integrity and loyalty' were the virtues inculcated by the headmaster, the Rev. Ernest G. Seale.[4]

In the late 1920s Portora was still a relatively small school, with under two hundred pupils, of whom roughly one-third were day boys. Newcomers, irrespective of where they hailed from, were allocated places in one of the school 'houses', named after Ireland's Four Provinces. Denis seems to have acclimatised well, attaining the status of prefect in his final year (1928), 'colours' on the rowing team and a place on the second XV of the school's rugby team. He also held the rank of sergeant in the OTC unit.[5] For reasons unknown, Tim and Sibyl took Brian out of Portora at the end of the 1925 summer term. His next station in education was Oswestry Grammar School in Shropshire. Since he remained there for one academic year only, the education on offer was probably deemed unsuitable. In September 1926 Brian entered Marlborough College, where he remained until his seventeenth birthday in June 1929.

There were some slight family connections with this elite establishment for young gentlemen. A John Hamilton Verschoyle (1854–1928), son of a clergyman in Omagh who went on to serve in the British Army in Egypt, attended Marlborough for a year. Two sons of W.H.F. Verschoyle of Dundrum, County Dublin, entered the Army as Old Marlburians and fell on the Western Front.[6] More importantly, Brian had a good neighbour with him at his new school, Francis Fforde, nephew of the sea-captain who owned Bruckless House near Dunkineely, 'got Communism' and visited Pat Breslin in Moscow.[7]

Located just off the High Street of the market town set in the middle of the North Wessex Downs, Marlborough College was an assortment of Queen Anne style buildings. Founded in 1843 at the seat of the Dukes of Somerset, the academy had gone through stormy years, including an open rebellion of the boys in 1851. A period of consolidation is associated with the name of Dr Cyril Norwood, who became headmaster in 1916. Jeered at first by the snob element among the boys because he had come from a grammar school, Norwood made his mark as one of Britain's best educationalists and was appointed chairman of the Secondary Schools Examination Council in 1921.[8] Among the new boys that autumn, five years before Brian's arrival, were Louis MacNeice (another Ulsterman, son of a clergyman who later became Bishop of Down and Connor) and John Betjeman. MacNeice's best friend there was Anthony Blunt, later the infamous 'Fourth Man' of the best-known Soviet spy ring in England. Although Brian arrived at his new boarding school just after the three aesthetes had left with university scholarships in 1926, MacNeice's memoir of the learning establishment, insightful and free of rancour, portrays a whole era.[9]

An elite British boarding school like Marlborough was characterised by conditions of physical discomfort (mainly unheated rooms), arcane rituals and a system of social stratification based on age and class. While the younger boys were servants ('fagging') for their seniors and were regularly caned for their omissions, the worst was over when, at the age of fourteen, they passed the School Certificate and transferred into Senior House. The boys reflected the class-obsessed world whence they came – the 'bloods' from the top aristocratic social bracket or those, for example, from the Home Counties with Army connections, whose parents played bridge, insisted on 'breeding' and went to the local Hunt Ball. Many pupils belonged to neither group and got on just as well because the school also had a highbrow tradition and cherished academic excellence. MacNeice found at least half the teaching body 'insignificant, pleasant enough but incurably trivial, fawning on their seniors [and] backbiting each other in the Common Room'. Brian Goold-Verschoyle, of 'black hair and reddish complexion', was described by his friend Fforde as 'cheerful and wilful and very clever academically'. Both disliked their housemaster and Brian's form master in the Science Upper Sixth.

Most of a pupil's day during the first year of Senior House was spent in Upper School, a vast barn-like structure in which the boys did their homework after the last meal in the great dining-hall (6.30 p.m.). Anyone who was out of his place at 7.15 p.m., or had not closed the lid of the desk so that it was flush, was caned by one of the four 'Captains'. These were 'hearties', athletes aged about sixteen grouped around the large open fire, who staged other scenes of mass sadism. 'Roman holiday' was the practice whereby an 'undesirable' was stripped of most of his clothes, covered in paint and pushed around the hall in a huge wastepaper-basket. Teachers considered this a fine old tradition and did not interfere; anyone 'basketed' lived subsequently under a cloud. The whole spectacle was accompanied by howls of approbation from the serried rows of boys. The culprit or victim was generally disliked for good reason, it was thought, and 'innate justice' was seen to be done. In MacNeice's words, it was 'Government of the mob, by the mob, and for the mob'.

We can only speculate on what Brian or Francis Fforde thought of all this brutality, but since Goold-Verschoyle was in Senior Sixth at an early age, the school atmosphere does not seem to have hindered his progress as a budding scientist. One other possible indication for his relatively smooth adjustment to Marlburian realities was his service, from entry to the school, in the local OTC. He was in the Signals Section, a pointer to his interest in radio. At home in Dunkineely, a family council was held on the future of the younger boys, Denis and Brian. Mother Sibyl wished to consult their stellar constellation and ordered an expertise (a 'fuller reading' cost two guineas, a 'special reading' three) from R.H.T. Naylor of Conduit Street in London's West End. He was later Britain's most famous astrologer, noted for his column in the *Sunday Express*. Naylor ruled out a career in the Army for Sybil's youngest boys and held that Brian was too idealistic for business but was likely to show a scientific or literary bent sooner or later. Brian, 'somewhat of a dreamer at heart', had a complex character: 'a love of adventure difficult to square with the gentle manners and somewhat nervous temperament'.

Brian did what he wanted to do, embarking on a career in science. He secured an apprenticeship leading to engineer status with the English Electric Company Ltd. in Stafford. His wage during apprenticeship was 29 shillings a week, which was augmented by an allowance from home of £72 p.a. English Electric had been formed in 1918 from the merger of a number of companies in the heavy electrical industry which included the Stafford works of the German firm Siemens Bros. The starting capital of £5 million was impressive, but the profits in the early 1920s proved modest and at the onset of the world depression the prospects for the firm did not look good.

In 1930, a year after Brian Goold-Verschoyle's entry, a new managing director was installed, George Horatio Nelson, formerly of the Metro-Vickers works in Sheffield. In the decade up to the outbreak of World War II, he managed to turn around the fortunes of the company, not least because of large public-sector orders, primarily trains and airplanes. During Brian's apprenticeship (1929–33) production centred almost exclusively on heavy electrical equipment: water and steam turbines, generating sets, switchgear, transformers and electrical equipment for electric and diesel-electric locomotives, ships, trams and trolley buses, industrial diesel engines and rolling mills.[10] Towards the end of his apprenticeship Brian was working as a 'tester's assistant'.

When Brian moved to Stafford in September 1929, his brothers had left Dunkineely. Neil had been living in London for some years, working for the schools programmes of the BBC after receiving a BA in Philosophy and a BSc from London University. Denis went to Trinity College Dublin (TCD), where he studied forestry. Sheila returned to Donegal in 1928 after four years at the Slade Art School in London. In 1930 she married Gerald Fitzgerald, an Anglo-Irish 'outdoor' type, who owned Charleville House near Castlebar, County Mayo. They set up a guest house, mainly for game shooting enthusiasts. Eileen's husband was a local man, Gerald Simms of Lifford. His father had been Crown Prosecutor for County Tyrone and the agent of Lord Abercorn; his mother the daughter of a naturalised German. Gerald was a brilliant student at Winchester and New College, Oxford. After a successful career in the Indian Civil Service he made his name as an expert on the Williamite war in Ireland and taught history at TCD from the 1950s. His brother George Otto, held in fond memory by many Irish people, was TCD Chaplain, subsequently Church of Ireland Archbishop of Dublin, and later of Armagh, and a noted scholar of Old Irish.

While Sheila remained basically apolitical, if strongly pacifist, Eileen tended towards the Left, describing herself in later life as a

'Gandhiite Communist'. She supported de Valera's neutrality policy during World War II and took up the study of Irish and Russian after her return from India in 1949. The three boys became communists. All siblings were influenced by the liberal atmosphere of the home and rejected the imperialist attitudes still adhered to by many of their class and religious creed in post-1922 Ireland. The War of Independence had been low-key in Donegal, mainly because of high emigration to Scotland in the summer months and disputes among local IRA commanders, but the Civil War executions (four Kerry Republicans at Drumboe in March 1923) were not forgotten. It is doubtful if Sibyl's sons were immediately radicalised by the freedom struggle, because of their youth and absence from home. However, there was stark poverty in rural Donegal after the foundation of the Irish Free State. The Goold-Verschoyle family may have discussed a worldwide campaign launched by the Comintern front organisation Internationale Arbeiter-Hilfe (International Workers' Relief – IAH) to alleviate near famine conditions in north Mayo and Donegal in 1925. The relief fund was the brainchild of the German Communist Willi Münzenberg, who also managed an empire of left-wing newspapers and periodicals and had founded the international 'Anti-Imperialist League' in 1927. The IRA, its female auxiliary Cumann na mBan and youth section Fianna Éireann were affiliated to the Berlin-based League. Münzenberg's campaign to help the hungry Irish in 1925 was the subject of harsh condemnations from the Catholic clergy. From February to the end of May, local Republicans distributed £724 collected by the IAH internationally to hundreds of families – foodstuffs, seed potatoes, coal, fishing nets and balls of cloth. In the Killybegs district just west of Dunkineely, twenty-five families received assistance.[11]

Joining the Communist Party, however, was a conscious step taken by very few of the many concerned citizens who were appalled by endemic poverty and the misery of mass unemployment after the Wall Street Crash of 1929. Neil, as eldest brother and mentor of Brian, was one catalyst. He was involved in intellectual and Christian Socialist circles (Ethical Church) in London and travelled widely. He left for the Soviet Union on 2 October 1930, a fact duly noted by the Special Branch at Scotland Yard.[12] Neil worked as a journalist on the English-language magazine *Intourist* for foreigners and also did freelance translation work in Moscow before returning to London in January 1933.[13] Although not a Party member in

Britain or Russia, in letters to Brian he praised the achievements of the First Five-Year Plan.

Another influence on the boys' drift towards Marxism was a popular neighbour, Thomas Roderick Fforde, the 'Red' sea-captain, who had bought Bruckless House in 1922, following his retirement, with Commander rank and on half-pay, from the Royal Navy.[14] To locals, Mr Fforde was something of an enigma – living the life of a country gentleman and propagating communism, often from a soapbox during the market in one of the local towns. He was held in esteem and affection not because of his politics – when he died in 1949 he was cycling home from a Fianna Fáil meeting – but on account of his philanthropy, whether employing locals directly as farmhands or servants, or indirectly by selling wood from his estate to a local sawmill. His local popularity was also enhanced by his sailing skills: Tom Fforde won the Killybegs Open Pleasure Boat Cup on four occasions between 1922 and 1936. The couple was childless, but any child who called to the door got either fruit or sweets, and all primary school classes in the area received a box of apples from Mr Fforde's extensive orchard at Christmastime.

Tom Fforde had been radicalised during the Boxer Rebellion in China (1900), or rather in its aftermath, by the brutality of the imperial powers in suppressing it. His last naval posting, as a torpedo officer, was Murmansk during the Russian Civil War, where he formed a rapport with his Russian counterparts in the port.

The Goold-Verschoyle children were frequent visitors to Fforde's home and would have seen his collection of books and pamphlets on Russia, the maps of the USSR on the walls of the dining-room and his study, or heard his comments about the programmes of Radio Moscow. Interestingly, he was not disillusioned by his stay in Stalin's empire in 1932–33. He probably put his experiences there in a kind of 'dialectic' perspective when talking to the Goold-Verschoyle boys: his cabinet-making tools were stolen in Leningrad and the only work he could find in Moscow was not fulfilling: making screws in a metal factory. After an injury to his hand which subsequently became infected, he despaired of Russian medicine and returned to his spacious house beside the sea in Donegal.

Denis, who had a great interest in local history and probably spent evenings discussing politics with his Bolshevik seafaring neighbour, joined the Irish offshoot of the Comintern, the Revolutionary Workers' Groups (RWG), in the early 1930s. In mid-1932 the Dublin branch of the RWG numbered seventy-three, of whom fifty-eight were active. Nineteen were unemployed, eleven were members of the IRA and three students.[15] The last were members of the University Marxist Group at TCD, which, as Denis had reported at a closed meeting at 206 Pearse Street at an earlier date, were in the red to the sum of £6.[16] Denis had a room in 63 Eccles Street, the site of the Workers' College, initiated by the veteran suffragette Charlotte Despard. When a Catholic mob singing 'Faith of our Fathers' attacked the house in March 1933, Denis and other comrades threw bricks from the roof, keeping the raucous hymn-singers at bay until the police arrived.[17]

Brian, who was very close to Denis, was influenced politically by both brothers. However, Neil and Denis did not get on well together, perhaps because Neil had been educated in Britain and spent skiing holidays on the Continent as a child with a rich cousin, thus laying the foundation for an interest in foreign countries. Denis, on the other hand, was firmly rooted in Ireland and involved in the local community, even saving part of his university allowance to restore a local castle with the help of other Dunkineely men. According to Denis, the last amicable conversation he had with his elder brother Neil was on the eve of Sheila's wedding in 1930, when they went for a swim at Bruckless. Neil admitted that, in comparison to his brother, he knew next to nothing of Donegal or of the local people outside the Protestant landed gentry. This difference in outlook was due to age and location, for Neil spent his formative years in Britain, and Denis had grown to manhood in the new Irish state. The political radicalisation of the two older Goold-Verschoyle boys, while reaching the same conclusions, therefore sprang from a variety of sources. Neil, who never lost his ascetic bent, came to Marxism from a Christian viewpoint, but Denis, who liked to mix and drink with friends in Donegal and Dublin, went from republicanism, selling the IRA newspaper *An Phoblacht* around Dunkineely in the early 1930s, to communism, a common path for radicals in the closing years of the Cosgrave administration (1922–32).

Brian Goold-Verschoyle first came to the notice of the British police in Stafford in July 1931 after he had made a written application to the British Communist Party for membership, since all correspondence to its headquarters at 16 King Street in the Covent Garden area of London was opened and photographed by the police. After making enquiries as to the habits of the young Irishman, the Staffordshire Chief Constable wrote to the Special Branch:

He came to reside in Stafford in September 1929 and has since worked as an engineering apprentice at the works of the English Electric Company. He is studious but very reticent. He keeps to himself and most of the time, when not at work, is spent at this lodgings reading Russian literature and Communist papers. It is believed that he has a brother in Russia. He has not been seen to mix or have any connection with the people of Stafford known to have Communist sympathies and in this connection I mention that although most of the persons who originally formed the Stafford Group are still living in the town, they appear at the present time to be quite inactive.[18]

At this juncture Brian was certainly of one mind politically with Denis, his senior by two years. According to the statement made to the British secret service (MI5) by a family acquaintance, T.D.B. Kempton, the behaviour of Eileen, Denis and Brian was anything but conventional: Eileen raised eyebrows because she believed in state as against private education for her children, whom she, as an adherent of the Montessori schools, 'allowed a great deal of freedom'; furthermore, she had insisted on having a native doctor at one of her confinements in India. Whereas Eileen, at least, had engaged Mr Kempton in conversation when she was at home on leave from India in 1933, both Brian and Denis had refused to meet him or his companions when they visited Dunkineely. Denis, 'an extreme Irish nationalist who spoke Gaelic in preference to English', and Brian did not deign to grace the teatime party with their presence because Kempton was an Englishman and another in the group an Irish-born officer serving in the British Army.[19]

The activities of the youngest Goold-Verschoyle son in the CPGB probably date from August 1932, when the party local branch in Stafford was reformed. Seven months later he was Local Organiser and asked King Street to send all circulars to his address. Colonel Sir Vernon Kell, creator and director of MI5, referred to Goold-Verschoyle's letter (duly photographed) when he enquired of the Chief Constable in Stafford as to the workplace of the 20-year-old Irishman. Lieutenant-Colonel Hunter replied that Brian was a 'premium apprentice, well thought of in the works and is likely to remain with the firm after the completion of his apprenticeship' in September 1933.[20] By this time the young engineer had also come to the attention of the Cadres Department of the Communist International, the recipient of his long biographical report dated 18 March 1933.

Goold-Verschoyle's main activity in the CPGB cell was distributing literature and organising training classes. He was now the only communist in the factory since two comrades, whom he had recruited, had left shortly before. He was also a member of the Amalgamated Engineering Union, Stafford Labour Club and the Stafford Industrial Co-operative Society. More impressive was his reading and learning programme: the ability to read French, German and Russian, and the study of Marx, Lenin (including 'What Is To Be Done?' in the Russian original), Bukharin and Plekhanov.

That Goold-Verschoyle penned his data in the style of Soviet questionnaires (social position and origin; intellectual development and education; political life, including reprimands or expulsion from the Communist Party; participation in social life; repression and prosecution) four months before his first visit to Moscow in July 1933 suggests that he may have contacted the Soviets earlier, via the CPGB. Another pointer to a job-seeking rather than a social visit to the USSR was that Neil, the brother to whom he was devoted, was not in Moscow, having returned to Britain in January 1933.

Observation by the British police continued. In June 1933, Birmingham CID informed Kell that the Birmingham Communist Stephen Jacoby was to give a talk on the First Five-Year Plan in Stafford and that Brian Goold-Verschoyle would accompany him.[21] Then the track grew cold, and the Irishman's departure from Britain was not recorded.

NOTES

1. I am indebted to David Simms for explaining his family's history. Seamus McShane, Dunkineely publican and a rich source of local history, also shared his memories of the Goold-Verschoyle family with me over well-pulled pints in July 2003. On the family background and the personality of Neil Goold-Verschoyle, see Uinseann MacEoin, *The IRA in the Twilight Years, 1923–1948* (Dublin 1997), pp. 919–23. Sheila Fitzpatrick also furnished details of family life when I visited her home in Wexford in July 1995.

2. Sheila Fitzpatrick, *A Donegal Summer. A Young girl's sketchbook of the 1920's*. With an Introduction by Pauline Bewick (Dublin 1985). See also the articles by Dermot Bolger: 'The Lady in the Fields', *The Irish Times Magazine*, 20 January 2001, p. 82; 'Last Rites for My First Audience', *Sunday Independent*, 3 September 2000.

3. The outline of Brian's biography is taken from what he wrote in his own hand for the Comintern bureaucracy (RGASPI, f. 495, o. 198, d. 1324, ll. 5–8).

4. James Knowlson, *Damned to Fame. The Life of Samuel Beckett* (London 1997, paperback), pp. 36–46.

5. Communication from William L. Scott, the Librarian/Archivist of Portora, 2 October 2003.
6. R.T. Smith MA, Secretary of the Marlburian Club, to the author, 1 September 1995.
7. Francis Fforde to Sheila Fitzpatrick (née Goold-Verschoyle), 30 June 1989.
8. Jon Stallworthy, *Louis MacNeice* (London 1995), pp. 72–105.
9. Louis MacNeice, *The Strings are False. An Unfinished Biography* (London 1965, 1996), pp. 80–101.
10. www.marconi.com/html/about/englishelectrichistory.htm
11. RGASPI, f. 538, o. 2, d. 27, ll. 67–86.
12. Public Record Office London (PRO), KV2/817, note 320/FRS/2189, 2 October 1930.
13. Ibid., Letter to Passport Office, 27 February 1936.
14. Clive and Joan Evans, the present owners of Bruckless House, kindly provided me with valuable information on the history of the Fforde family and their wonderful home.
15. RGASPI, f. 495, o. 89, d. 78, l. 30.
16. RGASPI, f. 495, o. 89, d. 83, l. 35.
17. Joe Monks, *With the Reds in Andalusia* (London 1985), pp. 9–11.
18. PRO, KV2/817, Chief Constable Stafford to Special Branch, 24 July 1931.
19. Ibid., Note on the Goold-Verschoyle family, 6 November 1940.
20. Ibid., Kell to Lt. Col. H.P. Hunter, 31 March 1933; Hunter to Kell, 12 April 1933.
21. Ibid., Birmingham CID to Kell, 1 June 1933.

Insistent Recruit

Brian Goold-Verschoyle received his first passport on 3 June 1933, two days before his 21st birthday. In it he is described as being 5 feet 9 inches, with black hair and brown eyes.[1] In July he travelled to the Continent for the first time. His destination was Moscow, his contact address there that of Olga Ivanovna Dobrova, Neil's wife, who was then pregnant and gave birth to a son, Pyotr, in September.[2] Brian hoped to work as an engineer in Moscow because his contract with English Electric had almost expired. Olga was very kind to him, introducing him to Irina Adler, the wife of an engineer and a member of the Central Committee of the Komsomol, the Party's youth section. The youngest Goold-Verschoyle brother had no idea that Olga was a secret police agent and he probably suspected nothing when a meeting was arranged with uniformed officers, since she emphasised that any foreigner seeking work had to be screened by the police.

Olga was a recruiting agent for the Foreign Department (INO) of the NKVD, and Brian, who believed he was being interviewed for an electrician's job in a Moscow factory, listened carefully to the conditions of employment. The men in green made a great secret of the meeting, saying that he, as a disciplined communist, should agree to serve the Soviet Union in any capacity and to wait in England until he was contacted. Furthermore, he was to sever all links with the CPGB and would, in the course of time, be granted his wish to settle in Russia. Brian Goold-Verschoyle then signed some form of contract, presumably an oath of confidentiality, and returned to Britain.

He subsequently abstained from political activism, an understandable security measure. He informed the CPGB that he had done enough for the working class and would in future work for his own. Now unemployed, he lived more or less as he had in Stafford, studying at home in furnished rooms near King's Cross, and later in Kensington. Idealistic and lonely, Brian had lost his political comrades and his only friend was his brother Neil, who was desperately trying to return to his wife and child in Moscow. Before Neil finally succeeded in obtaining a Soviet visa in 1934, he arranged a job for Brian at the BBC, in the schools programmes' department.[3] Two telegrams sent by Neil to his brother's address in London in June 1934 indicate that Brian was impatient, and hoping that Neil, through Olga, could expedite his first involvement with the secret organisation he had joined the previous summer. Neil was evasive, cabling that the possibility of such help was 'remote' since he and Olga were considering applying for jobs with a Soviet company or institution in London.[4] This may have been a ploy to keep Brian 'standing at ease' and was no doubt coordinated with the people in Olga's network who had scrutinised the insistent young Irishman the previous June. In any case, Brian Goold-Verschoyle did not take the hint but travelled again to Moscow on a tourist visa in the summer of 1934.

He was reprimanded by his NKVD contacts for coming of his own volition and told brusquely to return and await orders. Nonetheless, the short sojourn with Neil and Olga, and with the freshly divorced Irina, left him enthusiastic and more determined than ever to make his life in the Soviet Union. Once more in his London bedsit, Goold-Verschoyle lived for the letters from Moscow, from the voluble Olga and Irina, to whom he had become very attached. This almost subterranean and solitary existence changed in the autumn, when he fell for his German teacher, Margarete Charlotte (Lotte) Moos.[5]

Lotte was born in Berlin, the second of three daughters of the merchant Samuel Jacoby and his wife Luise (née Baumann) in December 1909. The Jacobys were prosperous Jews living in the upper middle-class suburb of Charlottenburg in the west of the German capital. Like many German Jews in business, they had far-flung relations all over Europe, including the United Kingdom. Mrs Jacoby admired the German-Polish socialist Rosa Luxemburg. Conversations within the family about the murder of Luxemburg and other leaders of the Berlin Spartacist Rising of 1918–19 probably laid the foundation for Lotte's interest in left-wing issues. Her father seems to have been less assertive than her mother. His great interest were the works of Goethe and he lectured on his idol to night-school classes. After secondary school Lotte took private training as a portrait-photographer at a studio on Berlin's fashionable Kurfürstendamm. In October 1931 she matriculated at the Humboldt University, where she studied Economics for eighteen months.

In 1929 she met Siegfried (Siegi) Moos, and they married in Berlin in October 1932. Siegi was five years older, from a Jewish family in Ulm. After his father had deserted the family to become an artist in Paris, Siegi moved to Munich, where his Uncle Hermann was part-owner in a firm producing fine liqueurs. Following his PhD graduation in Economics from the Technische Hochschule in Munich, he worked at a variety of jobs – as a bank clerk, and as a manager trainee in the drinks' business in Munich and Berlin. His intellectual passions were Marxist economics, dramatics and literature, and he met Lotte through a common interest in workers' agitprop theatre groups. Lotte wanted to be an actress and she wrote poetry, like her husband. Siegi Moos wrote sketches for the fit-up (travelling) troupes of the KPD, the German section of the Communist International, a mass party with a third of a million members which gained almost 17 per cent of the vote at the last free elections held in Germany before 1949 (7 November 1932).[6]

According to the Gestapo, Siegfried Moos was 'a convinced and active member of the KPD', and of the paramilitary communist organisation Roter Frontkämpferbund.[7] Siegi broke with his Jewish past in 1929 by resigning from his synagogue community and was active in the proletarian-secularist movement. By late 1932 he was an experienced and trusted communist, a member of the national executive (Reichsleitung) of the communist faction of the working-class Freethinkers (Proletarische Freidenker).[8]

Lotte Moos left Germany for Paris with the help of the communist underground in July 1933, five months after Hitler's accession to power. Her husband joined her there, and she proceeded to Britain with the intention of obtaining an entry permit for Siegi. When she landed at Folkestone on 9 December 1933, the immigration officer was convinced that she was no ordinary refugee from German fascism: she had £45 on her person and a letter from her maternal aunt, Martha Jacoby, in Brighton, promising to support her during a proposed course of studies at the London School of Economics (LSE). Lotte was allowed to disembark on the condition that she register immediately with the police, that her stay would be no longer than two months, and that she was not to take up any kind of employment.

British immigration control procedures for anti-fascist Germans were very tight. By the end of 1937 only roughly 5,500, or 4 per cent of all Germans who had fled their homeland by that date were permitted to settle in Britain. The situation did not change until 1939, following the Nazi occupation of Austria and Czechoslovakia, and the collapse of international negotiations held on the refugee problem at the French spa of Evian in the summer of 1938. Pressure on the British government to admit more Jewish refugees also grew because of the November 1938 pogroms in Germany and the imposition of the immigration embargo against European Jews by the British Mandate authorities in Palestine. When war broke out in September 1939, 74,000 German-speaking immigrants were resident in Britain, many on temporary residence visas before travelling to a third country.[9]

Whatever the Conservative government might decree, public opinion in Britain, especially the liberal, left-wing and intellectual sections of the population, remained sympathetic towards the plight of European refugees as the 1930s progressed: more and more Britons saw that Hitler could not be 'appeased'. London humour made gentle fun of Germans who missed their central heating or cuisine, dubbing them 'Bei unsers', as the German grouch often prefaced his or her grumble with 'Bei uns in . . .' (At home in . . .). Self-important German immigrants were ridiculed by fellow German-speakers, receiving the title 'Herr Emigranz' (His Emigrence).[10] The Committee for German Refugees had its seat in Woburn House in London, where Lotte registered following a one-night stay with her Brighton aunt.

She was exhausted after living on her wits in Germany and France, bewildered because her English was far from perfect and soon experienced a major disappointment when the LSE administration refused to recognise her credits from Berlin University, which meant that she had to matriculate all over again. Furthermore, she was not successful in obtaining one of the scholarships for refugees offered by the Students' Union at the LSE. Through another refugee assistance group, in Great Russell Street, Lotte Moos met the McKinnion Wood couple at a New Year's Party. He was an engineer at the Royal Aircraft Establishment at Farnborough in Hampshire, and later stood as a Labour County Council candidate. Lotte stayed in Hampshire until the arrival of her husband in 1934.

Mr McKinnion Wood was prepared to take responsibility for both and vouch for them to the immigration authorities. However, Lotte and Siegi had some money and he was in receipt of 200 Reichmarks (£20) monthly from an uncle in Munich, so that they did not want to burden generous hosts when most refugees had no money at all.

In February 1934 Lotte Moos's residence permit was extended to August, as was that of her husband, who had landed at Folkestone from Paris on 13 February. Siegi gained entry to the United Kingdom on the strength of a recommendation from the Scottish socialist MP Jimmy Maxton. The British authorities were still being very cautious: the Chief Constable of Hampshire, who reported on the stay of Mrs Moos in Farnborough, complained that she had not deregistered when leaving the area and advised that her particulars should be forwarded to Colonel Kell of MI5. The Home Office, although regarding her as a genuine student (she wanted to take entrance examinations for London University in May), believed that 'the case needs watching'. The couple's mail was being opened and read as from 12 March, but the Home Office reported that Siegfried Moos was also registered at the LSE and was 'no doubt' a genuine student. In late August, MI5 informed the Home Office that it had no further information on the couple.

The security service had nothing to report on the Moos family for another full year. Lotte took short courses in English and Population Studies at the LSE, and French and English at the Linguists' Club in Kingsway, a private school managed by the Oxford graduate A.T. Pilley, a friend of Lotte's parents. She was soon giving German classes there, very successfully according to Mr Pilley's letter of recommendation:

> Her gifts as a teacher are really outstanding and she has the rare quality of establishing immediate contact with her pupils, both with individuals and with classes. She has, of course, a complete mastery of her subject, and to a marked degree the faculty of imparting her knowledge to others.[11]

One of Lotte's pupils in the autumn 1934 class was Brian Goold-Verschoyle. The atmosphere in adult education has a peculiar erotic *frisson* when the natural authority of the teacher goes with good looks. Lotte – for Brian the older, sexually experienced woman – was just under five feet, dark-haired and slim, with large blue eyes and regular facial features. Initially she and Siegi held the Irishman to be a trifle odd because he was obviously lonely, nervous and so intense.

They grew to like and respect him after hearing from a German couple who had fled to Britain in 1933 that Brian had allowed them to live in his room and had vacated his bed for the hard floor. Teacher and pupil became lovers for a variety of reasons. Lotte was not happy in her marriage, and she separated from Siegfried Moos in March 1935. Both were frustrated that their programme of study could not be continued with the requisite application because of lack of funds. Put another way, they had a problem less common then than now: the husband, his studies long finished, had a foot on the career ladder, while the wife, burdened by household chores and lack of time and funds, still had to complete a primary university degree.

Alongside her teaching hours at the Linguists' Club and her courses at the LSE, Lotte Moos earned some money by typing for another foreign couple, Dr Béla Menczer and his German aristocratic companion, Ruth von Schultze-Gävernitz. Menczer, born in Budapest of Calvinist parents from a Jewish background, was a journalist and political scientist with influential friends in the British Labour Party because of his anti-fascist credentials (ten months' imprisonment in Hungary in 1922 for his opposition to the Horthy regime) and writings against the restoration of the Habsburg monarchy in Central Europe.[12]

The book he was dictating to Lotte never got written – it was about the English exile of Lajos Kossuth, the Hungarian folk hero of 1848 – because Menczer later came around to a more impartial view of the Habsburgs. The couples became friends for a while. Because Menczer was then a fiercely independent and non-Marxist socialist and Brian fairly scathing about the collapse of German communism in 1933, they may have influenced Lotte's estrangement from the political world of her husband and, indeed, the couple's separation. An undated report to Moscow (c. 1934–35) about the London KPD group characterises sixteen comrades, most of whom were the subject of an impending expulsion motion because of their dissenting views. Siegfried Moos (Party name: Herbert) is the most prominently named, and positive, exception: elected as group-leader, 'the only active and willing Comrade'.[13]

The separation of Lotte from Siegi seems, in retrospect, gradual. He remained attached to her despite the relationship with her Irish friend, which started slowly by Goold-Verschoyle accompanying his teacher home after class. She lived in a single room at 19 Lawn Road, near Belsize Park tube station, in north London.

Brian was forever talking of the Soviet Union, which he idealised. He often went home to Donegal and must have felt bereft when the Manor House was evacuated in 1935, for Sibyl, plagued by arthritis in the wet Irish climate, had moved with husband 'Tim' to the more clement weather of Oxford.

In May 1935, Brian Goold-Verschoyle travelled to Moscow, once again unsolicited. It was a rash move because it jeopardised his 'sleeper' status. It came to the knowledge of the Special Branch after British deciphering experts had decoded a radio-telegram dated 7 May from Moscow to the Soviet Embassy in London: VYDAITE VIZU TURISTAM... GOOLD VERSCHOYLE BRIAN (Issue visa to the tourists... Brian Goold Verschoyle). On this, his third, visit the Donegal-born engineer got into serious trouble with his prospective 'handlers'. He was threatened with arrest for staying in a normal hotel for tourists, told never to come back to Moscow without permission, and was given an address in Paris to which he could turn if he needed information or assistance. No use could be made of him now, they continued, because the 'organisation', as had been stressed on previous occasions, had as yet no structures in Britain. While the latter statement was untrue, the reprimands were justified since Goold-Verschoyle, by going through the 'normal channels' for this third Moscow trip, had recklessly exposed his identity, thus devaluing any worth he might have for his Soviet spymasters. The Russians had the highest respect for the British police and MI5, knowing that the Special Branch watched all ports and termini for boat-trains in Britain. The identities of those embarking on, or disembarking from, the Russian steamer to Leningrad at the London docks, for example, were established and passed on to the secret service.[14]

The two Soviet officials on this occasion were different from those Brian had talked to in 1933 and 1934. The most senior of the new duo, called Felix, was in all probability Feliks Gorski, a Pole who had been an important officer for Soviet military intelligence (GRU) in Berlin and Vienna before returning to promotion at headquarters.[15] His assistant, later christened 'Stachelschwein' (Porcupine) by Brian and Lotte because of his crew-cut, has not been identified. The officers were very interested in two topics, which their recruit dealt with fairly summarily: the nature of his recording work with the BBC and his 'aristocratic connections'. The Irishman said he had none. These presumed links to the top social cachet were a product of Olga's babbling on about the 'aristocratic' status of the Donegal Goold-Verschoyles.

Goold-Verschoyle broke another sacred rule when he was back in London – he informed Mrs Moos of his involvement with the Soviet secret service. Already extremely worried about the discrimination and daily humiliations faced by her Jewish family in Hitler's Berlin, Lotte felt that Brian, whom she considered to be highly strung, was unsuited for the stress and tension of cloak-and-dagger espionage. She also feared the consequences for herself and her German friends, who were very much guests on sufferance in pre-war Britain. She implored him to break with the Soviets, arguing that his pledge to them, given at such an early age, was morally indefensible. Goold-Verschoyle attempted to allay her fears by saying that he would never work for the USSR when they lived together in England, that he had never envisaged working in Britain in any case and that he was serious about one thing: living in Moscow like Neil and taking Lotte with him, where she would regain everything she had lost – work, security and a family.

The real danger of unwittingly disclosing his 'cover' to Scotland Yard in 1935, however, did not come from Brian's peregrinations but from Lotte's contacts. After all, he had dropped out of political life, had a respectable profession, a 'good' family background and had gone to Moscow, to all intents and purposes, to visit his brother. If seen by the Special Branch as an individual and not as an operative in a subversive network, his 'Bolshie' period in the latter Stafford years could be dismissed as an aberration which befell 'the best of families'. However, Brian Goold-Verschoyle became a second-line suspect in the summer of 1935 when renewed doubts about the *bona fides* of the Moos couple emerged.

In August, the Home Office received an anonymous letter, possibly from a disgruntled insider, about the KPD exile group in London: five persons were named as 'Communist agents and agitators for the KPD', including Siegfried Moos. MI5 was not alarmed and thought Moos relatively harmless.[16] A few days later, however, Sergeant A.M. Smith wrote to his superior, Inspector Kitchener of the Special Branch, that Brian Goold-Verschoyle and Margarete Moos 'will soon occupy large unfurnished rooms at 9 Lawn Road, Hampstead', where 'Moos will occupy a room next to Verschoyle's'. This information was the result of discreet questioning and observation, for plain-clothes detectives had observed Brian and

Lotte visiting a house, 158 Haverstock Hill, just around the corner from their new address.[17]

The tenant of one of the three flats in the building was an old acquaintance of the Special Branch, the photographer Edith Tudor-Hart. Edith, née Suschitzky, was born in Vienna in May 1908 into a middle-class family which owned a left-wing bookshop and a publishing firm. She emigrated to Britain in 1925 to work as a governess and Montessori teacher, joined the CPGB two years later and acted as a Comintern courier before she attracted the attention of Scotland Yard in 1930. Expelled from Britain in early 1931, Edith gained re-entry to Britain in 1933, after she had married the doctor Alex Tudor-Hart in August 1933. Her marriage in the British Embassy in Vienna also freed her from the custody of the Austrian police following her arrest in May 1933 on suspicion of acting as a contact person between the provincial cells and the Central Committee of the banned Communist Party of Austria (KPÖ).[18]

In analysing her importance for the history of Soviet espionage in Britain, one has to distinguish clearly between what the British authorities knew about her in the mid-1930s and what they collated over the next twenty years. Since the opening of the former Soviet archives we know that Edith Tudor-Hart 'talent-spotted' Kim Philby and brought him to his first meeting with his 'handler' Arnold Deutsch in June 1934.[19] She was implicated in the Woolwich Arsenal spy case of 1937–38 because she had purchased a Leica camera for the NKVD agents working with the prominent CPGB member Percy Glading, who photographed military and navy blueprints.[20] Finally, in the late 1930s, following the annihilation of the great majority of the best NKVD and GRU foreign personnel in Moscow which left the Russian espionage station in London without staff, she acted as a courier between the 'Ring of Five', CPGB headquarters and the Soviet Embassy.[21] When questioned in 1947, she admitted working for Soviet spy rings in Austria and Italy fifteen years before, and to her friendship with Litzi Friedman. Litzi, too, was from Vienna, and the first wife of, and Edith's first contact with, Kim Philby. In 1951 one of her acquaintances interviewed in the War Office characterised Edith Tudor-Hart as being 'now as a sick woman, highly neurotic and suffering from persecution mania'.[22] Over a decade later, when MI5 in the aftermath of Philby's defection was trying to reconstruct the history of Soviet espionage operations in Britain, Edith Tudor-Hart refused to talk.[23]

By reading her post from Vienna to Britain in the years 1931–33, MI5 knew that she was active in the KPÖ and worked as a press photographer (a good cover and a necessary skill for a spy) in the TASS (Soviet news agency) offices in Vienna.[24] During 1935 the British secret service also learned that she had sent money to an Austrian communist in Switzerland, who, it transpired twelve years later, had worked with her in a Viennese spy-ring of the Russians in 1932–33.[25]

Edith, who kept an open house in north London for German (and later) Austrian communist refugees and had some of them live in her apartment as sub-tenants, met Lotte and Siegi Moos for the first time in the summer of 1934. They were introduced to her by Dr Edith Hoyos, a comrade of Siegi's from Berlin days who had entered into a marriage of convenience with a British communist.[26] The Moos couple lived nearby in a single room and were glad of the opportunity to take a bath or wash their clothes in Edith Tudor-Hart's flat. She was very hospitable and, like many Viennese women, an excellent cook. Lotte, likewise a trained photographer, had hoped for some work from Edith, but little came of it. On one occasion, when Edith was on holiday in Cornwall, Lotte and her husband lived in the large flat. They could not fail to notice the two mackintoshed men posted at a corner out of hearing distance.

Special Branch officers, at the behest of MI5, were now observing Brian and Lotte at their new abode.[27] Nothing of note was to be reported from 9 Lawn Road for some months; the Home Office, despite the suspect acquaintances of the Moos couple, renewed both residence permits to the end of 1935. The decision could have gone the other way, for it had been established that Siegfried's studies at the LSE had terminated in April, that husband and wife had not re-registered for further study and that the amount of time they had spent actually attending classes had amounted only to a few hours weekly. Nevertheless, they still had £75 to their good at Barclay's Bank and were obliged to adhere to the terms of their residence – no employment, study only. Their case, however, still needed 'watching'.[28]

In the autumn of 1935 Brian Goold was activated by his Russian contacts. What kind of an organisation was he joining and who were to be his closest collaborators? Soviet intelligence abroad consisted of two branches – military intelligence (GRU) and the secret service proper (INO-NKVD). Britain was seen as classical INO territory, whereas most GRU operations were based in countries bordering on the Soviet Union and in Central Europe, or in lands which posed a direct military threat to the Soviet regime (Germany, Japan, Italy). INO-NKVD was active in three main fields in the 1930s: infiltrating White Russian émigré circles, stealing industrial secrets (especially in Germany) and acquiring government documents and cipher code-books in order to read diplomatic and military radio-telegraphic traffic (Britain).

After the police raid on the Russian Arcos offices in London in 1927 and the subsequent suspension of diplomatic relations between Britain and the USSR, Russian espionage efforts in London produced little until 1934. The level of the intelligence supplied hitherto, mainly by journalists, was deemed to be too 'low-level' for the risks involved.

The British security establishment was reorganised to meet the threat. In August 1931, Colonel Kell of MI5 was asked by the government's Intelligence Committee to take over all intelligence duties connected with civil security, with the exception of Irish or anarchist matters, which stayed in the realm of the Special Branch of the Metropolitan Police.[29] Captain Guy Liddell and others were transferred from Scotland Yard to MI5 at Cromwell Road (South Kensington), where `B' Division was made responsible for counter-espionage and subversion. Staff were increased in 1934 and four years later the total number working at MI5 consisted of 30 officers and 103 secretaries and registry staff. This was far too few for the task in hand. The Comintern radio-telegram traffic, which was deciphered in the mid-1930s, for example, could not be analysed or studied in any great depth because of lack of staff.[30] Most of the foot-slogging and dreary observation work was carried out by tough CID and Special Branch men, hardened veterans prized by the Army officer types in MI5 because they could talk to the 'working classes'. Only the police, of course, could arrest, and as it was peacetime in a democracy, suspects could not be detained on suspicion alone: they had to be caught *in flagrante*, as was the case with Percy Glading and his Woolwich Arsenal confederates in 1937. Surveillance resources were highly limited – as late as 1942 MI5 had only thirty-eight watchers and could tap a total of merely forty telephone lines at a time – so that observation of known subversives or Soviet agents was sporadic at best.[31]

Despite that, any Russian agent, mindful of the watchful British police and strict immigration controls at harbours, found it extremely difficult to provide himself with a cover ('boots') and a passport ('book') which would pass muster in Britain. Whilst the 'legal' *rezident* (spymaster) was attached to the Embassy in an ostensibly innocuous function (usually as a member of the Trade Delegation) and enjoyed diplomatic status, he could not supervise the spy-rings in any direct fashion. That was the function of the 'illegal residents' like Alexander Orlov, the Austrian Arnold Deutsch or the Hungarian Theodor Mally. Deutsch (another LSE student), who lived in London under his own name, could stay for an extended period in Britain because his papers were genuine. In contrast, the travel papers of his superior officers, Orlov and Mally, were, or proved to be, unsuitable. Orlov had a genuine American passport, but that of his wife was a forged Austrian one, and an international scandal had arisen in connection with forged and stolen Austrian documentation. Mally could never spend very long in Britain because he, too, went under an Austrian name and carried an Austrian passport.[32]

Under the guidance of this trio of 'great illegals', three major spy-rings in Britain were active or being set up by the mid-1930s: the net around Percy Glading (military and naval secrets from Woolwich Arsenal), the 'Cambridge' group (with Philby as the first recruit) and John Herbert King of the Foreign Office. King had a predecessor, Ernest Holloway Oldham, who offered his services to the Soviets in 1930. Oldham's 'minder' was Dimitri Bystrolyotov ('Hans', 'John'), who used Czech, Greek and British identities. Despite the valuable cipher material and lists of future contacts among underpaid and indebted Foreign Office staff he provided, Oldham was more than a 'handful'. A raging alcoholic, he committed suicide in September 1933.[33] His successor, John Herbert King, was recruited by Henri Christian Pieck, a subordinate of Bystrolyotov's, in 1934. King was a cipher clerk with the British delegation at the League of Nations in Geneva before being transferred to the headquarters of the Foreign Office. He was a man with Irish forebears and a salary too small to support a wife and student son. His interests were purely mercenary, and he had believed for some time that Pieck sold the information he provided to a major bank.[34]

Pieck was a 40-year-old Dutchman who posed as a painter and man of the world. He lived in Switzerland and Britain under his own name, but the Dutch police had informed Scotland Yard as early as 1930 (the year he was recruited by Soviet espionage services) that Pieck had been a communist since 1920, designed posters for the

Dutch Communist Party and had taken part in a delegation to the
Soviet Union in 1929.[35] Henceforth his entries to and exits from the
United Kingdom were registered and Dutch friends (or fellow-
agents) who visited him in London were tailed by the Special Branch.
The first batch of documents smuggled out of the Foreign Office by
King gave grounds to believe that the new agent had golden hands:
the verbatim report (29 March 1935) of a meeting between Hitler
and British Foreign Secretary Sir John Simon. Although security at
the Foreign Office had been tightened up considerably following the
Oldham affair, King proved resourceful, bringing with him to
meetings on the Continent the flimsies of deciphered ingoing and
outgoing diplomatic telegram traffic for Pieck's masters. By October
1935 he had a key to the safe controlled by the head of the cipher
department, thus gaining access to top-secret material not included
in his previous deliveries.

The Soviets were now in a quandary. King was producing so much
material on a daily basis that somebody was needed permanently on
the spot to process it. But Pieck's cover was anything but waterproof
since his first wife's husband, who had hired a private detective to
follow him, was threatening to expose him to the British. Neither
Orlov nor Deutsch could help out because they were fully occupied
with their own networks. However, Pieck's superior, Mally, while
reluctant to go to Britain (the ISLAND in NKVD parlance) because
of his ragged cover, did so in January 1936, in the hope of digging
deeper into the lode being unearthed by King and acquiring codes
and ciphers.

This was the scenario which prompted the summons longed for
by Goold-Verschoyle, who now became an important sub-agent in a
very intricate and dangerous operation. To understand what he did
it is necessary to explain how the system worked. For reasons of
security, there was no *direct* contact between operatives of one ring
and another, between NKVD or GRU agents or between the 'illegal'
spymaster (Mally) and the Embassy. Money from the Soviet
Embassy for operative costs went through many female hands before
Deutsch or Mally collected it. The role of messengers was vital:

> Usually the job of one paid agent was to visit six or seven addresses
> daily to collect messages for Mally. I bought a book for 10/6, meant
> meeting at 10.30 but there was always a previous arrangement that
> the real time indicated as the result of a subtraction or addition of the

agreed number to the figure put down in the letter. Only in urgent cases did any agent communicate by phone. Mally's chief agents would know that at certain times on certain days of the week he could, in cases of emergency, be found near a particular spot.[36]

Paris was the venue where Brian met his Soviet handlers in early October 1935. Against all the rules of conspiracy, he took Lotte along for a 'romantic weekend'. At his urging she vowed not to mention the trip to anybody, then or later. She noticed that the porter in the Hotel Massenet greeted Brian as an acquaintance, an indication that it was not Goold-Verschoyle's first trip there for the Soviets. On the second day his contact man rang the hotel. He met Bystrolyotov in the Café de la Paix and they later visited the Folies Bergères, where Brian drank more than was good for him. A second, more important, meeting took place in Amsterdam in early November, when Bystrolyotov, an unidentified Belgian woman and Mally entertained the young Irishman and took him to Holland to meet Walter Krivitsky.

Krivitsky was administrator and cashier for the Russian secret service in Northern Europe, with headquarters in The Hague.[37] His cover there was that of an antique dealer and art connoisseur. Meeting Krivitsky for the first and last time, the young Irishman made 'a wonderful, pure impression' on this seasoned spy. Goold was treated as a 'friend' – that became his official appellation within INO-NKVD – and he got on especially well with 'John' (Bystrolyotov), with whom he recited passages from Shakespeare on a platform at Amsterdam railway station. 'John' promised that Brian would be granted his wish to stay in Russia, a country he praised in the highest tones but without going into any details about the nature of his novice's work there. Then Goold-Verschoyle took heart and asked, without mentioning that he was living with her in London already, whether or not he could take Lotte to his Land of Promise. The affable Russians assented (they had no right to make such a spontaneous promise without consulting Moscow) and merely wanted to know: can the lady dance and put on make-up properly? The Dutch visit left Brian in an exultant mood and he expected to go to Moscow in the near future.[38]

Young Goold-Verschoyle's function in the organisation was that of a courier, firstly, between London, Paris and Amsterdam, and secondly, within London and Britain as a whole. Pieck had set up a

business with an unsuspecting Englishman called Parlanti at 34a
Buckingham Gate, near Victoria Station. In the evenings he photographed King's daily delivery of Foreign Office documents, but his
business partner became suspicious and broke into the locked room
when Pieck was away. When Parlanti asked the Dutchman about the
Leica secured over a large table, Pieck said he had been photographing 'dirty pictures'.[39] Mally arrived in England on 4 January 1936,
staying until 4 March to direct the Pieck-King operation.[40] Goold-
Verschoyle was now the contact man between Pieck and Mally, both
of whom he had met shortly before in Paris. He was given an address
in Hampstead through which he could contact Mally in London.[41]
Brian telephoned Pieck on many occasions and met him in
restaurants,[42] but his contacts with Mally were sporadic at first. This
changed when Pieck had to leave Britain temporarily in early
February, following threats and a veiled offer of recruitment for MI6
uttered by one of his party guests, the commercial attaché at the
British Embassy in Amsterdam, who had seen through the cover of
the firm at Buckingham Gate.[43] Mally rented a house where King
deposited the papers on his way home from work; Goold-Verschoyle
collected the documents and he passed them on, perhaps through
another agent, to Mally. Brian did not know what the packages
contained, thought he was dealing only with political matters but, on
one occasion, as Krivitsky remembered, he saw some of the papers
and that they were marked 'Secret' and was 'very shocked indeed'.[44]

According to Lotte Moos, the only visitor to the flat at 9 Lawn
Road between September 1935 and February 1936 was Brian's
brother Denis Goold-Verschoyle, probably on his way to South
Africa, where he was to settle and become a successful town-planner
in Cape Town. Brian visited his parents regularly and had three to
four days off work every fortnight. He came home to Hampstead
very late every third week.[45]

The Special Branch gave a more detailed picture of the activities
of the flat's occupants, mentioning that Edith Tudor-Hart's flat was
a contact address for Austrian communists, and that in November
1935 Lotte had attended a Young Communist League conference in
Commercial Road, Stepney. Brian's movements, while suspect,
continued to mystify the police:

> Discreet enquiries have failed to reveal the nature of this man's work.
> He spends a good deal of time at his private address but his outside

movements and hours are very irregular – he occasionally leaves the house between 4 a.m. and 5 a.m. and visits the provinces from time to time. He was in Manchester during the week ending 27th October 1935.[46]

Brian Goold worked in three shifts, collecting material, photographing it and developing the film. Since MI5 had no hard intelligence on Mally until 1938 and nothing to link him to his Irish technician until 1940, we know little about how often they met and where. Moreover, the small amount of information that Goold, in violation of his service oath, did impart to Lotte Moos about his clandestine activities, were distorted half-truths, told to soothe, rather than enlighten, her: he acted as a kind of receptionist for Mally and the Belgian woman, showing them London from a taxi since the 'friends' had not yet set up an organisation in Britain.

In December 1935 Brian told Lotte that he would be leaving for Moscow very soon. He broached the subject of her joining him there with Mally, who professed he had never heard of this woman, but she could take a normal Intourist ticket and once she was in the Russian capital the matter would be decided. Scotland Yard also knew of Brian Goold-Verschoyle's impending change of air, writing to MI5 on 11 February 1936 that he 'is leaving England to take up a position on the continent during the coming week'.[47] At the beginning of April the Special Branch had established that he was indeed gone, but did not know where.[48]

NOTES

1. PRO, KV2/817, passport application, 31 May 1933.
2. The account of Brian's visits to Moscow in 1933, 1934, 1935 and 1936 is taken from what he told his lover, Margarete Charlotte (Lotte) Moos, who made a lengthy statement to MI5 in 1940. See PRO, HV2/1241, report dated 27 April 1940. For summaries of this confession, see also PRO, HV2/817, 62a, 62b. Another source is Brian Goold Verschoyle's prosecution file held in the Central Archive of the Russian Federal Security Service (TsA-FSB, file No. R-36981).
3. The personnel files of Brian and Neil at the BBC are no longer extant, but records show that they definitely worked there in the early 1930s (Samantha Walker, BBC World Service, to author, 31 October 1995).
4. PRO, KV2/817, Telegrams (extracted by MI5 in 1953) dated 4 and 26 June 1934.
5. Unless otherwise noted, all information on Lotte and Siegfried Moos was taken from her MI5 files (PRO, KV2/1241, 1242). Their daughter Merilyn also provided valuable details of her parents' background.

6. Ian Kershaw, *Hitler 1889–1936: Hubris* (Penguin London 1998), pp. 389–90, 404–5.

7. Politisches Archiv des Auswärtigen Amtes, Bonn (PAAA), Inland II- A/B, Band R 99802.

8. Stiftung Archiv der Parteien und Massenorganisationen der DDR im Bundesarchiv, Berlin (SAPMO), RY1/I2/3/114, 116.

9. Gerhard Hirschfeld, 'Deutsche Emigration in Großbritannien und ihr Widerstand gegen den Nationalismus', in Klaus-Jürgen Müller and David N. Dinks (eds), *Großbritannien und der deutsche Widerstand 1933–1944* (Paderborn-Munich-Vienna-Zurich 1994), pp. 108–9.

10. J.M. and M.J. Cohen, *The Penguin Dictionary of Modern Quotations*, 1978 ed., p. 244.

11. PRO, KV2/1242, extract from letter of A.T. Pilley, Secretary of the Linguists' Club, 5 June 1937.

12. Menczer subsequently converted to Catholicism and became an adherent of the 'conservative revolution' as symbolised by Francoist Spain. See: Lee Condon, 'The Evolution of a Conservative. Bela Menczer (1902–1983)', *The Hungarian Quarterly*, vol. XL, no. 153, Spring 1999 (www.net.hu/hungq/no153/100.html).

13. SAPMO, RY1/I2/3/360, p. 68.

14. For instance, the October 1930 visit of Kathleen and Tamara Rust, wife and daughter of the British communist Bill Rust, to Russia (PRO, KV2/1048), or when Elisabeth Glading, the wife of Percy Glading (sentenced as a Soviet spy in March 1938), went on board the Soviet steamer *Rykoff* at London docks in July 1930 (PRO, KV2/1020). Her husband was a student at the International Lenin School at the time.

15. See the numerous references to him in the memoirs of Elisabeth K. Poretsky (*Our Own People. A Memoir of 'Ignace Reiss' and His Friends* (Ann Arbor 1969).

16. PRO, KV2/1241, Cross-reference, 12 August 1935.

17. PRO, KV2/817, letter of 16 August 1935.

18. Duncan Forbes, 'Politics, Photography and Exile in the Life of Edith Tudor-Hart (1908–1973)', in Sulamith Behr and Marian Malet (eds), *Arts in Exile in Britain 1933–1945. Politics and Cultural Identity* (Amsterdam and New York 2005), pp. 45–87.

19. Christopher Andrew and Vasili Mitrokhin, *The Mitrokhin Archive. The KGB in Europe and the West* (London 1999), p. 76.

20. The SIS infiltrator Olga Gray, who worked first at CPGB headquarters and later for Glading's spy-ring, was instructed to destroy all invoices for material purchased. She kept one addressed to Edith Tudor-Hart for the purchase of a Leica – PRO, KV2/1012, note to Inspector Thompson, 26 February 1938.

21. Nigel West and Oleg Tsarev, *The Crown Jewels. The British Secrets at the Heart of the KGB Archives* (London 1998), p. 182.

22. PRO, KV2/1014, report 24 February 1947; Interview with Source, Room 005 War Office, 3 October 1951.

23. Peter Wright with Paul Greengrass, *Spycatcher* (Heinemann Australia 1987), p. 249.

24. There is some uncertainty about her party record. According to an index-card of the CPGB dated September 1949 and photographed by the Special Branch, she was then a member of the St John's Wood Branch and had joined in 1927 (PRO, KV2/1014).

25. PRO, KV2/1012, report dated 31 May 1935; KV2/1014, report dated 16 August 1947.

26. Later known as Edith Bone, she was imprisoned as a 'spy' in post-war Hungary and survived seven years of solitary confinement. See Francis Beckett, *The Enemy Within. The Rise and Fall of the British Communist Party* (London 1995), p. 134.

27. PRO, KV2/817, Note to Superintendent Canning, Special Branch, 23 August 1935.

28. PRO, KV2/1241, Special Branch Report, 5 September 1935; extract from HO file 1308.

29. PRO, KV4/126, undated memoranda; Scotland Yard Circular, 14 October 1931.

30. PRO, KV4/1, History of SIS (Draft of March 1946), pp. 50, 72, 114.

31. Miranda Carter, *Anthony Blunt. His Lives* (London 2001), p. 289.

32. John Costello and Oleg Tsarev, *Deadly Illusions* (New York 1993), pp. 143–45.

33. West and Tsarev, *Crown Jewels*, pp. 64–75. In 1950 the wife and son of Oldham also committed suicide (PRO, KV2/808).

34. For the most comprehensive account of King's collaboration with Pieck and Mally, see West and Tsarev, *Crown Jewels*, pp. 81–102.

35. PRO, KV2/809, Cross-reference, 24 March 1930.

36. PRO, KV2/804, 27 January 1940.

37. PRO, KV2/802, SIS extract, 25 April 1938.

38. PRO, KV2/817, copy of report received 27 April 1940.

39. PRO, KV2/809, Information from C. Parlanti, 15 September 1939.

40. PRO, KV2/1008, extract from Special Branch report, 29 December 1937.

41. PRO, KV2/817, SIS extract, 1 May 1950.

42. Ibid., extract from report on Hans Christian Pieck, 18 September 1939.

43. West and Tsarev, *Crown Jewels*, pp. 92–93.

44. PRO, KV2/804, interview with Walter Krivitsky, 24 January 1940.

45. PRO, KV2/1241, report, 27 April 1940.

46. PRO, KV2/817, Special Branch report, 19 November 1935.

47. Ibid., Special Branch to MI5, 11 February 1936.

48. Ibid., Special Branch to MI5, 1 April 1936.

With Lotte in Moscow

When sub-agent 'Friend' took the Dover-Calais route on 18 February 1936, Lotte saw him off at Victoria Station. Chatting in the compartment before his departure, they were startled by a knocking on the window. A white-bearded old man, flourishing a tube-like parcel, asked Brian Goold-Verschoyle in a matter-of-fact fashion to post a portrait of young King Edward VIII in Paris. The younger man took the roll and the stranger disappeared in the crowd. Lotte Moos thought all this very strange but Brian just laughed. It was her initiation into his world of work, the first time she had glimpsed one of his collaborators.

Goold-Verschoyle travelled on to Paris, where he deposited his passport and received a new one. It was a forgery, made out in the name of a Norwegian and containing an entry stamp for Calais, as if he had landed there from the USA. The American connection was necessary since he knew no Norwegian and had to pose as the American-born son of Norwegian immigrants. The further details of his journey to Moscow are unknown, save for a stopover in Zurich, where he wrote to Lotte. Weeks passed without news from him and then Olga sent a postcard, writing that Brian was awaiting her arrival impatiently. He was in hospital at the time, recovering from an attack of mumps.

The Moscow reunion of Goold-Verschoyle and Mrs Moos was delayed. The Home Office now held the Moos couple to be 'undesirables' and gave them three weeks to quit the country. Siegfried decided to sit it out and appeal. In April 1936 he found, on the recommendation of Lord Hirst, a friend of his uncle, a post as caption-writer at the Continental Picture Service in the London office of the *New York Times*. Mrs Moos applied to the Soviet Embassy for a one-week Intourist visa to Moscow. The visa had not arrived by the time the expulsion order from the Home Office was about to come into effect, so she left Britain via Folkestone on 17 March for Austria, hoping to pick up the visa in Vienna. The

Intourist office there was dismissive and the visa was refused with no reasons being given. Lotte, now with literally nowhere to go, sent frantic telegrams to Olga. After about three weeks, the seven-day visa was approved and issued in the Austrian capital.

The correspondence of Lotte Moos to her husband from Central Europe in March–April 1936 demonstrates that her decision to follow Goold-Verschoyle to the USSR was not solely an affair of the heart. She was curious about the Soviet experiment and knew that her husband would come to her aid should she wish to return to Britain. During a stopover in Brno on her way to the Austrian capital she met her father, telling him she had left London because it was impossible for a foreigner to earn a living there. Painting her career prospects in Moscow in the brightest colours, Lotte explained that Siegi had similar problems with British employment restrictions, but was still in London because he had to complete a scientific study. If something did not turn up soon, she continued, Siegi would join her in Moscow shortly. This account probably did not reflect the true intentions of the couple, but since Lotte Moos was not at all sure she would receive the visa for Russia in Vienna, she was mentally prepared for all eventualities for herself and her husband, even an attempt to gain re-entry to the United Kingdom.

On 2 April she sent Siegi a postcard from Vienna depicting Rembrandt's *Singender Knabe* (Singing Boy) from the Kunsthistorisches Museum, informing him of her address and her 'jealous dreams'. She enlarged on the latter in a letter two days later, a chatty piece about excursions to the Vienna Woods with a communist she had met at Edith Tudor-Hart's apartment in London. The letter also contained a request to send her money (again). Lotte was obviously disturbed, but hardly devastated, that her husband had been in a love affair for the preceding half-year, a relationship he allegedly refused to talk about. She was obviously afraid of losing her hitherto ever-reliable spouse. Despite her jealousy, Lotte signed off on the cheery note that they would meet in Moscow should Siegi be expelled from Britain. The next letter from Vienna was full of effusive declarations of love and gratitude; Lotte had just collected her visa from the indolent Russians in the Vienna Intourist office and learned that it had been lying there for a week unnoticed because the 'responsible comrade' had been on holiday.

Lotte Moos arrived in Moscow in mid-April 1936. In the preceding weeks Goold-Verschoyle's masters had denied any knowledge of his companion and ridiculed the idea that Mally had given permission for Lotte to join 'Friend' in Moscow. Their joyous reunion was over-shadowed by a series of confrontations prompted by her arrival. Brian had a stately room in the Hotel Moskva, a modern building near the Bolshoi Theatre and opposite the Kremlin, while Lotte was lodged in an Intourist hotel, the Novaia Moskva. Two days after the arrival of his unwelcome girlfriend, his bosses had him ejected from the Hotel Moskva and transferred him to the 'hostel' wing of the old-world Hotel Metropol across the road. His room was without windows and contained two beds and a chair. As Brian was suffering from angina, Lotte insisted on moving him to her hotel.

This was when the baleful Muck (not identified, a nickname probably taken from the popular German folk tale by Wilhelm Hauff about 'little Muck', whose enemies were afflicted with donkey's ears and long noses) entered their lives. He came to the hotel, told Lotte to leave the room and shouted abuse at Goold-Verschoyle in German. When Lotte was called in, Muck told her that she had no right to be in Moscow and that her companion had not been permitted to send for her or change his room unilaterally.

Goold-Verschoyle was to be taught how to use modern long-range radio equipment by Pankratov, a Russian who had spent years in the USA. The teacher was taken up with other business so that his pupil had hardly anything to do between April and July. A colleague from headquarters, however, came every week to the hotel room and handed over Brian's wages, 500 roubles. During the hot Moscow summer of 1936 Brian Goold and Lotte Moos had the opportunity to visit acquaintances and explore the countryside. In May they travelled out to Bystrolyotov in his ramshackle *dacha*. Living there with his aged mother, Czech wife Maria and son, 'John' was embittered that he was now 'on ice', suspended from duty and without proper medical care for his tubercular spouse. While he had monitored espionage teams in Europe in the preceding years, Maria managed the network's passports and money from a sanatorium in Davos.[1] They asked Lotte her opinion of life in the Soviet Union and were apparently annoyed by what they heard from the opinionated and forthright Berliner. Bystrolyotov, a Clark Gable look-alike, castigated her for her heresies, which he probably shared, and intimated that she, 'Frau Doctor', could end up in Siberia.

Brian and Lotte, officially 'on leave' before a decision was reached on their predicament, had to report regularly to Shenia, by telephone or by weekly visits to her guarded apartment in a new block of flats near NKVD headquarters on Dzerzhinskii (now Lubianka) Square. Shenia was the sister of Lydia, the wife of Theodor Mally. Mally passed himself off in Britain as the Austrian Paul Hardt and was known to his service colleagues as 'The Long Fellow'('Der Lange'). He was a saturnine and sybaritic Hungarian who had treated Brian to dinners at The Savoy and at a noted Hungarian restaurant in London. According to the defector Hede Massing, Mally had fallen in love with one of his German subordinates, Gerda Frankfurter, but was forced by headquarters to marry Lydia. She functioned as nurse and watcher, trying to keep his heavy drinking in check.[2] A more fleeting new acquaintance of Goold-Verschoyle's was Georg Miller, the head of the Lubianka's forgery workshop. All passports of incoming agents were in his care and he was especially interested in the format of the customs stamps impressed on the documents, which he duly photographed.[3] Miller's real name was Georg Killich, another Austrian, a typographer by trade and a former councillor for the KPÖ in the village of Deutsch Wagram (scene of Napoleon's victory in July 1809) outside Vienna. The stages of his career were fairly typical for foreign-born staff of the Foreign Department (INO) of the Soviet secret police: in 1926 responsible for smuggling literature for the Romanian Communist party through Czecho-slovakia, then between 1927 and 1930 courier of the Soviet Embassy in Vienna, whence he was summoned to Moscow and appointed to work at the Lubianka.[4]

In July Muck announced that Goold-Verschoyle would soon be sent to Germany on a mission and that his girlfriend would have to stay in Moscow. The Irishman refused, fearing the prospect that his companion would become a hostage in the USSR. Lotte wanted to go back to Britain should they be separated. An impasse was thus reached which was not resolved for months. The pair also drew suspicion on themselves because of Siegfried Moos's letters to his wife, which he sent to the address of Neil Goold-Verschoyle and his wife Olga. When Olga was in hospital this arrangement broke down, for Lotte and Brian had fallen out with Neil. The reasons for the break with the older brother (Lotte thought he was 'mad') were due to lack of trust on both sides: Olga worked for the NKVD, and Neil, notwithstanding his gentle personality, was unhelpful. We may surmise that he wanted to avoid anything that would jeopardise his stay in the USSR or threaten himself, his wife or his child. The problem, after all, was not Brian, but his German lover, who had come 'without permission', an unwelcome development which Brian had brought upon himself. The letters from Siegfried Moos, writing from London, generally dealt with Lotte's impecunious state, and she used Siegi's KPD contacts in Moscow to get translation commissions with the Deutsches Theater. So Lotte had his letters rerouted to the address of Irina Adler, Brian's former intimate friend, who lived with her parents and brother in a north Moscow suburb. Irina, it transpired, was a secret informant (*seksot*) of the secret police and told her contact officer of the foreign mail she was receiving. The incriminating letter from London read:

> When you go to Schulz in Hotel C. and bring him greetings from Comrade Meyer, he will certainly give you journey money. He has a fair amount of money from Comrade Meyer from the last stay.

Shenia was furious with her charges, calling Lotte Moos 'a Nazi agent with something to hide'. She also turned on Brian for defending somebody who had been 'chased out of two countries'.

After the incident with the letters, Brian and Lotte were trusted even less. The suspicion of the NKVD was scripted. The first of the three great Moscow show-trials (August 1936) was about to begin and three of the defendants were members of the KPD, sacrificial victims for the prosecution case, a farrago linking former members of the Politburo with Trotsky and, even less plausibly, with the Gestapo. Franz David, one of the sixteen accused who were shot at the close of the courtroom drama, had been on the staff of Wilhelm Pieck, the Chairman of the KPD in Moscow exile. So the German party leadership was compromised as well. The examination of all foreign communist cadres in the USSR was intensified, especially in the German section of the Comintern.

Lotte Moos experienced the fallout from the purge of German leftists in the USSR. Fritz, a young Berlin comrade now living in Moscow who had helped her leave Germany in 1933, refused to meet her after their first appointment on a Moscow square – he obviously feared that she was some kind of informer. The climate of fear and suspicion led to a cessation of all links to German-speaking colleagues of Lotte.

One exception was Erna Kolbe, a typist in the German section of the Comintern who lived with her engineer husband in Kuzminki, a south-western suburb of Moscow. Lotte knew Gertrud Denecke, Erna's sister, from Berlin and had met her again in London exile. In the summer of 1936 Gertrud was staying with her sister in Moscow to help her with the new baby, since there were no child-minding facilities in Kuzminki. Gertrud had done the same in 1933, before Erna's first child had died. At that time, the whole family was either in a Nazi prison, in hiding like Erna, or under Gestapo observation, but Gertrud, who had been expelled with her husband from the KPD for 'deviation from the Party line' in 1929, was not on the wanted list of the Gestapo. Gertrud's stay in the USSR (she returned to Britain in September 1936), while obviously an act of sisterly solidarity, aroused suspicion. Gertrud Denecke and her companion Helmut, a student, were dissident communists and at odds with the leadership of the KPD group in London. Erna, an equivocally loyal communist, had dutifully informed the Comintern of her sister's views when arranging for her entry visa to the USSR in 1935. Lotte Moos remained in close contact with Gertrud Denecke after the latter had left Moscow for London.[5]

Since Lotte and Brian could not find any friends among the native-born population, the pair became increasingly isolated. The only people they had any kind of worthwhile conversations with in the initial stages were his cynical NKVD colleagues, who had the couple tailed within the city.

Apart from the confession Lotte Moos made to the British secret service in 1940, the only other source for her sojourn in the Russian capital (April–October 1936) are personal letters to her husband Siegfried and a manuscript she wrote shortly after her return, a collection of pastiches, with the names of the dramatis personae slightly changed but recognisable all the same: Bystrolyotov is 'Shakespeare', for instance. Her accounts of everyday life in Moscow are plausible and correspond to what other Westerners have written.

A constant source of frustration was getting enough to eat, buying food for breakfast and finding a cheap restaurant in the evenings. Lotte was initially the breakfast scavenger during the hot summer of 1936. There were three queues in front of the dairy around the corner from the shabby wing of the Hotel Metropol: for the cashier, for milk, and for butter and eggs. The shopper had to pay in advance for the goods, and Lotte frequently found that when she had reached the top of the second or third queue, the dairy products had been sold out. There was a great deal of pushing and obscene swearing;

women, especially small females like Lotte, were shoved and pushed aside by male queue-jumpers. On several occasions she returned exhausted and almost in tears to the hotel, and Brian took up the challenge. But he, by now adept at cursing in Russian, also found the daily scrimmage extremely trying.

Their attempts to strike up conversations with Muscovites generally led nowhere, either because their interlocutors were afraid to talk to strangers or because Goold-Verschoyle, and especially Mrs Moos, made no secret of their political opinions: a mélange of intellectual attitudinising which found fault with Soviet social reality but advocated support for the Soviet Union as a bastion against fascism. Such differentiation went over the heads of their listeners, who saw the capitalist West in black and white terms. The NKVD characterised this kind of 'Western' argumentation as 'Trotskyist' and held most foreigners, in particular German émigrés, to be potential Fifth Columnists: how come these people had escaped from the fearsome Gestapo without being 'turned around' and sent to the USSR as agents?

Apart from the mounting terror, the general political context in which Moos and Goold-Verschoyle found themselves was the return to conservative attitudes with regard to women and children. The less objectionable side to this retreat, from the ostensibly emancipatory relations between male and female of the 1920s towards more 'settled' role models for women, was the emphasis on *kulturnost* – people keeping themselves clean, going to night classes, listening to good music, visiting the theatre and cinema. The Westernisation process manifested itself in the craze for modern dancing, especially the foxtrot, and the use of make-up by younger women.[6]

For Lotte, and to a lesser extent Brian, a reprehensible aspect of the return to traditional social values was the June 1936 law banning abortion and making divorce more difficult. The Soviet regime, and the general population, were concerned about the huge problems posed by the break-up of families, a serious phenomenon since the Civil War and exacerbated by the destruction of rural communities during the forced collectivisation of agriculture. Large towns and cities swarmed with gangs of orphaned or unsupervised children who engaged in petty theft and, when older, in more serious crime. Following a series of murders and violent assaults in Moscow by two 16-year-olds who received only five-year sentences, the Politburo cracked down, passing the law of 7 April 1935 'which made violent crimes committed by juveniles from 12 years of age punishable as if they were adults'. That meant Gulag sentences or the bullet instead of a juvenile correction colony.[7]

Parents were now made responsible for their offspring and the days of the 'postcard' divorce were over – to date a notification from the feckless husband to the registry office had sufficed. The authorities published a draft of the new 'anti-abortion' law in *Pravda* on 26 May 1936, with a call for readers' reactions, and issued the preliminary law text as a pamphlet. Now abortion was permissible only when the woman's life was in danger; abortionists, or their accessories, were subject to two years in prison. Punishments for the non-payment of alimony were increased, as were the registration fees for new divorces. The Kremlin tried to profit from the discontent of harassed mothers by promising better child-care facilities, longer maternity leave and generous payments to large families. At the top of the scale a mother with eleven children was to receive 5,000 roubles per additional child for one year and 3,000 roubles for the next four years. The draft legislation, practically unchanged, became law at the end of June.[8]

Politicised younger women held the law to be reactionary, while Lotte Moos may have felt it smacked of Nazi eugenics – in Germany prolific child-bearers were given the *Mutterkreuz* (Mother's Cross) medal. The ban on abortion surfaced in conversations she and Brian tried to initiate during a fine June day in central Moscow. Both were pleased to have made the acquaintance of Alexander, a student and member of the Komsomol, in the Alexandrovsky Garden just beneath the Kremlin walls. Sitting on a park bench eating cherries, the foreign couple tried to draw out the young man. He had very conventional ideas about marriage, made little of the problems young couples had in getting an apartment and said divorce and abortion did not impinge on him: young Russian men 'went' with their girlfriends for a long time before marriage and, in any case, one loved only once in life. Alexander was interested only in the attractive young German woman and forced awkward intimacies on her later that day when the trio went to the circus.

The other occupants of the bench, an old woman in a cape and a haggard young mother rocking a pram with her foot, joined in the abortion discussion. While the old woman welcomed the legislation and praised the wisdom of Stalin, who 'always appears in a plain military tunic without medals', the younger woman emphasised that worthless husbands were naturally against the law. She was embittered that 'speculators' had driven up the price of baby clothes, which she could not now afford.

Other conversations took a 'wrong turn' or ended abruptly, partly because Brian and Lotte really wanted to know what their companions *thought*. But they made themselves suspect by underlining their own political stance (members of the Young Communist League, the British pendant to the Komsomol), or risible by realising too late that their prying was being met by gentle ridicule. An instance of snubbing on their part happened during a chat with a friendly couple in a Moscow park. The husband, a well-paid engineer enthusiastic about jazz and modern dancing, asked the foreigners if they liked dancing. The answer was like an icy douche: the comrades in the West have neither the time nor the wish to indulge in such pastimes, both inventions of decaying capitalism which have no place in a really socialist society. They dismissed the engineer's reply that the Party was in favour of such 'positive achievements' emanating from bourgeois society, thus terminating the exchange of opinions.

On another occasion they took issue with a young female civil servant reading a book on the history of English literature on a park bench in front of the Marx-Engels Institute. She held that all workers in the Soviet Union had opportunities of advancement if they, as in her case, were prepared to attend night classes. In her reply to Brian's objection that mass production in the Soviet Union and elsewhere would always need unskilled labour for tasks at the conveyor-belt, she changed tack, stating that workers in Britain were persecuted, beaten by the police and shot, and that the Communist Party was banned there. She left when Brian said that her views on Britain were uninformed: she could read the fully legal newspaper of the British Communist Party, the *Daily Worker*, in the library of the institute behind them.

A guarded conversation with two Moscow textile workers in a railway compartment was more productive. They opened up gradually, after saying 'the walls have ears'. Brian and Lotte, with two real members of the Russian proletariat on the opposite seat, wanted to know about working conditions in Soviet factories. What they heard was sobering: since 1928 real wages had fallen and the workers now had to keep their mouths shut. After enquiries about England – mill girls' wages, the price of a kilo of bread (a measuring-stick for all Russians) or how much it costs for an ordinary worker to open a small business – the atmosphere relaxed. When Lotte demurred by saying that life in Britain was hard, she heard the clinching argument: 'They let you out, though. They won't let us out.' Although they categorised the visitors from Britain as hopeless idealists for believing in socialism, the Russians gave the address of their textile mill, inviting the pair to visit it on their day off. While fascinated by the prospect of seeing a Soviet factory from the inside, Brian and Lotte dropped the idea, not wishing to endanger themselves or their sardonic rail companions.

Lotte Moos realised over time that such encounters could also undermine her own revolutionary zeal. Often accosted by women because of her well-cut British clothes, Mrs Moos had a depressing conversation in a cobbler's shop. The daughter of a doctor caressed the fine cloth of Lotte's coat before asking how much chocolate or oranges cost in England. Hearing her answers, the cobbler said that was the land for him and, in an angry aside, asked: 'What are you doing here if life is so good at home?' Her qualification that hundreds of thousands were living there on the dole and without hope prompted more questions: 'Have they bread and margarine?' 'Have they shoes?' The conversation broke off in mid-sentence when the house porter, probably one of the countless informants, the 'eyes and ears' of the NKVD, entered the shop. Lotte felt she had acted like a counter-revolutionary, talking to people who knew only hatred towards their own government and believed that capitalism was the best of all worlds.

The few carefree days, when concern about their future receded somewhat, were spent in places like Pushkino, with its woods and lakes a popular recreation spot for Moscow day-trippers. The beautiful surroundings prompted a reverie about living outside Moscow, starting a family, tending the garden and commuting to the city by the *elektrichka*, the suburban railway. When Lotte broke the spell by saying all that could have been organised much more easily in London, and Brian replied that was the fate they ran away from, both succumbed to a fit of laughter. However, even deep within the woods minatory reality was never far off – a man shooed them away from a riverbank because it was near a 'secret institute', youths played ball with them in a clearing for hours without addressing them, and a peasant woman allowed them shelter in her house during a thunderstorm and remained silent.

No rapport could be forged with Goold-Verschoyle's colleagues. Bystrolyotov considered the couple gormless or gullible intellectuals, but 'minder' Shenia gradually softened. She dutifully asked what they had been doing and if they had received mail from home (Siegi or Brian's parents). She was really more interested in talking to Lotte about women's fashion and the scarcity of silk stockings in the USSR. They visited her modern flat, and were always served tea only, although they were usually ravenously hungry. Shenia was obviously not enthusiastic about her custodial role and regularly made scathing comments about everyday Soviet life. Comrades Moos and Goold-Verschoyle knew that Shenia, like Bystrolyotov, was testing them and they offered her no ammunition for a negative report. In the sultry weather, she often took the couple to a tiny park near the Lubianka. The patch of greenery was packed with badly dressed and undernourished Muscovites unable to sleep in the torrid night. Here, on the park bench, their conversation, full of banalities now, tapered off and they parted – Shenia back to her apartment, they to the mice-infested hotel room.

Conversations with Shenia's secret service colleague 'Stachelschwein', a blocky Russian with red hair cropped tightly, were one-sided affairs and monotonously distasteful. Holding forth in a broad Canadian accent, he regaled his captive audience in Brian's room with tales of sexual licence in Canada: how 'fast' Canadian girls were and how the Mounties liked to frequent the best brothels. When they broached the subject of leaving Moscow, 'Stachelschwein' shuffled off without a word. The only person who was invariably friendly and communicative to the couple was Irina Adler, Brian's old flame. Shenia hinted that Irina had lost her seat on the Central Committee of the Komsomol, a ticket to the *nomenklatura* life, because of her volubility. Despite her bubbly personality, Brian and Lotte found Irina tolerable in small doses only. They knew she had a covert agenda for her friendship – reporting on them to the NKVD. In her Moscow manuscript, Lotte was obviously very jealous and spiteful about the woman's appearance – a prematurely aged and unprepossessing gossip feigning friendship with Brian's new woman. He, by the same account, was hurt by Irina's chiding of his unfaithful ways, perhaps wishing the past and present woman in his life to be friends.

Still, they accepted Irina's idea of taking part in a demonstration to Red Square to mark International Youth Day, 8 September 1936.

She had just enrolled in the History Faculty of Moscow State University, then located in the city centre and a few minutes' walk from the Hotel Metropol. On arrival, Irina was her usual effervescent self, kissing Lotte and reassuring Brian that they would be allowed to march with the students, even without a students' pass (*propusk*). The auditorium soon filled with noisy undergraduates, but the open and shutting of desks and the hum of conversation subsided when a student began an obligatory speech about the significance of International Youth Day. The next speaker on the podium was obviously a Party functionary since he was dressed in the unofficial uniform of his caste, a fashionable leather jacket. Striding back and forth across the stage he intimidated the audience, accusing the History Faculty of 'lack of vigilance', for one of their number had been arrested, 'a Trotskyist bandit, one of the scum who wanted to murder our beloved leader Stalin'. Warming to his theme, he continued to harangue:

> You have to leave your books and bags here and can collect them afterwards. When you reach Red Square, you are to keep your hands out of your pockets. You are all new, and we don't really know each and every one of you. I warn you, be vigilant, make sure that no stranger sneaks his way into your ranks. Persons not belonging to the Faculty are not allowed to march with you. The Professor was also one who sneaked his way in here. The agents of Fascism, the lowest Trotskyist mercenaries are well able to sneak themselves in anywhere. You have the responsibility of ensuring that this kind of reptile won't raise his head again. I say once more: Vigilance is your slogan. Now we are going to march past our beloved leader Stalin.

Each time the functionary mentioned the dictator's name, frenetic applause broke out. Brian and Lotte clapped with the rest, again and again, for the harangue lasted another half-hour. Flailing phrases rained down on the cowed students – danger of infiltrators, Trotskyist scum, beloved leader. Brian felt he had had enough and wanted to leave immediately, saying 'We are alien elements'. Lotte did not want to miss the chance of marching to Red Square, and Irina spoke with officials who said the foreigners could join the student columns. As a result of typical Russian disorganisation, the students had to wait for hours on the grass outside the university before moving off. Finally under way, Lotte was exhilarated, for this was her first workers' demonstration since 25 January 1933 in

Berlin. That night 130,000 members and sympathisers of the KPD had marched around Party headquarters, Karl-Liebknecht House, in the centre of the city, a cheering demonstration of solidarity in the biting cold. From the pavements, SPD workers shouted anti-fascist slogans to encourage their communist class brothers and sisters. It was the finale for a giant with feet of clay, for less than a week later Hitler was Chancellor and open season began on all left-wingers. The Moscow march was entirely different, slow and constantly halting; column after column joined at crossroads, ragged workers straight from the work-bench and rows of children, carrying the slavish slogan, 'Thank you, Comrade Stalin, for our happy life!'

The group around Irina was nervous because of the slow pace: the marchers might arrive at Red Square too late because Comrade Stalin always left at 8.30 p.m. Rerouted by traffic policemen still in their white summer uniforms, the columns finally stopped. In the long pause some students were dancing the foxtrot and humming the tune 'Who's afraid of the big bad wolf?'; others engaged Lotte in an argument about the collapse of the German labour movement in 1933. They parroted the Comintern line, that the Social Democrats were to blame for the rise of fascism. The discussion under a street lantern in the rain became very heated when Lotte, giving vent to her argumentative tendencies, said: No, neither the workers nor the rank-and-file were to blame; the KPD leadership did not know how to lead and it disciplined anybody in its ranks who dared to express a dissenting opinion.

The disputation ended shortly afterwards as the march resumed. In the vicinity of Red Square the stewards were going down the ranks, examining each demonstrator's *propusk*. They reached Irina's coterie and told Brain and Lotte to leave the column at once. Caught in no-man's-land, with the marchers in front and the empty street behind them and all junctions and side roads blocked by police cohorts, the foreign couple found all exits closed. Feeling trapped and fearing arrest, they were finally allowed to squeeze through after Brian protested that he was a British citizen on his way to a dinner engagement.

The lovers had plenty of time to ponder on their reckless adventure during the coming weeks. The Moscow autumn had arrived, with constant rain and low temperatures. Since the heating in Moscow was turned on centrally by a given date and no sooner (*tempus fugit...* it still is), the hotel room was clammy and cold.

Lotte fell ill with coughing and fever. Brian tried to heat their quarters by drawing electrical wires from the fuse box; they crackled and hissed for a while and then blew the fuses. Because of Lotte's illness, they rarely went out, save for Brian's daily expedition for food. His bosses were still being evasive and every phone call was a source of frustration: the 'responsible comrade' is still on holiday, but you will be rung back in a few days. Then, like a sickening blow, Brian and Lotte realised that, for months past, they may have been overheard by means of a listening device. If so, the NKVD knew that they even contemplated going to the British Embassy as a last resort. That was treason in any political system – defection – even if the notion was half-baked and soon discarded: the police would stop them at the gates; the British might not believe the story of a couple without papers, for Miller still had their passports. Brian held his colleagues to be too incompetent or indolent to 'bug' the room of a technician like himself. But Lotte was insistent, repeating a story that some prison-cells were 'bugged' by a device hidden in the electric light bulb. The lamp was examined, likewise the telephone – nothing. Then Brian examined all the holes in the wall and, poking into one above the window he received a slight electric shock and jumped from the chair. So there was no evidence of a listening device, but one never knew for certain.

Underneath the blanket on the bed, Brian and Lotte tried to reconstruct all their 'counter-revolutionary' remarks of the past months. The content of the whispering was a closed circle: no mission abroad unless Lotte could travel back to England. Brian tried to reassure himself and Lotte with the argument that they had not really been treated badly by the Russians, who might still have trust in his skills and loyalty. But what if his superiors had been listening in to the lovers' conversation? On the other hand, Siegfried Moos knew of their dilemma and promised to raise a scandal in Britain should Lotte be refused an exit visa.

Lotte's illness persisted; she was now becoming desperate despite Brian's forced sanguine attitude. One night, in early October 1936, the phone rang. It was Miller, the keeper of passports, who wanted to meet Brian in the street. She was afraid that an arrest squad would arrive when Brian had left the hotel. He was expectant, since he now had a chance to talk to a 'responsible comrade' and put his case. Still, he came back almost immediately and told Lotte to lock the door and not to admit anybody in his absence. The waiting for his return seemed endless; downstairs the jazz-band started to play, so she knew it was 10 p.m., roughly the time when the police started their nightly arrest operations. A man argued on the telephone in the corridor, a footfall near the door, but the sound receded.

When Brian returned and woke Lotte from her feverish sleep, he had good news to impart. He had summed up his case well to Muck and Miller:

> My wife does not want to stay here and you will understand that I do not want to take the responsibility for her if she is held here just because of me. If you can't send us away together then you have to separate us. And if I am to work for you I must have the reassuring feeling that she is in good hands wherever she wants to go.

Lotte, while immensely relieved, wanted Brian to go straight to Britain on his release, and only after he had received a telegram from her that she had crossed the Russo-Polish border safely. He saw the conversation with his officers as a mark of confidence in himself and was prepared to undertake the (as yet undisclosed) foreign mission. On its completion, he pledged, he would return to London and the waiting Lotte. She said she would wait for years, but once again she pleaded with him to forget whatever commission he might receive and head straight for England. From Lotte's manuscript, it is evident that Brian was not prepared to take the latter course; he was proud to work for 'such a serious organisation' and was relieved that he had regained its trust, despite the long waiting game and the suspicion to which he had been subjected. A party to these 'negotiations', if only in a consultant role, was a tall, pleasant Englishman, who had introduced himself to Brian and Lotte as 'Fisher'. He told them of his English childhood, how he had emigrated to Russia with his parents and had worked as an electrician in the Kremlin, where he met Lenin and Trotsky.

William Genrikhovich Fisher was a native Londoner who had left Britain with his parents in 1920 at the age of seventeen. He joined Soviet espionage in 1927, served in several European cities and may have known Brian from his 1935–36 stint in Britain. Fisher became a household word in the USA in 1957 after his arrest by the FBI and subsequent trial. As Rudolf Abel, he was sentenced to thirty years in a penitentiary on espionage charges. Five years later he was exchanged for the U-2 pilot Gary Powers, the last prisoner to be incarcerated in the Lubianka before 'Inner Prison No. 1' was pulled down.[9]

Two NKVD doctors arrived the day after the talk with Muck and Miller and declared that Lotte Moos was not yet fit for travel. Miller appeared, ostensibly to enquire about her state of health, leaving with the jocular and ambiguous remark: 'You are in a hurry, that is clear'. When Muck rang to fix an appointment, old fears resurfaced: they have changed their minds, Muck does not believe us, he'll give us a thorough going-over. But Muck, now attired for the winter in riding boots and fur hat, was polite and solemn. Miller accompanied him, remaining silent and smiling in approval of his superior's arguments. Muck explained to Lotte that she had had the chance to stay in Moscow and marry her Irishman, in which case she would have become the wife of a 'comrade', and the 'organisation looks after the wives of our comrades'. However, he continued, she wanted to return and since she was not 'one of us', he had no right to tell her what she should do. The other part of the arrangement, he emphasised, was that Goold-Verschoyle must cut off all links with her. Her emotional interruption – whether she could write to Brian – raised a low and haughty laugh: 'You won't know where to write and you won't have any chance of finding out his address.'

The conversation then turned to Goold-Verschoyle. He reiterated the plea to Muck and Miller of some nights before, not avoiding Muck's steely stare. Lotte admired what she took to be his childlike falsity, but she may have been totally wrong because he was now being taken seriously again and was obviously needed. That interpretation is suggested by the course the meeting then took: the tearful Lotte, in her bed, was ignored and the 'comrades' talked in great technical detail about the new radio set that Brian would operate abroad. When the NKVD duo left after perfunctory handshakes, Lotte had mixed feelings. She now had what she wanted, but had shown her emotions to Muck, even asking him if she could send Brian a telegram from the border. He was taken aback by the question but said that was her affair. She also felt that Muck had contempt for her, that she had not been 'up to it', was not a proper communist after all but an emotional Western female. It also preyed on her mind that Brian was obviously very much back in harness and glad of it. As so often in the past, he now played the optimist and congratulated Lotte on the tactical use of her tear ducts.

Why did the Russians concede to the deal? For them Lotte Moos
was a troublesome interloper, a walk-on part at best, whereas Brian
Goold-Verschoyle was useful. The Spanish Civil War had broken out
in July and in the autumn the Soviets decided to intervene on the side
of the embattled Republic. With his technical and polyglot skills
Brian was a valuable asset to the NKVD in Spain. Other factors may
also have played in his favour. Despite the months of inaction, Brian
had never given his masters cause to doubt his fundamental loyalty;
his dissenting remarks were probably seen as Western belly-aching,
which may have been the drift of the argument when Krivitsky and
Bystrolyotov, as Lotte subsequently came to believe, spoke out in his
favour. Mally, now commuting between Paris and London, may also
have supported the further employment of the idealistic Irishman.
Two similar cases, that of Elisabeth Poretsky in 1937 and the
Massing couple in 1938, also had a – provisionally – happy ending:
they were allowed to leave Moscow for the West because the *apparat*
still needed them.

Pankratov appeared on the morning of Lotte's departure, 18
October 1936. Brian and he argued for hours about the workings of
the radio set before mastering its functions. In the afternoon the
couple went on their last shopping expedition in the Moscow rain,
to buy food for Lotte's train journey. They went to the food hall on
the Arbat, where everything edible was on sale, at exorbitant prices.
The place was full of well-dressed women ... and pickpockets. In
the evening the atmosphere in the restaurant matched their sombre
mood, for the female singer sang forlorn Russian melodies, including
the popular '*Chërnye Glasa*' (Black Eyes). They repeated the text of
the telegram which Lotte would send from Negoreloe, where
travellers had to change trains from the wide Russian gauge to the
narrower European one. Their hurried farewells at the station were
full of practicalities: where to hide her dollars from the Soviet
customs, the text of the telegram from Negoreloe, how to
communicate in future.

Lotte sent Brian the reassuring wire from Warsaw, after leaving
Russia without incident. She could return to 9 Lawn Road because
Siegi had continued to pay the rent, posing as her brother. She heard
Brian's voice in November, when he rang the London number
Primrose 3430 from Paris: he was not coming back for an indefinite
period and was on his way somewhere else.

NOTES

1. West and Tsarev, *Crown Jewels*, pp. 64–69.
2. Hede Massing, *Die Grosse Täuschung. Geschichte einer Sowjetagentin* (Freiburg-Basel-Vienna 1967), pp. 130–33.
3. Poretsky, *Our Own People*, pp. 186–87.
4. RGASPI, f. 495, o. 187, d. 651, ll. 3–6.
5. Information from Dr Meinhard Stark, Berlin.
6. Sheila Fitzpatrick, *Everyday Stalinism. Ordinary Life in Extraordinary Times: Soviet Russia in the 1930s* (Oxford 1999), pp. 67–88.
7. Ibid., p. 151.
8. Wendy Z. Goldman, *Women, the State and Revolution. Soviet Family Policy and Social Life, 1917–1936* (Cambridge 1993), pp. 331–36.
9. PRO, KV2/1241, Statement of Charlotte Moos, 27 April 1940. MI5 could not identify the mysterious Mr Fisher in 1940 (Ibid., manuscript 62b). For his biography, see Helmut Roewer, Stefan Schäfer and Matthias Uhl, *Lexikon der Geheimdienste im 20. Jahrhundert* (Munich 2003), p. 9f.

Spanish Imbroglio

Participation by non-Spaniards on the republican side in the Spanish Civil War has long been seen as a romantic crusade. The anti-fascist cause was legitimate, for sections of the regular Spanish Army had staged a putsch against the elected republican Government in July 1936, an attempt to stifle social reforms and conserve the power of the landed elite. Very soon the internal Spanish conflict became a proxy war between the totalitarian powers – Germany and Italy on the fascist side, the USSR on the anti-fascist. Soviet aid was decisive in the early stages. Stalin's interest in the Spanish struggle, however, was to wane by late summer 1937, after a series of military defeats and a civil war within the Spanish Left, orchestrated in no small part by his legates. After that date the arms supplies from the USSR were reduced, with roughly only one-third of the total supplies arriving after December 1937.[1]

The decrease in the level of Soviet aid to Spain was also caused by other preoccupations of the Kremlin, in particular by Japanese expansionism in China. In the autumn of 1936, Chinese communists received almost the same number of rifles that Moscow shipped *in toto* to Spain.[2] Stalin held his hand for another reason – he feared that more direct involvement in the Spanish struggle would endanger his hopes of a European anti-German alliance. Soviet assistance to the Spanish government thus never reached the level afforded Franco by Germany and Italy.

Soviet participation in the cause of republican Spain had a sinister side: the attempts of Stalin's plenipotentiaries to run the republican war-machine and to purge the Spanish Left of perceived enemies. The new evidence, primarily from Russian archives, confirms what anti-Stalinists like George Orwell in his *Homage to Catalonia* wrote about the machinations of the Soviet advisers and their Spanish satellites. When Brian Goold-Verschoyle arrived in Valencia in November 1936, the former London *rezident* of the NKVD, Alexander Orlov, was already in the city. Orlov supervised the transportation of Spanish gold reserves to the USSR in October 1936.[3] The bullion shipment was not Stalin's initiative, rather the decision of the Madrid government fearful of fascist victory. According to Moscow, the Spanish reserves ran out and Soviet loans were used to finance the last arms shipments, However, there is strong evidence that the Soviets overcharged for their military hardware by manipulating currency rates.

Orlov then turned his attention to counter-intelligence. His efforts in that sphere were directed not only against real enemies of the Republic such as fascist Fifth Columnists, but also against the libertarian Left, foremost the anarchists and the communist breakaway party POUM, which he, and all Stalinists, incorrectly dubbed 'Trotskyist' – Trotsky had broken with the POUM in 1936.

The NKVD teams under Orlov collaborated with Republican Military Intelligence (SIM), the Cadres Department of the International Brigades and counter-intelligence agents (mostly Germans) in the Central Committee of the Spanish Communist Party (PCE) and its Catalonian offshoot, PSUC. Orlov also established training schools to train guerrilla fighters and Soviet agents for missions in their own countries.

Brian Goold-Verschoyle's place in this plethora of networks is unclear. There is no personal file on him in the Moscow archive of the Russian Foreign Intelligence Service.[4] The letters he wrote to his mother from Valencia, along with the summaries of his correspondence to Lotte Moos, were sent to the British Foreign Office, but were subsequently destroyed with the official correspondence, save for two slim folders from the early 1950s.[5] Finally, the originals of the letters which Brian sent to Lotte from Valencia were seized by MI5 in 1940 and have not been located.

One account holds that Brian worked for Radio Barcelona as a technician,[6] another that he transmitted messages for the Soviet Ambassador in Valencia,[7] a third that he worked 'in his profession and instructed members of the International Brigades in this skill'.[8] The last version probably comes closer to the truth. Valencia, his base, was the fulcrum of the anti-fascist war effort, following the evacuation of government ministries there from Madrid in November 1936. The Soviets in the new capital, officially attached to the Soviet Embassy (Orlov was 'political attaché'), were involved in all sections of the war effort, frequently as military advisers.

Following their experience in helping to ward off the direct fascist attack on Madrid, Soviet army officers set up the first guerrilla training school in late 1936.[9] Orlov also pursued this diversion and sabotage strategy ('D-line' in Russian parlance) and he established two saboteur schools for about two hundred men each in Madrid and in Benimamet, a small town to the north-west of Valencia. The candidates were taught marksmanship, demolition work and how to carry out attacks deep within hostile territory.[10]

Such partisan hit-and-run missions behind enemy lines are the framework for Ernest Hemingway's gripping *For Whom the Bell Tolls*. Since the guerrilla groups were sometimes supplied from the air by Soviet transport planes, it is possible that Brian taught them how to use radio transmitters and codes. Their base was Benimamet, in 1930 a holiday resort with just over three thousand inhabitants. It had been part of Valencia Municipality since 1882 and served as a resort for wealthy holiday-makers, who lived in the summer chalets. Most of these homes were nationalised during the Civil War and handed over to public authorities or the military. Bombed-out families from Valencia were housed in the smaller chalets, while Soviet staff occupied some of the bigger ones. The headquarters of the guerrilla units was in Chalet Banach, a large house in its own grounds in the town centre, near the tramline to Valencia. Goold-Verschoyle shared a house in Benimamet with his colleagues, 'Marko' and a Czech couple who went under the names Andy and Maria Novotny.

'Marko' was probably Slavomir Vukelich, a Croat who used the service-name 'Andrei Markovich' after joining the espionage department of the Red Army in 1933. He was an engineer by profession and worked as a radio operator in Spain.[11] The Novotny pair later moved to Barcelona, possibly to the spy school which Orlov had set up to train members of the International Brigades. This school was operated clandestinely and its existence was concealed from the republican authorities. Its graduates, personally chosen by Orlov, were to be infiltrated back to their home countries to work as NKVD agents. While there is no direct evidence that Goold was involved in this enterprise sited near Barcelona, the training programme of what Orlov called his CONSTRUCTION scheme – underground work, secret communications and espionage – were skills the Irishman had learned. The security at the school was so tight that the pupils were known by numbers only. One of the alumni was the New Yorker Morris Cohen, who later operated in the Los Alamos atomic spy ring and was finally arrested, with his wife, in Britain. Under the assumed identities Peter and Helen Kroger, they were sentenced to twenty years in 1961 for their part in the Portland naval secrets case.[12]

Goold-Verschoyle probably thought his remit on the Iberian peninsula was to fight fascism, rather than support Soviet aggrandisement. He never intended to honour his pledge of breaking off contact with Lotte: he wrote to her regularly, and to his mother, from Benimamet, using the address of a Spanish friend for the replies. The 24-year-old Irishman therefore committed the security breach of not going through 'official channels', if there were any, in posting and receiving letters. He may have felt that, as long as he did his job well, his private affairs were nobody's business. Underlying these service 'transgressions' was a deeper malaise and he soon clashed with his superiors on the nature of Soviet policy in Spain.

Two interrelated aspects of Soviet policy evidently caused the Irish radio expert to break with Stalinism: the role of Soviet military advisers and the systematic surveillance and persecution of dissidents, especially members of the POUM. Goold-Verschoyle would have been privy to reports, which he transmitted by radio or had conveyed to Moscow on tiny rolls of film. Why was the POUM targeted?[13] The anarchists, being libertarians, were anti-Marxist and anti-Soviet. As the largest indigenous current within the Spanish labour movement, the anarchists were too numerous a force to be suppressed outright at the behest of Moscow. The POUM, on the other hand, was a small party founded in 1935, with only 5,000 members at the outset and roughly 30,000 at the end of 1936. Its very existence provoked the visceral hatred of Moscow because it grew from a coterie of left, communist groups consisting mainly of Trotsky sympathisers who had been expelled from the PCE. Its most prominent leader during the Civil War was Andrés Nin, who was kidnapped by Orlov's agents in June 1937, murdered the following month and buried, in the presence of Orlov, in a field near Alcalá de Henares, west of Madrid.[14]

But the war strategy of the communists was undermined by another, comparably lesser known, manifestation of their tactics: in-fighting within the corps of Soviet experts. The most prominent of their number, the Soviet Civil War veteran Manfred Stern, alias General Emilio Kléber, was sidelined relatively early in the conflict. He was officially attached to the Central Committee of the PCE as adviser, helping to build up the famous Fifth Regiment (Quinto Regimiento) of Communist Party militants. In propaganda terms at least, Stern was the outstanding commander in the defence of Madrid in late 1936. However, he was premature in demanding the removal of 'untrustworthy' Spanish officers and clashed on this issue with his Ambassador, Rosenberg, and with the head of Soviet military intelligence, Jan Berzin.[15] All this backstage cut and thrust was reflected in denunciatory reports to *la casa* (Moscow), in which actors in this internal Soviet squabble tried to cover their own shortcomings or deflect accusations of 'political unreliability' by pointing the finger at others.[16]

Alexander Orlov reported to Moscow about uncovering enemy spy-networks on the basis of copies stolen from the archive of the French Deuxième Bureau (secret service) in Barcelona. His other sources were papers purloined from the Italian consul in Valencia or confessions extracted from suspect members of the International Brigades.[17] In a missive to Moscow as early as October 1936, Orlov peddled the fantasy that the anarchists and the POUM were planning an armed insurrection against the republican government, adding that 'the Trotskyist organization POUM, active in Catalonia, can be easily liquidated'.[18] On 17 December 1936 *Pravda* warned that the purging of Trotskyists and anarchists was underway in Catalonia and would be pursued with the same energy as the purges in the Soviet Union.[19]

Orlov overstepped his commission by planting agents in key ministries of the Spanish Republic. Contacts in the Ministry for Foreign Affairs enabled him to read all cryptograms being sent and received by the foreign legations in the republican war zone.[20] In February 1937 he radioed Moscow, calling for the execution of deserters, 'putting an end to inter-party squabbles', and accused the Soviet military advisers Berzin and Gorev of incompetence because of their lack of battle experience.[21] Berzin retaliated by informing Soviet Defence Commissar Voroshilov about outrage in higher circles of the Valencia government because of Orlov's 'unwarranted interference and espionage in government quarters'. Berzin concluded by calling for Orlov's recall to Moscow.[22]

Goold-Verschoyle cannot but have known about these developments seeing that he worked for Orlov and knew several of his sub-agents. Many of these were Germans, Austrians or Poles, figures from the shadowy world of republican counter-intelligence.

The first of the multinational anti-espionage units was the *Servicio extranjero* (foreign service) of the Catalan Communist Party (PSUC), a sub-unit founded by the German communist Alfred Herz and the Polish Bolshevik Szaja Kindermann. They worked with Orlov's *apparat*, set up provisional prisons (*checas*, as the Spaniards called them) in confiscated Church property (e.g. Santa Ursula Convent in Valencia), where they interrogated members of the International Brigades and other foreigners. They also observed anti-Stalinist socialists like George Orwell and his wife Eileen,[23] the young Willy Brandt or the Irish Trotskyist Paddy Trench, who put his journalistic expertise at the disposal of the POUM.[24] In the autumn of 1937 the PSUC counter-espionage unit was dispersed, mainly owing to pressure from the Socialist International and Spanish politicians. However, the collaboration of foreign communist agents with Orlov's people continued, and counter-espionage activities remained largely a fiefdom of the Soviets, despite the expansion of republican intelligence agencies led by Spaniards.[25]

When off-duty in Benimamet, just a tram-ride away from Valencia, Goold-Verschoyle generally consorted with German-speakers. In late March 1937 he went with a certain Max, an Austrian whom he had got to know through 'Marko', to Café Levante in Valencia. There they met another Austrian, a portly man in his 40s who invited them back to his apartment in a large house in the city centre.[26] The man was probably Julius Deutsch, the former leader of the Schutzbund, the military formation of the Austrian Social Democratic Party, and now a general commanding the coastal artillery in the republican zone. Deutsch was held to be 'a suspicious element' by Orlov's German agents because he was still a convinced, and prominent, socialist and an opponent of Stalinism. His secretary, Reventlow, a German socialist, was, by the same lights, a 'spy' and his adjutant, Menzl, 'an agent of the Austrian police'.[27]

The mysterious Max was another Austrian, a so-called 'Mexican', that is, a non-Russian communist who had volunteered for service in Spain while a political immigrant in the USSR; hence the pseudonym behind the real name, Franz Löschel. Löschel had been to the Lenin School in Moscow and entered 'the special service attached to the Russian friends' some time in 1937, after being wounded at the front.[28] Brian Goold-Verschoyle was presumably *au fait* with the work of Löschel and others and thus realised how spy-scares, normal in any war, were being invented or inflated by the Soviets in order to repress the non-communist Left, thus undermining the anti-fascist struggle.

In Valencia, a bastion of the PSOE left-wing, their newspapers and leading functionaries began to publicly denounce the unscrupulous drive for hegemony by the communists. Lotte's letter of 9 March 1937 to Brian Goold-Verschoyle implies that both were following these events closely, and that he had made the decision to break with *la casa*:

> Your letter of the 5th has made me very glad. I am looking immensely forward to your announced review of your life etc [....] I am glad about the change of your opinions and your becoming mature. Not only because of you, but because it reflects your environment [....] Don't specialise too much on the 'Jewish' question, which is only one aspect of the picture. I think the Pomade is all right.

The 'Jewish' reference applied to Trotskyism, the 'Pomade' hardly to hair-cream, for Brian's hair was thinning out and, in his mother's words, 'he used to wear a beret, and was rather Spanish-looking, tall and slender.' The politics of the POUM was what Lotte meant. The single extant communication from Goold-Verschoyle to Lotte at this decisive turning-point in his life is a postcard of the medieval town walls of Valencia (Torres de Serranos), post-marked 12 April 1937:

> Dear Lotte,
> While waiting in cue [*sic*] for stamps I wrote this. I have just been for my first bathe in the sea for this year. During the next couple of weeks I won't be very busy, and after that. You know I am waiting for your reply to my last letter with impacience [*sic*].
> Your Grisha

Not that Brian had nothing to do: if anything, Orlov's operations were at full throttle. The civil war within the Civil War was in preparation. It culminated in the 3 May attack by the communist-led police on the Barcelona Telephone Exchange, a bastion of the anarchists. Goold-Verschoyle's postcard message, written not long before the communist *coup de main*, can only mean that he had been suspended from duty, or had decided to leave the service of the Soviets or had asked for a transfer to other work. He may have been already in contact with the British Consul in Valencia, for his mother heard subsequently from that source that her son had had a disagreement with the Soviet Ambassador: Brian denied he was a communist and stated he had come to Spain 'to help the Government to win the war against the Fascists'. Sybil also learned that Brian had been sent by the Russian Ambassador to Barcelona and had never been heard of again.[29] Another version, which Goold told his fellow-prisoner Karlo Štajner in 1938, was that in view of the disturbing growth of NKVD influence within the republican army, he had approached his commanding officer with the following argument: he was a Republican and not a communist, and as he realised that the present struggle was for a communist Spain rather than a Republican one, he requested that he be discharged from his duties. The commander listened without comment, merely stating that Goold would have to wait until a replacement was found.

In late April the Spanish vessel *Magallanes* was moored in Barcelona harbour. Built in Cádiz in 1931, her most famous mission was to Mexico in the autumn of 1936. Despite being attacked twice by Italian planes, *Magallanes* landed 20,000 Mauser rifles and 20 million cartridges at Cartagena, the first cago of Soviet shipments to Spain. Later *Magallanes* plied the Russian route, transporting Spanish trainee pilots to the Soviet Union and bringing back military hardware. Its passage was guarded by republican naval vessels off the North African coast and in the Dardanelles.[30]

Shortly after the talk with his commander (as related to Karlo Štajner), Goold-Verschoyle was asked to report at Barcelona harbour, to repair a ship's radio. Embarking on *Magallanes* with his tool-bag, he was escorted to the radio cabin. The door was locked behind him. There was no radio to be seen, but two Russians, fellow-prisoners. Their names were Hurdis and Shubodev, members of the Komsomol. Their exact date of departure is unknown. The three 'dangerous criminals' landed on Soviet soil on 6 May.

NOTES

1. Soviet aid was offered either in the form of armaments (648 airplanes, 347 tanks, 1,186 pieces of artillery, 20,000 machine-guns and almost half a million rifles during the course of the Civil War) or military advisers like Manfred Stern ('General Kléber') – Iurii Rybalkin, *Sovetskaia voennaia pomoshch' respublikanskoi Ispanii (1936–1939)* (Moscow 2000), pp. 44–45.

2. Jung Chang and John Halliday, *Mao, the Unkown Story* (New York 2005), pp. 179–80.
3. Costello and Tsarev, *Deadly Illusions*, pp. 257–64; W.G. Krivitsky, *I Was Stalin's Agent* (Cambridge 1992), pp. 123–25 (ed. Mark Almond); See also G. Howson, *Arms for Spain. The Untold Story of the Spanish Civil War* (London 1988).
4. Fax from the Russian Foreign Intelligence Service to the author, 9 February 1995.
5. M.J. Faulkner, Records Branch Foreign and Commonwealth Office, to the author, 18 November 1994.
6. Karlo Štajner, *7000 Tage in Sibirien*, Vienna 1975, p. 74.
7. PRO, KV2/817, Sibyl M. Goold-Verschoyle to Walter Krivitsky, 8 May 1939.
8. TsA-FSB, NKVD prosecution file No. R-36981 Brian Goold-Verschoyle, l. 42.
9. E.M. Primakov (ed.), *Ocherki istorii rossiiskoi vneshnei razvedki, tom 3, 1933–1941 gody* (Moscow 1997), p. 136.
10. Costello and Tsarev, *Deadly Illusions*, pp. 269–71.
11. A. Kopladiki and D. Prokhorov, *Imperiia GRU. Ocherki istorii rossiiskoi voennoi razvedki. Kniga vtoraia* (Moscow 2001), p. 332.
12. Primakov, *Ocherki*, pp. 144–45; Costello and Tsarev, *Deadly Illusions*, pp. 275–78; *The Guardian*, 30 June 1995 (obituary of Peter Kroger).
13. Unless otherwise mentioned, all references for the POUM are taken from the following exhaustive study: Reiner Tosstorff, *Die POUM im spanischen Bürgerkrieg* (Frankfurt am Main 1987).
14. For the details, see Costello and Tsarev, *Deadly Illusions*, pp. 287–92.
15. Walerij Brun-Zechowoj, *Manfred Stern – General Kleber. Die tragische Biografie eines Berufsrevolutionärs (1896–1954)* (Berlin 2000), pp. 70–98.
16. See the numerous documents from the Moscow Military Archive RGVA in Ronald Radosh, Mary R. Habeck, Grigory Sevostianov (eds), *Spain Betrayed. The Soviet Union in the Spanish Civil War* (New Haven and London 2001), especially the denunciation of Antonov-Ovseenko, the Soviet Consul in Barcelona (p. 154) or of Ambassador Rosenberg (p. 94).
17. Costello and Tsarev, *Deadly Illusions*, pp. 268–69.
18. Ibid., p. 281.
19. Pierre Broué and Émile Témime, *Revolution und Krieg in Spanien. Geschichte des spanischen Bürgerkrieges. Erster Teil* (Frankfurt am Main 1978), p. 293.
20. Costello and Tsarev, *Deadly Illusions*, p. 272.
21. Ibid., pp. 264–66.
22. Krivitsky, *I Was Stalin's Agent*, pp. 117–18.
23. RGASPI, f. 545, o. 6, d. 149, l. 46 (report of Alfonso, 29 May 1937, Barcelona), l. 99 (July 1937); d. 62, l. 37 ('Liste der POUM-Leute').
24. RGASPI, f. 545, o. 6, d. 62, ll. 27, 41 (Brandt), l. 31 (Trench).
25. Peter Huber and Michael Uhl, 'Politische Überwachung und Repression in den Internationalen Brigaden (1936–1938)', *Forum für osteuropäische Ideen- und Zeitgeschichte*, 5. Jahrgang, 2001, Heft 2, pp. 121–59.
26. NKVD prosecution-file Goold-Verschoyle, ll. 61–2
27. RGASPI, f. 545, o. 6, d. 69, ll. 13–15.
28. RGASPI, f. 545, o. 6, d. 74, l. 27.
29. As footnote 7.
30. J.L. Alcofar Nassaes, *Las fuerzas navales en la guerra civil espanola*, Barcelona 1971, p. 67 ; idem, *La marina italiana en las guerra de Espana*, Barcelona 1975, p. 284; Howson, *Arms for Spain*, p. 103.

Prisoner No. 500

Magallanes sailed east, passed the Bosporus into the Black Sea and docked at Feodosiya, a port in the south of the Crimean peninsula, on 6 May 1937. An officer from the INO office in the Lubianka, Zerebrennikov, who had organised the kidnapping and transporting of Goold-Verschoyle to Russia, was also on board. He confiscated 'Friend's' passport, his notebook and wallet, which contained $20 and 1,495 Pesetas.[1] These objects were enclosed with an order to the local NKVD office, transferring the Irishman to Simferopol, where directives from headquarters about the transport to Moscow would arrive in due course. The prisoner was escorted to Simferopol the following day. A conditional order to arrest was issued and confirmed by the NKVD chief in the Crimea and a local public prosecutor. At the foot of the directive was the typed line that 'Verschoyle had been exposed, for carrying out espionage activities for a foreign power'. A Morse code alphabet, written in pencil and found on Goold-Verschoyle, was attached to the documents.

He and the Komsomol suspects were handed over to INO staff on 10 May. They arrived in the capital two days later. Goold-Verschoyle was put through the usual routine in the Lubianka isolation block: completing the questionnaire for prisoners, in which he gave details of his family and his present non-Party status, signing receipts for the belongings seized (foreign currency, passport, watch, wallet, braces, tie, films for a Leica camera, fifteen postage stamps) and posing for frontal- and side-view photographs. In captivity, Brian was known as 'Hamilton' or 'Gold', since his name was a tongue-twister for prison staff and his fellow-prisoners, and almost impossible to transcribe adequately in Russian. For our purposes, he is now 'Goold'.

The formal arrest warrant was issued on 15 May and confirmed by Frinovsky, the deputy of Nikolai Ezhov, People's Commissar for Internal Affairs. It was based on a report from Abram Slutsky, the head of the 7th (Foreign) Department of the Main Administration of State Security. For the INO boss, it was an open-and-shut case:

At the beginning of April 1936 Mrs. Margarita Charlotte Moos arrived in Moscow. According to Brian Goold-Verschoyle, she had a relationship with him since July 1935 and was the wife of Siegfried Moos, a German Communist immigrant in England. In October 1936 Margarita Charlotte Moos returned to London to her husband after divorcing Brian Goold-Verschoyle. Goold-Verschoyle himself was sent by us in 1936 to work in Schwed's [Orlov's] rezidentura. In the period when he worked for us Brian Goold-Verschoyle was forbidden to disclose his address. Despite this, he remained in contact with Margarita C. Moos and corresponded with her. We have learned from this correspondence that Brian Goold-Verschyole, Margarita C. Moos and Siegfried Moos are active Trotskyists. In addition, Brian Goold-Verschoyle was very curious about matters which had nothing to do with his own work, which is further proof that he had links to a Trotskyist organisation and probably to a hostile intelligence service as well.

Slutsky informed Weinstock, head of the Prisons' Department of the NKVD, that Frinovsky had ordered that Goold was to be held without name in prison, under the alias 'Prisoner No. 500'. Furthermore, the memo continued, only Slutsky's direct subordinates, namely Major Kaminsky and Lieutenant Nikultsev, were allowed to escort the prisoner from his cell and to interrogate him. This was a highly unusual measure since it was usually officers from the 3rd Department (counter-intelligence) who acted as inquisitors and torturers. It is probable that Slutsky was protecting his rear and keeping Spanish secrets 'within the family' now that a clean-out of high-ranking NKVD officers had begun under the new landlord of the Lubianka, the vicious dwarf Ezhov.

The first interrogation of Goold took place on 15 May, most probably a preliminary joust dealing with formalities, ending with Nikultsev completing the questionnaire of twenty questions about the family of the prisoner. Goold signed his name under the sentence 'the protocol was taken down correctly according to the words and formulations made by me'. Walter Krivitsky, in Moscow from March to May 1937, heard that a report on Goold-Verschoyle's 'Trotskyist sympathies' had reached headquarters from Spain. One officer in the INO department answered Krivitsky's queries evasively, but the Hague *rezident* asked other acquaintances in headquarters and learned about the circumstances of the kidnapping on board the ship in Barcelona and the voyage to the Crimea.[2]

On 29 May Nikultsev summarised his findings to date, holding that prosecution case no. 11993 against Goold justified further investigation:

> During the period in which he worked as an operative for the NKVD abroad on an important mission he joined a Trotskyist organisation and carried out active work prejudicial to the interests of the working people. Charged under Article 58/§1a, 58/§10 and 58/§14 of the Criminal Code of the USSR.

Each charge could result in the death penalty – high treason, anti-Soviet propaganda and agitation, and counter-revolutionary sabotage.

On 2 June 1937 Brian Goold had his first exhaustive interrogation with Lieutenant Nikultsev. Since the prison file of Goold-Verschoyle could not be found in the Russian Federation (searches for it in Moscow and Orenburg Province drew a blank), one cannot know how often he was interrogated, for how long and when exactly he was transferred from one place of incarceration to another. The protocol of the 2 June grilling, while not verbatim, gives a general picture of the contents of the verbal pummelling. The prisoner began by rejecting the charges and denying adherence to Trotskyism. He admitted being critical of Comintern policy in regard to the KPD before 1933, in particular its 'social-fascist' slandering of the Social Democrats and its policy, after Hitler's accession to power, of urging its members to join the fascist trade unions. He finished his initial statement by describing his disillusioning experience with Soviet reality during visits to Moscow in 1933 and 1935, which convinced him he could not live there permanently: no political freedom, the gagging of free expression and no free press.

Nikultsev then wanted to know about the political views of Lotte Moos. Goold answered by saying that she was a former member of the KPD, but now, as letters from her had shown, supported the group around Heinrich Brandler. Suspended from his post as a secretary of the Politburo of the KPD in 1924 because he had condemned the armed putsch in Germany organised by the Comintern the previous year, Brandler became a prisoner-at-large in Moscow, shunted off to work in the Krestintern. He was finally given an exit visa in 1928, but was expelled from the Soviet and

German parties. In the years to follow, he was seen as the unofficial leader of 'Right' or 'conciliatory' communists in Germany, an opposition group with substantial numbers which formed the KPD-O (KPD-Opposition) and later became part of a loose international federation of expelled communists (IVKO) who rejected the sharp ultra-left turn ('social fascism', 'class against class') in the politics of the Communist International after 1928. The KPD-O had considerable intellectual punch: August Thalheimer, one of the first theoreticians of the KPD and an early analyst of fascism, plus the Reichstag deputy Paul Frölich, who edited the writings of Rosa Luxemburg. With its differentiated critique of Soviet socialism, unequivocal anti-fascism and notable support among industrial workers in many German regions long before 1933, it is not surprising that the KPD-O held attractions for Lotte Moos. Indeed, she may well have met Brandler and his exiled circle in Paris before she landed in Britain in 1933. In London, Lotte was in contact with scattered KPD-O supporters, such as Gertrud Danecke and her companion Helmut.[3]

Nikultsev was not interested in long explanations, for him 'right' or 'left' opposition to Stalin from novice or veteran communists was 'Trotskyism'. He brushed aside Goold's correct interjection that Brandler had no time for Trotskyists and *vice versa*. The attack then turned to Lotte's support for the POUM and her alleged urging that Goold support its policies. Once again, the Irishman's objection that, contrary to what Nikultsev had said, the POUM was not 'Trotskyist', provoked another verbal onslaught. At the end of this exchange Goold 'conceded' that Lotte Moos was a Trotskyist, he himself as well, as early as 1935, without being a member of a 'Trotskyist' organisation.

He then signed the protocol. It was perhaps at this juncture that he hesitated to put his signature under the distorted and mangled version of his views penned in black ink on five pages by Inquisitor Nikultsev. Perhaps a 'heavy gang' entered the office, perhaps Nikultsev waved the truncheon in his face. Sizing up his chances, Goold signed, as he put it later to cell-mates in a humorous understatement, 'because being an Englishman, I cannot allow violence to my person'.[4] Despite this sympathetic flourish of self-depreciation (Continentals know that Englishmen are notoriously eccentric), his signing was logical: the 'organs' had read his correspondence, seized Lotte's last letter to him, which he carried in his pocket for weeks, and there was obviously no sense in arguing about the finer points of Marxist politics in the Lubianka. In other words, this part of the charge sheet was 'proven'; it was more important to fight the other accusations, especially the lethal ones like 'high treason' and 'espionage for a foreign power'.

After a pause, Nikultsev resumed the interrogation, a marathon session that went on for three days. The ten pages that it generated are Nikultsev's version, hammered out in acerbic exchanges. Brian Goold, like anybody under interrogation by the omniscient NKVD, had to sign beneath each answer and the entire protocol at the conclusion of the exhausting bout. The questioning began by Goold stating that he knew none of Lotte Moos's acquaintances in London, merely that she moved in German and English communist circles. He was able to fend off the expected riposte – that her political activity endangered his cover – by arguing that 'John' (Bystrolyotov), after being approached on this matter, had no objections, seeing that nobody knew the Goold-Moos pair were cohabiting, save Siegfried Moos. The next accusation ended in a draw: yes, Lotte Moos knew that Goold was a NKVD courier as early as 1935, but she had no fixed idea of what her lover actually did since the material was kept in a locked case in the house when he was absent. And she knew nobody from the London network, meeting 'John' only in 1936, in Moscow.

Then Nikultsev produced the trump card Goold feared: that he had deliberately stayed in contact with Lotte Moos, although 'categorically forbidden to do so'. His answer, although cast in the dictated form, was the truth:

> I confess that I committed a crime by staying in correspondence with Charlotte Moos, despite being ordered not to do so. I remained in contact with her because of my feelings for her.

According to the totalitarian subtext that all acts are basically political, Nikultsev insisted that the emotional argument was irrelevant: the uninterrupted correspondence was pursued because Lotte was 'a member of a counter-revolutionary, Trotskyist organisation'. Brian Goold restated his reason for not breaking with her:

> I admit once more that my personal feelings for Charlotte Moos were much stronger than I thought when I promised to break with her in

Moscow. Afterwards I felt the need to communicate my thoughts, my political ideas, to her.

The interrogator then wanted to know about contacts with the POUM. Goold reiterated that he had not been a member of a political organisation in Spain, had no contacts with the POUM, but might have joined the party had he stayed longer in Valencia.

Nikultsev then switched attention to the Goold-Verschoyle family, specifically to Neil and his wife Olga. Neil had nothing to do with the prosecution case, which was based on transgressions in Spain and the letters between London and Benimamet. Brian Goold's extremely negative comments on his eldest brother are a surprise. They can be interpreted as a line of narration prompted by Nikultsev, who may have hoped that it could lead to 'linking' the Goold-Verschoyle brothers to the British Secret Service. In any case the dialogue that followed (that is, as written down by Nikultsev) is rarely punctuated by questions, almost a monologue about Neil's biography and Brian's comments on it. There is a ring of truth in the account: that neither he, nor Lotte, nor his bosses in the Lubianka could understand how an upper-class Englishman (as Neil was perceived) with a good education could tolerate such appalling conditions in Moscow, the untidy room he shared with Olga and Pyotr; or that Neil, when again in London in 1933–34, for all his professed communism, wrote for the liberal press (*Manchester Guardian, Adelphi*) and consorted with wealthy intellectuals. The insinuation was that Neil at that time in London was a bit of a sham, with a conservative doctor for a mistress, while the pregnant Olga lived out her life in a run-down *kommunalka* room. According to Goold, Olga warned him about telling anything about his NKVD recruitment to Neil, whom, she stressed, had also been seen as a prospective candidate for Soviet espionage until she explained that he was not temperamentally suited for such missions and already had too many acquaintances in Moscow.

When asked why he had not relayed his doubts about Neil's political reliability to his NKVD superiors, Goold replied that he was sure that the matter had been looked into since Neil was living with Olga, an agent of the secret police, and had been issued with an entry visa for the Soviet Union again in 1934. This part of the interrogation ended with information about Neil's friends in Moscow, fleeting acquaintances about whom Goold could say nothing of note. The next stage concerned the key piece of evidence, Lotte's letter of 9 March 1937:

> Dear Brianchen,
> Only short in the P. Office. Got your letter to-day and it is now obvious that my letter from 17th got lost. Maybe because I put a newspaper in it. Meanwhile I wrote on the 3rd another one. I hope you have got that one. Don't write any more to the address of my aunt, she is cross with us because of it. I got your two letters, one from 20th, and one of the 22nd, and I answered them in my letter from the 3rd. Please write to the Club, that is all right. Your letter of the 5th has made me very glad. I am looking immensely forward to your announced review of your life etc.
> I think I will go in for an interpreter course in April. This is to learn English properly and get fluent in French.
> (P.T.O)
> That might be useful one day, and also when I come to Spain. Perhaps I will do that one day, when my scholarship is over. That means July. I am glad about the change of your opinions and your becoming mature. Not only because of you, but because it reflects your environment. Don't specialise too much on the 'Jewish' Question, which is only one aspect of the picture. I think the Pomade is all right. The paper I send [*sic*] belonged to H. Pity it got lost. I must stop. I embrace you dear friend, Brian.

Nikultsev wanted to know about 'H.', who had passed on the 'Trotskyist' newspaper (title unknown) to Goold via Lotte. Not that Brian Goold knew much about him – a certain Helmut, a German refugee in London whose wife Gertrud was a friend of Lotte's. She and Brian had visited Gertud's sister, an employee of Comintern headquarters, twice at her home south-east of Moscow. Goold subsequently read in a letter from Lotte to Spain that Gertrud's sister had been arrested by the NKVD. This passage referred to Erna Kolbe and her sister Gertrud Denecke, whose surnames Goold could not remember. Erna was subsequently fired from her post in the German section of the Comintern and sent to the Gulag, which she survived.

With that line of investigation exhausted, the interrogator turned to the obvious passages in the letter about the POUM ('Pomade') and Trotskyism ('Jewish Question'). Goold admitted that he had sympathy for the dissident Marxists led by Nin but he denied that

Mrs Moos had 'instructed' him to join up. The last section of the interrogation hinged on the technicalities of the postal communications between the lovers. Goold stopped writing care of Lotte's Brighton aunt because the women had argued – Lotte found her aunt insufferably 'bourgeois'. His letters were henceforth addressed to the Linguists' Club. Her letters reached Brian Goold via his colleague 'Marko', for Goold believed, wrongly as it turned out, that they would not be opened. He had made an even greater and gratuitous blunder by sending Lotte a photo of himself beside 'Marko' and 'Novotny', without disclosing what they did. This confession was seen as proof that Goold had betrayed his colleagues to the 'Trotskyist Moos'. The questioning ended with a scripted answer, a full 'capitulation' demanded over many sleepless hours and by means of threats. Brian Goold realised, in respect of the letters at least, that he had no exit strategy:

> I confess that I committed a crime by sending these photos to the Trotskyist Charlotte Moos, all the more so because she could imagine that the people in the photo were indeed NKVD operatives. I told her the surname of one of the operatives, namely that of 'Marko', whose address I used so that her letters to me would not be controlled. I did not disclose 'Novotny's' name to her. However, I did write her that he shared my political views.

The interrogations were interrupted for thirty-five days. When they resumed on 9 July, Major Kaminsky, head of the First Subgroup of the INO (7th) Department of State Security, teamed up with his subordinate Nikultsev. The first accusation referred to the incident, mentioned earlier, which had caused cynical amusement among hard-bitten INO staff in Western Europe: Goold's consternation when Foreign Office documents fell out of a parcel he was handling in London. The incident was now twisted to fit the charge of opening secret material against orders. Goold parried the accusation, saying that he had no recollection of such an incident and was, in any case, informed of the contents by a senior officer in the London *rezidentura*.

Presumably on the basis of reports from Orlov, Kaminsky wanted to know why the Irishman showed 'an unseemly curiosity' in his work in Spain, in other operations and in the contents of what he had to photograph. Following the prisoner's denial, Kaminsky demanded he 'admit' that he had kept secret papers in his possession for longer than was necessary, 'in order to learn of their contents'. Goold conceded that on one occasion he had forgotten to hand over a film which he had developed, and the photographs, immediately, as was the rule, but did so the following day. A similar incident had occurred in London, when he, the novice, had destroyed a film after developing, forgetting that a senior colleague should have been present when the film-roll was burned. This sin of omission was construed as evidence of espionage for the British:

Question: You are lying. The film allegedly burned by you was handed over by you to the organisation on whose directive you joined the NKVD in the first place. In the same way you also handed over the other film which you held for one day. You passed the film to our rezident only after you were ordered to do so.

Answer: I deny categorically that I handed over any film to any organisation and also deny that I belonged to any such organisation. I confess once more that I really did burn the film because at that time I knew nothing of the order that the second man in the rezidentura had to be present when material was destroyed. Regarding the film I handed over one day late, I did so by giving it personally to the rezident and without any such request from him.

The questioning then took a different direction, the probing of Goold's motives for learning Russian and his interest in the USSR. He mentioned the influence which Neil had exerted on him, his interest in the economic upsurge in the USSR at a time of mass unemployment in Britain, which he had followed in the left-wing press, and his intention to work at his profession in the USSR. As evidence of his earnestness, he stated that he had begun to learn the Russian language on his own but later took lessons from Rosa Meyer-Leviné in London, giving her a letter of recommendation from Lotte Moos. Rosa was a 'suspicious element', a Russian revolutionary and the widow of two KPD leaders, Eugen Leviné (leader of the short-lived Bavarian Soviet Republic and executed in 1919) and Ernst Meyer (died in 1930). She had attempted to hold a middle position in the KPD between the warring right and left factions.[5] Within the London exile group of the KPD, Rosa and her sons Genja and Rudolf were considered unreliable dissidents. In 1936, for example, she was forced to compose a three-page text on why she had reservations about the Popular Front tactics of the Comintern.[6]

Kaminsky and Nikultsev could not understand why Goold-Verschoyle and his relatives had not been hauled in and grilled by Scotland Yard because of their correspondence with Neil during his first sojourn in the Soviet Union (1930–33). The interrogation team then 'suggested' (that is the phrase in the protocol) that Goold confess to being an imperialist who had joined the CPGB, learned Russian and gone to Moscow at the instructions of British Intelligence, a Philbyite 'mole' in reverse. He denied the fabrication, and the variant that immediately followed, that both he and Lotte Moos were British spies and that she was the contact person between him and British espionage. The interrogation ended with inconsequential queries about Neil's visit to the British Embassy in Moscow (for purposes of registration) and his former adherence to Christian Socialist circles in London.

On 4 August 1937 the Special Board (OSO) of the NKVD sentenced Brian Goold-Verschoyle (in absentia) to eight years in prison on the charge of KRTD ('counter-revolutionary Trotskyist activities'). That was the acronym for 'terrorism', the most common verdict against 'politicals' in the Ezhov years (1936–38). The sentence is noteworthy because the prisoner was not to be sent into the Gulag Archipelago as a work slave, but to solitary confinement in a prison. Another striking fact is the relative speed with which the case was concluded. On the other hand, the prosecution case was not based on fiction but on facts, serious offences 'in the field' which in any secret service would have had dire consequences for the delinquent. In the case of Goold-Verschoyle, however, thoughtless or brash breaches of security were seen as proof of treachery, predestining him to the dungeon and not mere dismissal in disgrace. We can only speculate on the nature of the sentence, for it could have been harsher. Perhaps Kaminsky and Slutsky, like their counterparts in the Breslin case, could not underpin the spying charges and reckoned that eight years in isolation ensured the removal of a 'secrets bearer'.

Another unusual aspect of the investigation was supplementary questioning after sentencing. In an undated [August 1937] memorandum, Slutsky and Nikultsev summarised the charges ('suspicion of spying' and 'aiding the foreign bourgeoisie'), held as proven that the prisoner had close links to 'Trotskyists' in Britain

(Lotte Moos, Rosa Meyer-Leviné) and concluded that further interrogations were necessary to probe the suspicion of espionage for Britain and Germany. They recommended that the prisoner be kept 'completely isolated from foreigners', not be subject to forced labour and be forbidden to correspond with the outside world. All incoming letters to Goold were to be sent direct to Slutsky, who demanded that the prison authorities inform him of the Irishman's conduct in confinement.

The last meeting between Goold and INO officers was a perfunctory exercise, the tying-up of loose ends. The short confrontation on 28 August 1937 centred on Goold's colleagues and acquaintances in Spain and he identified the Czech Novotny couple from photographs. He was then transferred to Butyrka prison, an assembly point for those already sentenced and awaiting their transport to the Gulag or a high-security prison.

The Butyrka, still in use, is situated in the north of Moscow behind a screen of high-rise flats. In the 1930s it was Moscow's largest prison, a former barracks for Catherine the Great's Hussar Regiment, consisting of three-storied blocks containing collective cells in which the prisoners slept on bed-boards along the walls. It had a special wing (*spetskorpus*) for isolated prisoners where conditions and food were better than in the normal mass cells. Twenty to thirty thousand inmates were incarcerated there in 1937. Arriving prisoners found themselves in a hall as large as a railway station. Before the prisoner was officially registered, searched and taken to the bath-house, they were kept in narrow upright boxes (*sobachniki*) without a seat. Once the procedure of admittance was over, the prisoner was pushed into a large cell, full to overflowing with half-naked, sweating inmates, who momentarily stopped their discussions or arguments in order to size up the new arrival.

The Butyrka was a foretaste of hell in 1937 for two other reasons: the weather was unbearably hot and the inmates found it difficult to get a night's rest. Screams and whimpering from the interrogation cells above echoed across the courtyard and entered the cell through the tiny milk-glass aperture of the window high up on the wall. The Terror was gaining in momentum, and speedy confessions were necessary to expedite the backlog of cases; hence the thudding sounds of boot and fist on soft flesh, the scraping of chairs or the wet slap of whip or truncheon on bloodied backs. The screams of the tormented and the cursing of their torturers went on from nightfall to 3 a.m. Evgeniya Ginsburg, a transit prisoner in the Butyrka during that hot summer, borrowed cotton wool from a friend to plug her ears.[7]

Since we know next to nothing about Goold's prison experience, we can take, as a *vade mecum*, the moving account of a generous and indomitably courageous fellow-prisoner whose path through the system intersected with that of the Irishman on several occasions. Karl Steiner (Karlo Štajner) had an immaculate proletarian biography: apprenticeship as a printer in Vienna, joining the communist movement while still a teenager and later working for the secret *apparat* of the Yugoslav comrades. It seemed he had reached the climax of his career in 1932, on being appointed managing director of a printing works in Moscow. In the dead of night in early November 1936 he was arrested, a victim of the purge within the headquarters of the Communist International.

A month later Steiner landed in the Butyrka, in collective cell No. 61, measuring 45 square metres and designed for twenty-four prisoners, but now holding a tangle of 250 stinking bodies in the half-light, lying or sitting on bunk-slats or hunched on the floor. The doughty Steiner soon accustomed himself to the daily routine: rising at five, inadequate rations in the morning, at noon and the evening (watery soup, tea-water, soggy bread and buckwheat porridge). Other natural breaks in the monotony were morning ablutions (*opravka*), the afternoon stroll in the exercise yard and the opportunity to buy rations in the prison shop every ten days. Those with money could spend 50 roubles at a time, usually on bread, butter, sugar, herrings and tobacco. The others, who had been arrested without funds or had no relatives to send them money, were allowed to partake in the short-lived bonanza (the rations were gone after five days at the most). That was a decision of the *bedkom* (committee for the poor) formed by the politically conscious inmates intent on strengthening solidarity, something that was kept secret because it would be interpreted as evidence of 'counter-revolutionary' combination.

Steiner's interrogators found him uncooperative. He rejected the charges and refused to leave the cell for a further nightly bout of senseless barraging, demanding the immediate presence of a public prosecutor. Since the guards and Governor Popov could not seize him over the expanse of prone figures, the cell was cleared, and Steiner, strapped in a straitjacket, was thrown into the punishment cells (*kartser*). He steadfastly refused to sign a confession, even after his transfer to Lefortovo, the high-security prison where the interrogation rooms were on the same corridor as the cells. The screams of the tortured kept the Austrian awake, but he still refused to sign on the dotted line, even after a mock-execution. On 6 September 1937 the Military Collegium came to Lefortovo and sentenced Steiner, in a hearing lasting less than 20 minutes, to ten years' strict isolation in prison.[8]

The following day, Popov, the Governor of the Butyrka, received an order from the NKVD in respect of Goold. He was to be sent in a 'single cell' railway carriage to serve his penitentiary sentence in Vladimir, leaving no later than 15 September. Vladimir prison, situated in the town of the same name 250 kilometres north-east of Moscow, was where revolutionaries had been entombed in Tsarist times. Under Ezhov a fourth block with single cells had been built. All cell windows looked north and, because they were bricked up to half-length, the inmates rarely saw sunlight.

During his sojourn in the Butyrka, Goold held conversations with his fellow cell-mate Heinz Neumann.[9] Already a confidante of Stalin's in the mid-1920s, Neumann was the archetypal Comintern agent, active from Canton to Catalonia, and a leading proponent of the ultra-left and disastrous policies of the KPD in the last years of the Weimar Republic.[10] Whether Neumann was amenable to Brian Goold's jaundiced views on communism, or had retained his Stalinist fervour, is unknown. After five months' imprisonment, the German had not yet succumbed to the pressure of his interrogators. He was executed in late November 1937.

The transit prisoners destined for Vladimir were kept in a former chapel in one of the Butyrka's courtyards. The building had been renovated and divided into cells of different sizes on three floor levels. The hygienic conditions were indescribable in the grossly over-crowded transit block, with two *parasha* per cell and one bucket of water for washing for eighteen inmates. Steiner was fortunate in that he did not sleep on the concrete floor but on the table that divided the cell in two. The transitees, having been sentenced, were left more or less in peace; they whiled away the time by recounting the books they had read or their biographies. Steiner's group, which may have included Goold, were brought under heavy escort to the railway station of the Kursk line on 17 September. Their destination was Vladimir, but the guards refused to disclose it. Speaking in the third-class wagons was forbidden, but the transportees commented in whispers on the waving women they saw through the heavy grille fixed to the carriage window – bereft wives and mothers who hoped to catch a glimpse of their loved ones before they left for planet Gulag.

Arriving in Vladimir before dawn, the prisoners were transported by lorry to the prison. They had to kneel for over two hours in the muddy forecourt before the gaol gates swung open. The new intake soon realised that Vladimir was a hard-regime prison: the guards were brutal, the rations paltry and the isolation almost total. During the daily fifteen minutes in the exercise-yard, for example, the inmates walked up and down a narrow corridor of gravel hemmed in by tall wooden walls; each cell had its own 'corridor' and anyone who infringed the rules (head down, hands held behind the back, no talking) landed afterwards in the punishment cells. That was Steiner's lot on two occasions because he demanded medical treatment and a special diet to cure his acute diarrhoea. Heartening moments were few, in Steiner's case a letter from his wife and a picture of the baby born in his absence, and the books distributed from the well-stocked library.

After two months the group was moved to a huge cell for two hundred prisoners. Many had familiar faces, old companions from Moscow's prisons, which suggested that a new transport was being planned. As in the Butyrka chapel, the prison rules were relaxed once more and the inmates knew that a change was imminent when they were ordered to hand back the lags' uniform and change into their own tattered clothing. The new route led back to Moscow, with friendly guards and enough rations for the 48–hour journey. The train did not stop at the Kursk station but continued to the Leningrad line, a sure sign that the transport was destined for the Far North, possibly to one of the many logging Gulags. The train stopped at Kem in Karelia, on the western shore of the White Sea.

The grey winter morning of 2 December 1937, the boundless grey sea and the grey faces of prisoners passing the railway siding were intimations for Steiner and his comrades: what awaited them could hardly be better than Vladimir, despite what the voluble guards had said on the journey north.

Soon a ship hove into view and Steiner knew it was their vessel from the letters SLON on its side – *Solovetskie lageria osobogo naznacheniia*, Solovetsky Special Camp. Soldiers with sub-machineguns at the ready formed a cordon and hurried the prisoners on board the ship which cast off and reached the main Solovetsky island, 70 kilometres away, seven hours later.[11] Solovetsky inspired dread and was known abroad since the 1920s. The archipelago, originally a monastic settlement, was where the Soviets perfected their slave empire since the island camps were run on a profit basis and became a show-piece ensemble.[12] By 1937, however, the economic schemes on Solovetsky, such as fox-farming, agriculture, fishing and forestry, were curtailed. This Soviet Devil's Island reverted to what it had been originally – an isolation prison camp for the 'most dangerous' political prisoners.

Senseless cruelty and random killing of prisoners were widespread. In 1930 an investigating commission from Moscow arrested scores of the most prominent sadists on the prison staff and had them sentenced to death or a Gulag term.[13] A famous massacre of prisoners occurred five years later on Bolshaia Muksolma, the second largest island. The victims were nuns and female members of religious sects who refused to 'work for the Antichrist'. They were shot out of hand before the assembled prisoners.[14] Steiner and Goold were oblivious of the camp's bloody history when they landed on the pier opposite the Solovetsky Kremlin. Their reception gave grounds for belief that conditions on the island hermitage were comparatively liberal: a well-heated and wooden-floored cell for ten men, sacks filled with straw for mattresses, and clean blankets, wholesome rations (potato soup, gruel, fish, plenty of bread), business-like guards and good hygienic facilities.

The illusion lasted no longer than a week. Steiner's entourage was frogmarched across the silted causeway to Bolshaia Muksolma, to the two-storied prison ruled with an iron rod by Commandant Bardin. The new prisoners were stripped, shorn and driven naked – it was 30 degrees below zero – across the courtyard into the bath-house, and then into their cells. Still wet from his shower and unable to sleep because of the cold, Steiner introduced himself to his seventeen cell-mates. In the weeks that followed the group divided into two camps: defenders of Stalin and those, like Steiner, who considered the dictator to be the gravedigger of socialism. Egorov, once Mayor of Stalingrad, explained to Steiner that the Stalin apologists were usually faking, in the hope that their loyalty to the system while in prison was some kind of insurance against the persecution of their relatives. On Muksulma the food was inadequate, the exercise period too short, but the odd letter from home and the occasional visit from the librarian with his trove or the opening of the prison shop were days to be treasured. Yet Bardin was always on the prowl outside, frequently snapping open the glass eye in the cell-door, eager to spy a transgression and withdraw the writing, reading or exercise 'privileges' because the prisoner had laughed, read aloud to his mates or exercised in the cell.

Steiner was just as pleased when he was transferred to a 'foreigners only' communal cell in March 1938. The inmates were communists, stranded remnants of cadres from the Communist International (*lavochka*, the huckster's shop, in Stalin's contemptuous phrase) who had been spared the executioner's bullet but who were now condemned to a slow death by starvation. Despite political differences, Steiner befriended Werner Hirsch, the former editor of the KPD daily *Rote Fahne* and one-time secretary to party leader Thälmann, with whom he had been arrested by the Gestapo in March 1933, tortured and sent to a concentration camp. Released a year later, Hirsch emigrated to the USSR. Receiving no financial support from outside the prison, Hirsch was dependent on Steiner for bread and cigarettes. Growing weaker by the day because of the meagre rations, Hirsch wrote a request to Bardin for extra portions, but to no avail. He then began a hunger-strike, thus incurring the wrath of the sadistic commandant, who henceforth sent him to the punishment cells on the slightest pretext. Having spent one-third of the year on the starvation rations (bread and water) in the *kartser*, by the end of 1938 Hirsch was too feeble to take advantage of the exercise walk in the courtyard.

Another striking personality in the 'communist' cell, in which Steiner spent one year, was the former Education Commissar of the German Volga Republic, a stolid Stalinist who refused gifts from the food parcels of people with whom he did not see eye-to-eye, politically if not personally. He generally had his nose stuck in a book, as may have been the case with Goold, whose story fascinated Steiner. Goold recounted his Spanish experiences and the circumstances of his kidnapping, but was dissembling as regards his real role in Spain, maintaining that he had been a volunteer in the Spanish People's Army seconded to work at Radio Barcelona as an expert. Disclosing the true nature of his assignment could have brought another sentence and by this stage the Irishman knew that it was dangerous to confide in anyone, for the secret police had their informers everywhere.

The other cell-mates were German journalists or workers, political refugees from Nazism sentenced by their erstwhile 'comrades' as 'Gestapo agents'. Communication with the other cells was initiated by placing scribbled notes under the petroleum lamp when the prisoners were brought to the sit-down lavatories in the morning. One of the notes was found on Steiner during an unscheduled inspection and he was punished with two five-day periods in a basement cell.

Like Hirsch, Steiner now became one of Bardin's pet-hates: he refused to hand over the money sent to the Austrian by his wife in Moscow but gladly gave him a letter from the same source, the last such missive and the one informing him of the death of his baby daughter. Steiner's most serious confrontation with Bardin ensued after the latter had ordered that the upper section (transom) of the cell window was to remain closed, save for two periods of fifteen minutes, during hot weather. The inmates felt they were suffocating, some fainted, and when it was time to troop out to the exercise-yard one afternoon, Steiner feigned illness and stayed behind. He swung the water bucket against the transom, shattering the glass.

Brought to Bardin, Steiner was confronted with the charge that his wilful act of destroying 'Soviet property' was the signal for a prisoners' uprising. His refusal to sign such a statement meant another spell in the *kartser*. When he returned to his home cell, Brian Goold and the others congratulated him on his courage because they could now open or close the upper part of the window as they pleased.

Steiner was uneasy, fearing that his act of rebellion would have another sequel, a final act, for Bardin had threatened him with Sekirnaia Gora, a lonely hill on the island near a lighthouse where prisoners were shot and thrown into the sea. He therefore feared the worst when, three months later, he was roused in the night and taken by heavily armed guards to the Kremlin on the main island. To his surprise, he was brought to the Governor's office in order to sign a decision passed by the NKVD Prisons' Administration in distant Moscow: twenty days in the Kremlin *kartser* and a 44 rouble fine for smashing the pane of glass. The tiny, windowless punishment-cell was damp and freezing; the daily diet consisted of 300 grams of bread and a mug of hot water. After eleven days a high-ranking commission arrived, a sign that the 'excesses' of Ezhov were being investigated and that the Terror was being wound down. Steiner complained of the barbarous treatment. He was moved to a spacious one-man cell with a wooden floor. On returning to his native cell after the twenty days, the Austrian's appearance shocked Hirsch, Goold and the others: a filthy, bearded wraith with elephantine legs, whom they had given up for dead. Each man broke off a piece of his bread ration for the apparition. The reunion was short, for during the same day Steiner was brought to the baths for a clean-up and sent to a new cell, a four-man room occupied by three Yugoslav Communists, one of whom Steiner knew from his days as a Comintern agent in Zagreb.[15]

Shortly afterwards Brian Goold shared biographies with another veteran from the Comintern, the 33-year-old Thomas Miksch from Vienna. A baker by trade before becoming a professional revolutionary, Miksch worked for the Western European Bureau of the Comintern before his cover was blown in December 1931. The Austrian CID arrested him in a Viennese *Kaffeehaus*, confiscating his attaché case and a loaded pistol.[16] Following his release from prison in Vienna, Miksch emigrated to the USSR in 1932 and worked at his trade, becoming director of a giant bakery in the Ukraine. Arrested for contacting the Austrian Embassy in Moscow in 1935, Miksch was let out on parole after a hunger-strike. Taken into custody again a year later, he was accused of emigrating to the USSR on the 'orders of the Gestapo' (although that organisation was not in existence in 1932), tortured and sentenced to five years in prison. He had sat in three Ukrainian high-security prisons before his transferral to Solovetsky in 1937.[17]

Miksch's recollections of the Irishman differed somewhat from Steiner's account. Now, the Donegal man is Hamilton Gold, a naïve BBC engineer who clashed with his Russian masters in Spain allegedly because of falling Soviet aid for the Republicans. Goold's account of the kidnapping in Barcelona covers the version he told Steiner, but was spiced with the story of why he had signed the confession under threat of violence.[18]

In May 1939 the unexpected happened. A medical commission examined each prisoner and listened to complaints. Bardin disappeared and the prison rules were relaxed. The daily exercise in the fresh air was extended and the prisoners were even allowed to talk in low tones while doing their rounds. Cut off from all news from the outside world because newspapers were forbidden, the Solovetsky inmates were suspicious since any change in prison routine could presage something worse. They did not know that Stalin was preparing for war against Finland, a costly offensive, with huge Red Army losses, which began on 30 November. The island was to be evacuated for the military, and in the summer months feverish building works (barracks, an airfield) were carried out by slave labour on the archipelago.

High-security prisoners like Brian Goold-Verschoyle or Steiner could only speculate when herded together for departure before dawn on 3 August 1939.[19] Solovetsky Prison, under direct Lubianka control since February 1937, was officially closed on 2 September 1939.[20]

The prisoners were scattered to the four winds. Steiner began an odyssey through the Gulag system and was allowed to leave the USSR in 1956. Hirsch died in the Butyrka in June 1941, allegedly after another hunger-strike, while Miksch, with hundreds of other German and Austrian anti-fascists, was handed over to the Gestapo in February 1940. Brian Goold-Verschoyle remained in prison, in Sol'-Iletsk (Orenburg Province), a town near the border with Kazakhstan. He died in confinement on 5 January 1942.

NOTES

1. This chapter is based on the documents in Brian Goold-Verschoyle's NKVD investigation file.
2. Krivitsky, *I was Stalin's Agent*, p. 116.
3. Theodor Bergmann, '*Gegen den Strom*'. *Die Geschichte der Kommunistischen Partei-Opposition* (Hamburg 1987).
4. Margarete Buber-Neumann, *Als Gefangene bei Hitler und Stalin. Eine Welt im Dunkel* (Frankfurt/Main 1993), pp. 190–91.
5. See her biography, *Inside German Communism* (London 1977).
6. Bundesarchiv Berlin, SAPMO, RY 1/I, 213/260, pp. 69–71.
7. Jewgenija Semjonowa Ginsburg, *Marschroute eines Lebens* (Reinbek bei Hamburg 1967), pp. 128–69.
8. Karlo Štajner, *7000 Tage in Sibirien* (Vienna 1975), pp. 28–47.
9. Buber-Neumann, *Als Gefangene*, p. 190.
10. Margarete Buber-Neumann, *Von Potsdam nach Moskau – Stationen eines Irrweges* (Berlin 1990), pp. 138–71.
11. Štajner, *7000 Tage in Sibirien*, pp. 47–65.
12. Anne Applebaum, *Gulag. A History of the Soviet Camps* (London 2003), pp. 40–58.
13. N.G. Okhotin and R.B. Roginskii (eds), *Zven'ia. Istoricheskii al'manakh, vypusk 1* (Moscow 1991), pp. 357–58.
14. Štajner, *7000 Tage in Sibirien*, pp. 84–85.
15. Ibid., pp. 67–81.

16. Austrian State Archives (ÖSTA), BKA/Inneres, 22/Bundesländer, Karton 5174, Zl. 239.111/31.
17. Hans Schafranek, *Zwischen NKWD und Gestapo. Die Auslieferung deutscher und österreichischer Antifaschisten aus der Sowjetunion nach Nazideutschland 1937–1941* (Frankfurt am Main 1990), pp. 72, 73, 150, 151.
18. Buber-Neumann, *Als Gefangene*, pp. 190–91.
19. Štajner, *7000 Tage in Sibirien*, pp. 87–89.
20. N.G. Okhotin and A.B. Roginskii (eds), *Sistema ispravitel'no-trudovykh lagerei v SSSR, 1923–1960. Spravochnik* (Moscow 1998), p. 396.

Lotte in Trouble

Not having heard from Brian for some weeks, Lotte Moos visited his mother in Oxford, as he had recommended in case of an emergency. Her Spanish addressee in Valencia wrote that Goold had gone to Barcelona and that she should not ask about his whereabouts again. During the initial period of her friendship with Sibyl Goold-Verschoyle, Lotte told the story of her adventures with Brian in instalments, since the old lady was distraught and helpless. In early summer 1937 both thought that Brian might have been killed in the May fighting in Barcelona or was still in a prison of the Soviet secret police somewhere in Spain. Copies of his letters to Sibyl and Lotte were made and included in the correspondence that Mrs Goold-Verschoyle now began with the Foreign Office.[1]

For the British authorities, Brian Goold-Verschoyle had been a suspect subversive since 1935. In June 1936 his name was added to a list of over thirty individuals, the majority of whom were communists (students at schools in Moscow, Comintern functionaries and agents, officials of the CPGB), who, although holders of a British passport, were not to be allowed to land in any part of the British Empire outside the United Kingdom. This was a measure to safeguard against communist subversion in the colonies, especially in India and the Far East.

Information on Brian Goold-Verschoyle's disappearance could hardly be expected from official Soviet sources. Consultations between London and Moscow about reciprocal notifying procedures in the case of the arrest or imprisonment of their respective citizens seemed close to conclusion in 1935, after a verbal assurance by Moscow. London baulked, however, when the Soviets insisted that the agreement should apply to the whole British Empire, because this might imply that the Dominions recognised the USSR regime. A compromise formula was reached in 1937, after the Foreign Office had asked the Dominion governments whether they wished to be parties to the proposed agreement. New Zealand and Australia, not having diplomatic relations with the USSR, concurred and requested that notification of arrest should be communicated to them via London. The South Africans did not wish to be party to the scheme; and Canada and Ireland did not reply to the Foreign Office invitation. The text of the Anglo-Soviet agreement of 14 July 1937 was of an informal nature since the Russians were against publicity: they were at a loss to understand that any agreement entered into by the British government could lead to 'questions in the House'. However, experience was to show that the Soviet Foreign Ministry consistently ignored the agreement, for as early as April 1938 the British Ambassador to Moscow complained to the Soviet authorities about non-notification concerning the arrest of three British citizens.[2]

Lotte Moos also turned to the Goold-Verschoyle brothers for advice. Neil, who had been expelled from the USSR and was now active in communist circles in Dublin, had broken off all contacts with his family. Although he did not resuscitate these links until his sister Eileen returned to Ireland in 1949, his mother had his Dublin address, which she passed on to Lotte. His reply to Lotte's letter was unequivocal: he had no idea where Brian was and, even if he did know, he would not tell her. Lotte's letter to Denis, far away in South Africa, was forthright. Writing to him on 29 June 1937, Lotte, 'in a terrible state [...] for months', stated that Brian had been 'thoroughly disillusioned with the Soviet Union' and had 'lost faith in Marxism'. She added that he had 'fully endorsed the Popular Front policy in Spain and thought very little of Trotskyists and POUM'. Although she, too, was in the dark about what Brian had actually done in Spain, she emphasised that he 'always expressed great satisfaction about the job he did'. Lotte, in contrast to Party member Denis, knew enough about Stalinist psychology to conclude that Brian wanted to escape from Spain but had reckoned without his host. She was also more realistic in putting greater faith in the diplomatic intervention initiated by Sibyl than in enquiries through the communist structures ('your friends') which Denis proposed.

Mrs Moos resumed her studies in England. She was especially interested in nineteenth-century French and English literature, studying at University College London and carrying out research for Columbia University on a freelance basis. Now in receipt of a grant from the International Student Service and the possessor of a stenography machine (paid for by the Refugee Committee at

22. Hamilton Frederick Stuart Goold-Verschoyle in court dress, 1890s.

23. Hamilton Frederick Stuart Goold-Verschoyle ('Tim'), Brian's father.

24. Sibyl Goold-Verschoyle and her children 1914, from left to right: Eileen, Sheila, baby Brian, Dennis and Neil.

25. Willi Münzenberg of the KPD at the 5th Congress of the Comintern, Moscow 1924.

26. The Goold-Verschoyle family in their limousine, c. 1920.

27. Edith Suschitzky, 1930.

28. Lotte Jacoby, aged fifteen, 1925.

29. Lotte Moos, London 1934.

30. Lotte Moos,
    Durham 1947.

32. Pyotr, the son of Neil
Goold-Verschoyle and
Olga Dobrova, 1947.

31. Siegi Moos, Paris 1933.

33. Olga Dobrova and Neil
Goold-Verschoyle, Moscow
1970s.

34. George Killich, aka Miller,
Moscow 1945.

35. Brian Goold-Verschoyle, arrest
photo, May 1937.

36. Brian, arrest photo, sideview.

7. The members of the Dublin Unemployed Committee in front of the Rotunda (now the Gate Theatre) which they occupied in January 1922. The figure on the right of the step is Jim Phelan. Sean McAteer, the secretary of the committee, is possibly the man in the hat on the extreme left.

38. Liam O'Flaherty and his daughter Pegeen, 1933.

39. Jim Phelan, aka Finchley, shortly after his arrest, Liverpool, June 1923.

40. Sean McAteer's clothen 'passport' for the Comintern. It is obvious that the pseudonym 'David Twist', under which he lived in the USSR, was chosen before he fled the United Kingdom.

15th June, 1923.

TO WHOM IT MAY CONCERN:

This is to certify that the bearer, David Twist, is a political refugee from Ireland. We commend him to the Committee for International Red Help.

Yours fraternally

Thomas Bell

Political Secretary.

Woburn House), she completed a shorthand course in London, and continued her studies in French language and French stenography during a four-week stay in Paris in August 1937. Siegfried, whose residence permit had been renewed in 1936, thanks to the good offices of the Society of Friends, had found an academic niche at last, as a research student at the Department of Social Biology at the LSE. He was writing on economics, on the connection between marriages and business cycles. According to data they gave the Home Office, Lotte Moos had joined the KPD in 1934 and dropped out two years later, while Siegfried Moos, a member since 1929, maintained that he had ceased to be a Party member in 1933 but was active in the Anti-Fascist Committee (a communist front organisation) from 1934 to 1937. This was untrue, since we know he was considered a leading cadre in the London group in 1934 and was still in contact with KPD comrades subsequently.

Lotte's 1937 Paris sojourn deepened her fear and loathing of Soviet agents. While staying in a small *pension* in the rue d'Assas, she was terrified by a Russian fellow-guest. A big man posing as a Latvian in Paris to buy musical instruments – although the specialist shops were all closed for *les grandes vacances* – he became too attentive and inquisitive for her liking. Sensing that he was a bloodhound from INO, she warned him she would disclose her experiences since 1936 if he did not leave her alone. He did, but the incident left her badly shaken.

Her description of the sinister Russian ('big, about 45, with streaks of grey hair') fits that of Sergei Shpiegelglas, deputy head of INO and now hunting 'traitors' in Western Europe. At that time all leading Soviet intelligence officers were being recalled, one after the other, to Moscow. That was a one-way journey to interrogation, torture and the executioner's bullet. Walter Krivitsky and his friend Ignace Reiss knew, especially in the wake of the execution of the Red Army generals in June 1937, what awaited them. After all, Elisabeth Poretsky, the wife of Reiss, and Krivitsky himself, had returned from Moscow shortly before, with searing memories of the general feeling of mistrust and suspicion, or the chilling certainty that many of their friends had already disappeared. Ignace Reiss made a fatal error before going underground – he wrote a corrosive letter to Stalin (17 July 1937), in which he pledged his allegiance to Trotsky's Fourth International. The letter was opened in the Soviet Embassy in Paris and Shpiegelglas and his gang of assassins went on the hunt. Reiss was tracked down near Lausanne, Switzerland, and murdered by two INO agents on 4 September 1937. Shpiegelglas accompanied the killers back to Moscow, where they both received the Order of the Red Banner.³ Krivitsky was also on the wanted list, now that Shpiegelglas knew that The Hague's *rezident* had been aware of the planned defection of Reiss and had read the latter's vituperative valediction to Stalin. For a while at least, luck was on his side. Through the assistance of exiled Russian Mensheviks in Paris, Krivitsky gained the protection of the French socialist Minister for the Interior, who provided him with a police escort. After commenting at length on the third Moscow show-trial (March 1938) for the Paris-based Menshevik press, which syndicated his articles, Krivitsky emigrated to the United States with his wife and child.

Theodor Mally, Brian's commanding officer in London in 1936, did not choose to go on the run. He was increasingly nervous about his shaky Austrian identity and business cover. Neither he nor his assistant, Bernard Davidowicz, knew very much about buying rags in Britain for the Polish market, as British Intelligence subsequently learned from their London business partners. Recalled by the Moscow Centre on 4 June 1937, Mally left London precipitately three weeks later, abandoning his well-furnished flat in Marylebone and £1,931 in his account at the Midland Bank in Russell Square.⁴ Implicated because of his friendship with Reiss and Krivitsky, and on account of his refusal to go to Canada straight from Britain,⁵ Mally was arrested in Moscow on 7 March 1938, charged with espionage for Germany and sentenced to death by shooting on 20 September. The sentence was carried out the same day.⁶ Mally's photographer in London after Brian's departure in February 1936 was Wolf Livent-Levit, recruited for INO in Germany.⁷ He and his wife, Stefania, were recalled to Moscow and executed in 1938.⁸ Brian's Shakespeare-quoting colleague, Dmitri Bystrolyotov ('John'), was also put through the Lubianka meat-grinder (*miasorubka*) in 1938, suffering broken ribs, a penetrated lung, a cracked skull and torn stomach muscles before 'admitting to espionage for four foreign powers'. After he was 'rehabilitated' and released from his twenty-year sentence during World War II, he learned that his wife and mother had committed suicide.⁹ Finally, INO Chief Slutsky, who had ordered Brian's capture in Spain, was ordered to be disposed of 'without noise' (Ezhov). In February 1938 he was drugged with chloroform by two of Ezhov's deputies in the Lubianka headquarters before being injected with poison. His successor, Shpiegelglas, was arrested nine months later and subsequently executed.[10]

While this campaign of annihilation went unnoticed in the West, the murderous activities of NKVD mobile units on the Continent in the years 1937 and 1938 did not: the 'disappearance' of Nin and other revolutionaries in Spain, the murder of Reiss and the arrest of the assassins' accomplices in Switzerland, the murder of Trotsky's son, Lev Sedov, and Rudolf Klement, administrative secretary of the Fourth International, in Paris, and, finally, the kidnapping of the White Russian General Miller in the French capital.

Lotte Moos was therefore constantly confronted with the detritus of her recent communist past and justifiably feared the long arm of Moscow. She concluded her summer sojourn in France with a hiking holiday on the French side of the Pyrenees. The invigorating air, friendly locals, cheap living costs (a bed for the night costing the equivalent of eight old pence) and pleasant walking companions improved her mood. Her choice of holiday retreat might indicate an intention to visit Spain, an eventuality she had mentioned to Brian. In a postcard to Siegi, she wrote that she was becoming happy again, but slowly, very slowly. Lotte Moos never did cross the frontier into Spain in a one-woman quest to look for her Irish lover, but returned to Britain, where she and Siegi seemed to have reconciled their differences.

Sometime in 1938 she settled with her husband in Oxford, but wanted to complete her education in the United States and bring her husband and parents there in due time. Siegfried Moos had found a new post in the Institute of Statistics at Oxford University. She gained entry to the New World by virtue of a job offer from the Federated Labour School in Philadelphia, to teach the German and French languages and European history. During 1938, while Siegi was working at his new post at Oxford University, Lotte spent much time in London libraries, collecting statistical information for an American economist, Arthur Mayer of Columbia University. Probably with his assistance, she left for America in January 1939. The German Embassy refused to renew her passport (Lotte and Siegfried Moos were deprived of German citizenship in July 1939)[11] but she was granted a Home Office identity card valid until February 1940. Besides teaching, Lotte also lectured on Nazism to the local branch of the American YMCA, but she really wanted to study.

Philadelphian friends in whom she had confided about her past and Goold-Verschoyle's disappearance told her of a series of articles which were to give her life another cruel twist: Walter Krivitsky's revelations of the Stalinist system, three pieces in the *Saturday Evening Post* (15, 22 and 29 April 1939).

Krivitsky's statements had appeared sporadically in the press (for example, *Daily Telegraph*, 9 December 1937), especially in Paris, but in his article of 15 April for the American magazine he mentioned Brian Goold-Verschoyle, as the radio engineer named 'Friend' from England, for the first time in an English-language periodical. Some of the details were inaccurate, perhaps intentionally so: that the victim had been brought by ship to Odessa, that he was in a Moscow prison by 12 April 1937 and that his brother lived in Leningrad.[12] Lotte wrote immediately to Sibyl Goold-Verschoyle, enclosing the article. Through friends in Philadelphia, Moos also contacted Isaac Don Levine, Krivitsky's literary agent and ghost-writer, explaining her interest in the case and enclosing a photograph of Brian, whom Krivitsky failed to recognise. Sibyl tried the same tack, repeating to Krivitsky on 8 May what she had told the Foreign Office:

> After reading your article sent me by a friend I am overpowered with grief to know that my poor son has possibly been thrown into a Russian prison or is still suffering more in a concentration camp. I would be so thankful if you could give me some clue as to what I can do to trace him and save his young life. He has many influential friends and relations in this country who would try to help if they knew on what lines it would be best to act. Knowing Russia so well you might be able to give me some advice. I am enclosing a photograph of my son which you may recognise. Please, please do what you can to help me find him – perhaps the person who told you later of the trick by which he was taken on the ship may know where he was eventually taken to.[13]

Siegi Moos had spent that evening with Sibyl in Oxford, three hours helping her draft the letter to Krivitsky and typing out copies of the *Saturday Evening Post* article. At midnight Siegi wrote an airmail missive to Lotte about his labours, a letter which implies that Sibyl originally thought that the German couple were the cause of Brian's disastrous involvement with the Russians:

She was quite distressed about the possibility that he is in a camp or not alive. I definitely think he is alive. If they wanted to get rid of him, there was no better and easier way than the April-May days in Spain [...] I also succeeded in convincing her not to tell anything to her elder son [Neil]. It is all so funny. A 100% alien explains to her that she could not trust her own son. [...] As far as she told me, he is more fanatic than ever. [...] She has been staying in bed for over nine weeks. She read so many books, she says, nearly exclusively on concentration camps in Germany, Russia, Spain, and that she is very distressed about the possibility that B. is in one of them. [....] I definitely had the impression that she does not think of me what you said she thinks (I can't forget that). She considers her daughter-in-law [Olga] as the responsible one. Petja's [the son of Neil and Olga] whereabouts are unknown to her, she thinks he is still there. And she thinks if her daughter-in-law has still any influence left, she will do everything to ease her brother-in-law's [Brian's] position.

When Lotte visited her uncle in New York in June 1939, Don Levine telephoned: would she be interested in writing an article for the *Saturday Evening Post* about her Irish friend? She said no, feeling it would harm him. Krivitsky, whom she met at Levine's house, was of the same opinion. According to Lotte Moos, Krivitsky did not know her and had never heard her name, and he questioned her closely. The defector, mentioning at the outset that he had written about Brian earlier, in a Russian newspaper in Paris, told Lotte that Olga's relatives in Moscow had been arrested. Krivitsky took Neil's expulsion from Russia as a good portent and surmised that he had made some kind of pledge to the Russians concerning his youngest brother before his forced departure from the USSR in 1937. This consideration is plausible and would explain Neil's uncooperative attitude towards his family and Lotte, behaviour in keeping with his wish to see his wife and son Pyotr at some future date. Krivitsky listened to Lotte's argument that the British Foreign Office was pleading discretion in the case of Brian before interrupting: the British were not doing nearly enough, Lotte should help Sibyl put more pressure on the Foreign Office and she, Lotte, could contact him in future for further advice.

Siegi Moos was now a frequent visitor to Sybil's house in Upland Park Road in Oxford. The meetings were draining, after a day's work at the Institute and writing his treatise about the Nazi economy. The atmosphere in the house was tense because Sibyl was terrified lest her highly strung husband, 'Tim', who was unaware of Brian's disappearance, might enquire about the content of her conversations with the German economist. Siegi typed out more copies of Krivitsky's article (a cable by Sybil to *The Saturday Evening Post* to send the 15 April issue was not acted upon), but his main task was to comfort the old lady and to convince her that her endeavours to date to find out more about Brian were inadequate. She seems to have relied on the offices of some Rt. Hon. Gentlemen, Sirs and Lords of her acquaintance.

One of her main supporters was Sir Christopher Lynch-Robinson, a resident magistrate and a relative. According to a letter he wrote to the famous left-wing scientist J.B.S. Haldane in June 1937, soliciting assistance in tracking down his missing Irish relative, it is clear that Lynch-Robinson had spoken to the British Consul in Valencia, who told him that Brian's work in Spain had been 'highly confidential' and that the young Irishman had had a conflict with the Soviet Ambassador, after which he had gone to Barcelona, where he disappeared.[14] Siegi favoured a more direct approach – to the Foreign Office – based on Krivitsky's disclosures, but he basically felt that little could be done.

Krivitsky finally answered Sibyl's entreaties at the beginning of August 1939. In her reply she stated that the British diplomats in Moscow had declined to make a disposition to the Soviets on behalf of Brian Goold-Verschoyle because of the pending Anglo-French negotiations in Moscow, the low-level talks led on the British side by Admiral Dax, which came to nothing. Any answer in connection with Goold-Verschoyle, the British Ambassador argued, would almost certainly take the form of previous Russian statements, made by Ambassador Maisky in London and by Russian diplomats in Spain in 1937: no Englishman of that name had worked at the Soviet Embassy in Valencia as a wireless operator. Sibyl then asked Krivitsky for details he either did not know or thought politic not to disclose – what name Brian employed in Spain and what passport identity he used in entering that country from France so that his movements after April 1937 could be traced – and a statement from Krivitsky that he had heard that Brian was in the Lubianka in May 1937.[15] He did not reply.

In summer 1939 Krivitsky's credibility was under fire, and Siegi Moos enlightened Brian's mother as to the political background of the campaign. The July number of *New Masses*, the literary journal of the Communist Party of the USA (CPUSA), gave Krivitsky's real name (Ginsburg), stated he was 'a denizen of Paris nightclubs' and implied he was in league with the French secret service and the American State Department.[16] Unknown to the lonely collaborators in Upland Park Road, the Northern Department of the British Foreign Office, which was responsible for the USSR, was equally dismissive, ridiculing Krivitsky's claim that a Soviet-German Pact, which was to become reality on 23 August, had been Stalin's wish since 1934. The official Foreign Office line was not shared by its diplomats in Washington and Moscow, but Britain had no experience with defectors and British officials felt that Krivitsky may have pepped up his chronicle of Stalin's evil-doing in order to justify the hefty $5,000 advance from the *Post*.[17]

Lotte Moos returned to Britain, landing in Southampton on 2 July 1939. Her homecoming was a bitter defeat, for she had just been granted a scholarship to complete a BA course in French and Economics at Swarthmore College, Pennsylvania, which, with her credits, she would have completed by June 1940. She was obviously concerned to have her and Siegi's residence permits renewed by the Home Office and, now that a war was looming, had family matters to attend to. Her sister Kätchen had just arrived, penniless, in England as an adult accompanying a Jewish *Kindertransport*. Furthermore, she and Siegi were responsible for little Ruth, the daughter of her eldest sister Annemarie, who had been an inmate of a German mental institution since 1934. Lotte had therefore been thwarted thrice (Berlin, London, Philadelphia) of a university education, had huge family commitments and little spare money to send (via Switzerland) to her parents, who were still in Berlin and desperate to leave. Her *bona fides*, however, still satisfied the British state. In November 1939 she was granted permission to stay in the United Kingdom 'for the present' provided she did not enter any employment, paid or unpaid. Her husband's residence permit was renewed on the basis of an application from the Institute of Statistics, Oxford University, where he now had permanent employment 'as a computer and research assistant'. Further good news was that the Oxford Refugees Tribunal found in late October 1939 that the couple should be exempted from internment and all movement restrictions.

Nevertheless, communists, ex- or active, were still a suspect category, primarily because of divided loyalty, since the Soviet

Union had a non-aggression agreement with Britain's enemy, Nazi Germany. That devil's pact allowed Stalin freedom of manoeuvre in extending his empire into the Baltic states. The onslaught he ordered on Finland, the 'Winter War' (November 1939–March 1940), led to a crisis between the Kremlin and the democratic powers, causing London and Paris to draw up plans to send an expeditionary force to assist the courageous Finns and bomb the Baku oil fields.[18]

The political atmosphere was therefore propitious for Krivitsky's book, *I Was Stalin's Agent*, published by Hamish Hamilton in London and serialised in the *Evening Standard* from 12 December 1939. Three months earlier, on the day Chamberlain declared war on Germany, the British Embassy in Washington had cabled Whitehall with disquieting news: Krivitsky had disclosed the names of Foreign Office 'leaks', including that of the cipher clerk John Herbert King, the mercenary traitor who had kept Mally (and Brian Goold-Verschoyle, temporarily) so busy in between 1935 and 1937.[19] King was arrested on 25 September and sentenced to ten years' imprisonment in a secret trial at the Old Bailey one month later.[20]

MI5 tried to reconstruct the ramifications of the Mally network in Britain, interviewing the business partners of Mally and Pieck (who was then in Holland). In obtaining hard evidence in order to arrest other Soviet agents, British Intelligence was hampered by the fact that none of the main operatives was in the country, save for Percy Glading. Sentenced to the relatively mild term of six years' penal servitude under the Official Secrets Act at the Old Bailey in March 1938 and now in Maidstone Prison, Glading rejected the blandishments of the Secret Service, refusing the offer of a partial remittance of his sentence if he would talk. The Special Branch and MI5 staff interviewing him on 16 October found an unrepentant and humorous inmate: he rejected the prospect of early release because his two co-defendants would still be in prison, and he bore no grudges against his erstwhile fellow-agent 'Miss X' (Olga Gray), who had 'set him up', reckoning that his arrest had been 'a fair cop'.[21]

After meeting that stone wall, Whitehall suggested that Don Levine be invited to London, but the British Embassy in Washington thought it better to invite Krivitsky himself, with the help of French Intelligence. The defector, who had given evidence at Washington's

Special Committee on Un-American Activity (then known as the 'Dies Committee', after its chairman Martin Dies, a conservative Texan Democrat), stated his demands, which were met: the Labour politician Herbert Morrison would be responsible for him in Britain, and the Canadian government must grant his wife Antonia and son Alexander temporary refuge. Krivitsky wanted, above all, to stay unnoticed in London, and he left Halifax, Nova Scotia, on 11 January 1940 on board *SS Duchess of Richmond*.

During the three weeks of interviews in his room at the Langham Hotel in London, Krivitsky ('Mr Thomas') told the British Secret Service a great deal: about the International Lenin School, the difference between the GRU and INO networks, how the operatives transferred secrets and money, and he listed the names of 85 agents and the physical description of others.[22] While much of this information must have been infuriatingly vague to the MI5 interviewers because Krivitsky's main field of operations had been Germany and not Britain, the disclosures on the Mally operations (Oldham, King) were highly illuminating. In one of the first interviews, on 24 January, he discussed the topical case of John Herbert King, Brian Goold-Verschoyle's function in the spy-ring and the correspondence with Sibyl following the articles in *The Saturday Evening Post*. He then gave his opinion of Lotte Moos:

> Another result of his article in the *Saturday Evening Post* was that he was called upon in New York by a woman who said she was a friend of Mrs Verschoyle. She was a German Jewess. Thomas is convinced that she was a member of the OGPU [Soviet secret police]. He knows that she is in this country at present, married to a German Jewish refugee. He thinks her name could easily be obtained from Mrs Verschoyle, but the greatest care would have to be taken in making enquiries as to her: he thinks she is important.[23]

What prompted Krivitsky to denounce Mrs Moos? One source for his extreme suspicion of the attractive young German woman may have been the feeling that she was hiding something. We may assume that both were extremely guarded when they met in America in the summer of 1939, at least at the outset. He was not giving anything away to somebody he did not know or who could not benefit his reinvention in the democratic world. Lotte probably posed as the young devotee of an aged Anglo-Irish lady in distress, but we do not know how much she told about her intimate relationship with

'Friend' or their purgatorial stay in Russia at the beginning of the Terror. For his own safety, Krivitsky's prime maxim had to be vigilance for, shortly before, in March 1939, he had escaped the clutches of a kidnapping-killer trio in New York. For all he knew, Lotte could have been a 'swallow', to entice him to a fatal rendezvous.

In the event, MI5 took Krivitsky at his word and set the investigation machinery in motion. The first move by the security establishment was the application for a Post Office warrant to read the mail of the Moos couple (159 Banbury Road, Oxford), because 'these individuals are strongly suspected of espionage on behalf of a foreign power'. The intercepted correspondence produced little of note: a card from Sibyl informing Lotte that the old people were down with flu, a letter from the Master's Lodgings of an Oxford University college refusing to sponsor Siegi's application for British citizenship on the grounds that the German was not known well or long enough by the correspondent, letters from several relatives recently arrived in the United Kingdom and airmail post from close friends in America, which said that they had managed to send 150 Reichsmark to Lotte's parents via Zurich.

On 15 March 1940 MI5 informed the Aliens Department of the Home Office that Lotte Moos was a Soviet agent who 'should not remain at liberty'. On 9 April the Home Office relayed the order to the Chief Constable of the Oxford City Police that Margarete Charlotte Moos was subject to internment, immediate arrest and transport to Holloway Prison in London, but that she should be allowed time to 'settle private affairs'. Two days later the police called to the house. Lotte was aghast when she read the detention order and asked for permission to ring her husband. She spoke to him in English and her escort waited until he arrived before leaving with their charge and two suitcases full of books, manuscripts and press-cuttings. MI5 Chief Kell, who evinced interest in the papers, was sent the suitcases in due course.

The conditions under which Lotte was held in Holloway were a tribute to the robustness of British democracy, to the civilised treatment of a suspected spy in time of war. In her first letter to her husband (12 April), Lotte wrote that she was in a bright cell and could write as many letters as she liked; she had not been told why she was in prison, but Siegi need not worry because the United Kingdom was 'a democracy'. The rules were indeed tolerable.

Prisoners could walk around until lock-up at 9 p.m., there was a prison shop with fruit, and a well-stocked library. Four days into her detention, the Governor wrote to Oxford that husband Siegfried could visit his wife every fortnight on receipt of a visiting order from her personally. Her first letters home detailed the strategy of her release petition (based on her true experiences since 1933), the later ones requests to Siegi for towels, stockings and cigarettes, the currency between all prisoners. She might well be in good fettle, seeing that she got on well with 'the other girls' and had received two letters and a parcel in her first week in custody from Siegi, who was allowed to see her for thirty minutes on Saturday, visitors' day.

Lotte soon had to revisit her haunted past, however, in interrogation with the MI5 officer Kay Archer, who had been one of Percy Glading's interlocutors in Maidstone Prison six months before. Archer had also been involved in bringing Krivitsky to England and in processing his disclosures. Her first questioning of Lotte Moos on 24 April produced a lengthy, typed text, basically the story of the German's life with Brian and its seemingly never-ending aftermath. The intelligence officer felt that Lotte was being, at best, disingenuous about her Communist contacts in England:

> I interviewed Margarete Charlotte Moos alone yesterday. She was extremely voluble and hysterical and it was difficult to make head or tail of what she was talking about [....] She had a plausible story for her association with Edith Tudor-Hart but apparently did not remember that she had ever met her until I reminded her. She said she was recommended to Edith Tudor-Hart, I gather, by the Refugee Committee because she had done some photography in Austria and she did some photography with Edith Tudor-Hart, whom incidentally she called a fool. She denied meeting anyone at Tudor-Hart's except the sister-in-law Helen, whom she said was a clever woman, and her husband Alexander.

Lotte was relieved afterwards, writing to Siegi that he must come on Saturday, for she had 'news for him' and was glad she was 'in the most humane country in the world'. The euphoric mood did not last. Mrs Archer called again with more questions, and to collect a manuscript in Lotte's handwriting since they had agreed that this was a better method than the dictated answers of their first sitting. That composition had brought back the past, Brian's fate and her part in it ('we have suffered so much'), and a day filled with tears.

Two days later she thanked Siegi for sending £2, expressing her relief after completing a 24-page manuscript, which she handed to the Governor for Mrs Archer. In the meantime her friends were being questioned. Mr McKinnion Wood, her protector in 1934, wrote about Lotte in the highest terms, emphasising that she had shown no interest in his work at the aircraft establishment at Farnborough and had confided in him, after her escape from Moscow, tales that he could compare with his own experiences, since he had visited the Russian capital in 1932 and 1935. Siegi supported his wife's appeal for release, penning a petition to the Home Office in which he blamed himself for his wife's contacts with the Soviets:

> Concerning the relation of my wife with Mr Bryan Goold Verschoyle I should like to draw your attention to the fact that the separation from my wife in 1935 was entirely due to my attitude. I could not get accustomed to the narrowness of refugee life, and was unable to work and to write. I, therefore, separated from my wife, against her will. It was my neglect which drove her to loneliness and despair and made her thankful for the friendly attitude of Mr Verschoyle who was a common friend of us and whom I esteemed very much. It was exclusively due to our permit to stay in this country not being renewed that we thought of going to Russia and that Mr Verschoyle offered help. Without the difficulties regarding our stay in this country my wife's journey to Russia would never have taken place. But in despair of not knowing what will happen in a few weeks time, a despair which drove to suicide so many a refugee, made my wife ready to accept any solution, especially as she expected that I could follow too [....] Since her return in 1936 she has never openly or secretly adopted another attitude. The references enclosed as well as the Russian diary written in German and in the possession of the Home Office can prove this fact.[24]

In her report to the Home Office of 1 June 1940, Kay Archer stated her belief that Lotte had given a truthful account of her 'association' with Brian Goold-Verschoyle, but with the Germans at the English Channel and British troops being evacuated from Dunkirk, the case could not be brought to its logical outcome:

> We believe her story that she has ceased to take any part in political work of any kind since the disappearance of Brian Goold-Verschoyle

and since various unpleasant experiences she has told us about. We would have been prepared to permit this woman's release on restrictions, but as Category B are now all interned, we see no alternative but for her to remain in internment during the present crisis period.[25]

She told Lotte as much, as Siegi read in his wife's letter of 5 June: 'They definitely said that I am not suspect.' He was interned for two months of the glorious 1940 summer in the Scottish Highlands, where the Army treated him well, inviting him to dine at the officers' table. Lotte was transferred to the Isle of Man in early June and quartered in the Perwick Hotel at Port St Mary. Before she left London, Lotte tried to extract the reason for her further internment from Mrs Archer. The MI5 officer was evasive, at one point arguing that because of the Hitler–Stalin Pact pressure could be exerted on Lotte because her parents were still in Nazi Germany. The German woman felt that this was a very feeble line of argument since Mrs Archer, in another connection, had admitted that no pressure had been exerted on Lotte, either by the Nazis or the Soviets, while 'Brian was alive'. 'Now that he is dead', as Lotte concluded in a letter to her husband, 'it is even more improbable.'

Her main problem on the Isle of Man seems to have been boredom and the presence of some committed Nazi women among the internees. She gave language classes and was in receipt of regular parcels from Siegi in Scotland. The release order, supported by Mrs Archer, finally came through in late October 1940. In Oxford once more, Lotte demanded her suitcases, which were returned in January 1941. The general course of the war and bad news from Germany drove her into depression. Years later she described her mood at that time:

> The blacked-out rooms of World War II and the horrors seeping over from the Continent finally boxed me in, making me fall back on something I had almost forgotten. Feeling guilty, almost sinful, I would sit at the table – like a clod – when everybody had gone off and, instead of clearing up, tried to give shape to the visions the night had left behind. A few stories appeared, were even broadcast. 'Let us have some more', I was told, 'when the spirit moves you.' But the spirit is a squeamish fellow: it feeds on tears.

Her grief was not confined to the loss of Brian. In January 1941 she learned from a family friend who had managed to emigrate to

New York that her eldest sister, Annemarie, was dead. As a long-term inmate in a mental asylum, the woman fell victim to the euthanasia programme of the Nazis. As regards Lotte's aged parents, only the worst could be expected. Her father Samuel died in Theresienstadt concentration camp, and her mother Luise, presumably of general weakness, in Berlin in August 1941.

After their release from internment, Lotte and Siegi Moos kept a very low profile, with Lotte looking after her niece Ruth and daughter Merilyn, who was conceived when the tide turned for the Allies in 1943. Siegfried Moos lost his university job to a returning soldier and the family moved to Durham in 1948. The year before, the couple had been granted British naturalisation, and MI5, on being asked in the line of duty, stated in July 1947 that neither had come to their attention since 1940. They remained in contact with old Mrs Goold-Verschoyle in Oxford. Brian's father was finally let into the family secret and died of a broken heart in 1942. Sibyl lived on in the house, with her sister, until her death in November 1946.

Brian's fate became public knowledge for the first time during the famous Kravchenko trial in Paris in 1949.[26] Kravchenko, a Ukrainian engineer, fled his post at the Soviet Embassy in Washington in 1943 and, immediately following his defection, issued a statement denouncing the tyranny in the USSR. He published an account of the Russian slave labour camp system in 1946. His book, *I Chose Freedom*, created a furore in the West and led to countless vicious counter-attacks in the communist press. Victor Kravchenko decided to sue on the basis on one such libel, that published in the French Communist *Les lettres françaises* in November 1947, which alleged that Kravchenko's book was written at the behest of the American Secret Service and contained hardly a line from his own pen. The trial in Paris (January–April 1949) was a battleground for Cold War invective and ended with a guilty verdict. Two communist editors were sentenced to hefty fines, a compensatory sum for the plaintiff and to payment of the costs of the long courtroom drama. It was seen as proven that the defendants had not produced any witnesses to contradict Kravchenko's claims or to prove that he had not written the book himself. The case went to the appeal courts twice, thus prolonging the heated debates, which incidentally led to a rift between Albert Camus and Jean-Paul Sartre.

On 22 February Margarete Buber-Neumann, the widow of Heinz Neumann, Brian's cell-mate in the Butyrka, took the witness-stand. A survivor of the concentration camps of Stalin and Hitler who had travelled from Sweden to give witness, Buber-Neumann told the court of her years of torment in Karaganda and Ravensbrück and made a deep impression on her listeners. In her statement she outlined the arrest and imprisonment of Mr Hamilton Gold (Brian), the details of which she had learned from an Austrian (Thomas Miksch) in Lublin in 1940, when both, along with hundreds of fellow Germans or Austrians, were in a Gestapo prison following their extradition from the USSR.[27]

The report on her disclosures in the *Manchester Guardian* (24 February 1949) prompted a letter to the editor signed by 'X.Y.Z'. The correspondent was probably Christopher Lynch-Robertson or a more immediate member of Brian's family, as he/she mentioned that the Goold-Verschoyle family was 'well known among Dublin music lovers'. Lotte Moos, who kept the press-cutting in her papers, would hardly have known this detail of family lore.[28] On the other hand, why should a family member or friend from Britain or Ireland, eager to fathom Brian's fate, wish to remain anonymous?

The last surviving documents pertaining to the fate of Brian Goold-Verschoyle are in the files of the Foreign Office, correspondence generated during the Attlee Labour government at the instigation of Brian's relatives. Probably at the request of his sister Eileen, who saw herself as the unofficial head of the family now that the parents were deceased, Christopher Lynch-Robertson approached Whitehall through the Conservative MP Richard Law in February 1949. In October the British Embassy in Moscow deposited an enquiry with the Soviet Foreign Ministry, noting that Brian had been known as Goold in Spain, was said to have been sentenced to ten years' imprisonment for alleged espionage, part of which he had served on Solovetsky Island. Because the prisoner should have been released eighteen months previously, the note concluded, HM Government requested information 'regarding the whereabouts of this British subject'. The official Soviet answer, transmitted on 2 January 1950, was the standard lie :

> The British subject Brian Goold Verschoyle died in 1941 while being transported by railway, as the result of an accident caused by a German air attack.

Richard Law was informed of the above contents, with the postscript that the Foreign Office had no means of ascertaining the truth of the Soviet statement. Finally, in 1951, the Oxford firm of solicitors dealing with Sibyl's estate and Brian's portion of the inheritance applied through the Foreign Office for an official Soviet death certificate. The civil servant was not sanguine:

> I am to add that previous experience in matters of this kind suggests that the Soviet authorities are unlikely to reply promptly to the application, and that they may indeed vouchsafe no reply at all.

His prognosis was correct.

Brian Goold-Verschoyle had a posthumous literary appearance in the late 1970s, in a short story by Danilo Kiš (1935–89), a remarkable Serbian writer from a Jewish background who chronicled the horrors of totalitarianism and its victims in lyrical prose. The piece was based initially on interviews with Karlo Štajner in 1976.[29] The title of the short story, 'The Sow that Eats her Farrow', shows the influence of Joyce: the father of Goold-Verschoyle is a former 'Parnellite', the son a fugitive, like Joyce, from 'phoney priests, poets and traitors'. Kiš adhered broadly to the stations of Brian's biography, omitting, however, London and Moscow. And the end he chose for the Irishman – shot in Karaganda while trying to escape in 1945, with his naked corpse trussed up in barbed wire and dumped at the camp gate – is derivative, a description taken from Štajner's account of the death of Rudolf Ondraček, a friend from revolutionary Vienna, who perished in Norilsk Camp.[30]

NOTES

1. This chapter is based on the MI5 files of Brian Goold-Verschoyle (PRO, KV2/817) and Charlotte Moos (PRO, KV2/1241,1242), and on private correspondence in the possession of her daughter Merilyn.
2. PRO, FO 371/111698.
3. Pavel Sudoplatov (with Anatoli Sudoplatov, Jerrold L. and Leona P. Schecter), *Special Tasks. The Memoirs of an Unwanted Witness – A Soviet Spymaster* (London 1994), p. 47.
4. PRO, KV2/1008.
5. West and Tsarev, *Crown Jewels*, pp. 120–21.
6. L.S. Eremina and A.B. Roginskii (eds), *Rasstrel'nye spiski. Moskva 1937–1941. Kommunarka, Butovo* (Moscow 2000), p. 261.
7. PRO, KV2/804, Note of Interview, 8 February 1940.
8. Eremina and Roginskii, *Rasstrel'nye Spiski*, p. 247.

9. Christopher Andrew and Vasili Mitrokhin, *The Mitrokhin Archive. The KGB in Europe and the West* (London 1999), pp. 106–7.

10. Marc Jansen and Nikita Petrov, *Stalin's Loyal Executioner. Nikolai Ezhov 1895–1940* (Stanford 2002), pp. 68–69.

11. Michael Hepp (ed.), *Die Ausbürgerung deutscher Staatsangehöriger 1933–1945 nach den im Reichsanzeiger veröffentlichten Listen, Band 1* (Munich-New York-London-Paris 1985), p. 195.

12. The newspaper cuttings are in PRO, KV2/802.

13. PRO, KV2/817, Sibyl Goold-Verschoyle to Dear Sir, 8 May 1939.

14. Marx Memorial Library London, International Brigade Archives, Box 39/6/20. I am grateful to Julian Hendy for this reference.

15. PRO, KV2/817, Sibyl Goold-Verschoyle to Mr Krivitsky, 10 August 1939.

16. PRO, KV2/802, SIS extract, 31 October 1939.

17. Christopher Andrew, *Secret Service. The Making of the British Intelligence Community* (London 1985), pp. 593–94.

18. Geoffrey Roberts, *The Soviet Union and the Origins of the Second World War. Russo-German Relations and the Road to War, 1933–1941* (Houndmills 1995), pp. 111–16.

19. PRO, KV2/802, telegram from British Embassy, Washington, 3 September 1939.

20. PRO, KV2/816.

21. PRO, KV2/1023, interview summary, 13 October 1939.

22. PRO, KV2/805.

23. PRO, KV2/804, interview summary, 24 January 1940.

24. PRO, KV2/1242, petition from Siegfried Moos, (?) May 1940.

25. PRO, KV2/1241, K.M.M. Archer to HO, 1 June 1940.

26. Wolfgang Kraushaar, *Linke Geisterfahrer. Denkanstösse für eine antittotalitäre Linke* (Frankfurt am Main, 2001), S. 33–45.

27. *Daily Graphic*, 24 February 1949 (PRO, KV2/817).

28. *The Manchester Guardian*, 11 March 1949, Letters to the Editor.

29. Danilo Kiš, *Homo poeticus. Gespräche und Essays. Herausgegeben von Ilam Rakusa* (Munich-Vienna 1994), pp 79–88.

30. Danilo Kiš, *A Tomb for Boris Davidovitch* (London and Boston 1985).

PART III
Seán McAteer

Border Man

The authorities were not really sure who he was. For the Sheriff of Shoshone County, Idaho, the suspect in 1920 was John McEntee. One year later in Dublin his comrades called him McIntyre, and in 1923 the Liverpool Police sought him urgently under the name John Francis McAteer. For the Soviets, who granted him political asylum, he was David Ivanovich (son of John) Twist, although he signed his Russian letters as Seán Twist. His exact date of birth is unknown. In Russian documentation the year is given as 1893, the place of birth as 'Edensobo, Dondok' (Edentober, Dundalk), but the British authorities described him as a native of Newry, County Down.[1]

McAteer, 'Mac-an t-Saoir' ('son of the craftsman'), is a very ancient clan name, derived, it is said, from Ciarán Mac an t-Saoir, the founder of the monastic settlement in Clonmacnoise in the sixth century. The Scottish version of McAteer is McIntyre. McAteer used the names McEntee, McIntyre, McGinty and Twist to deceive his pursuers, perhaps in the knowledge that the transliteration of Irish names into the English language was frequently haphazard, so that one version of a surname was difficult to distinguish from the next.

A search of birth registers and census returns did not clarify the matter. In his Russian depositions, McAteer names a village near Dundalk, 'Edensobo', which is most probably Edentober, a townland within the Barony of Dundalk Lower. In the last decades of British rule, Edentober was attached to the Dundalk Poor Law Union district, in the census area of Ravensdale and in the parliamentary constituency of North Louth. Edentober is the last townland on the Louth side of the present border to Britain's Irish enclave, at the tip of an extended finger surrounded by County Armagh to the north and west and County Down to the east.

The area was always a frontier, physically and politically. Edentober looks over the plain towards Newry, perching on the last high ground on the northern side of the Cooley Mountains at the

end of the beautiful Flurry river valley, a natural route to the north
flanked at its narrowest point by Dromad Wood and Ravensdale
Forest. Slightly farther on the main Dundalk–Newry Road, as it
emerges from the sylvan narrows towards the plain around Killeen,
there is a left turn which leads immediately to a junction of minor
roads, one of which leads to Jonesborough. At this point the border
dissects the cross-road settlement of Flurry Bridge. Less than a mile
to the north, the next turnoff leads east, passing through the
townland of Edentober in the direction of the Newry river channel.
The landscape is dominated by Slieve Gullion mountain in the north-
west.

Within this area John Francis McAteer grew up, between the
thriving towns of Dundalk and Newry, in an area of spectacular
beauty but poor land, hilly (drumlin) country of little farms. Several
searches in birth registers did not locate any John McAteer, who, in
his own words, was 'born in 1893 in a small village near to the town
of Dundalk Ireland'. The only similar entry is for 18 May 1893, the
birth of John McAteer, son of the farmer Patrick McAteer and his
wife Mary (née Keenan), who lived at Crieve (Creeve), a townland
on the eastern outskirts of Newry. According to the 1911 Census,
the couple had nine children and the 17-year-old John was the eldest
of five boys. The only McAteers registered in that year in the
townland of Edentober (35 houses, 128 inhabitants, all Catholic)
was a young, childless woman and two John McAteers, father and
son, who gave the Irish version of their Christian names (Owen, i.e.
Eoin). The 45-year-old John Jnr was married but childless. Our John
McAteer is probably the eldest son of the Crieve family of that
surname and he may have lived with relatives in Edentober while
attending school in County Louth. The densest concentration of
McAteers was around Newry, in the townlands of Ballyholland
Upper and Lower, where the McAteer 'clan' now hold their annual
reunion. In the 1901 Census returns these McAteers are often
described as 'illiterate', small farmers who frequently also worked as
stone-cutters. Most of them still spoke Irish; only a minority of the
older folk had not acquired a knowledge of English.

Despite the fact that the family farm consisted of only five acres,
John Francis McAteer was not born at the bottom of the social
pyramid. His mother worked the land and his father made his living
as a surveyor, mainly in neighbouring towns. Young John completed
his education at the local National School and was then sent to the

Christian Brothers in Dundalk. He left school at 16 (1909) to serve his time (five years) as an apprentice to a stone-mason in Newry. 'After having trouble with the master' he decamped to Birkenhead, where he had relatives, and began work as a machinist in the Cammell Laird shipyard, moving later to a similar job in Belfast. McAteer spent the longest period of steady employment in Ireland in the Dublin Dock Yard. There he joined the ITGWU and was elected shop-steward.

McAteer's home area was the fighting ground of Cúchulainn, the mythical Ulster hero against the invading Connachtmen, and a land steeped in story-telling and resistance to foreign rule. It was also a part of Ireland which had been conquered and colonised relatively late, in the early seventeenth century. Fireside tales and Irish poets also sang the praises of Redmond O'Hanlon, the rapparee leader who harried the new settlers for twenty years until his death in 1681. McAteer would have heard older people talking about the depredations of Lord Blayney from nearby County Monaghan, whose troops devastated the area in the 1790s.[2] Other factors reinforcing an acute sense of nationality in an area still clinging to Irish customs and culture were the sectarian tension in the neighbouring county of Armagh, where the Orange Order had been formed in 1795, and the defence of tenant rights against landlordism. However, McAteer's immediate home area was almost exclusively Catholic and had strong links to immigrant communities in Scotland and the north-west coast of England, especially in Liverpool.

These contacts sometimes fostered a kind of trade union or craft consciousness, if not a working-class one. It is significant that McAteer's father worked for a wage and that the son, like so many of his small-farm cousins, learned his trade in the hard craft of stone-cutting. As a some-time migratory worker, he would have picked up socialist ideas from waterfront colleagues across the narrow channel plied by the steam-packets sailing to Liverpool from Dundalk or Newry.

His first politically conscious step was initiated by a childhood friend, Patrick Mackey or McEvoy (the Russian transliteration is unclear), a sailor on a cutter craft in the port of Dublin who swore the young Edentober apprentice-fitter into the Irish Republican Brotherhood (IRB). This was the most dangerous secret society in Ireland, the staunchest upholder of armed separatism and known the world over as the 'Fenians'. According to his rather self-aggrandising autobiographical account written for the Comintern in 1925, McAteer also joined the Socialist Party of Ireland (SPI) and the Irish Citizen Army (ICA), the workers' self-defence militia set up in 1913. As a prominent dockyard trade-unionist, McAteer got to know James Connolly and, more importantly, James Larkin, with whom he formed a sporadic collaboration. Larkin, ever eager to deflate the sneers that he was a Liverpudlian, took pride in his Ulster roots, in the fact that both parents were of tenant-farmer stock from around Newry. He may therefore have looked upon McAteer as one of his own, a rough diamond activist like himself.[3]

In August 1915 McAteer was sacked from the dockyard because of his union activities and was blacklisted. He subsequently gave the Soviets two versions of the reasons for his escape to the USA in December 1915. Firstly, in his deposition to the Comintern, he stated that he had 'become active in receiving arms and munitions for the Irish Citizen Army' and was arrested, but released owing to lack of evidence; hearing that he was to be arrested a second time, he 'was told to leave by the Comrades', who arranged his illegal passage to the United States on the American ship *Sheen*. Secondly, while under interrogation by the NKVD, McAteer maintained that the RIC had found a hidden arms cache for which he was responsible, and on the advice of the IRB he fled to America.

No trace of such a find could be located in the RIC County Inspectors' reports in this period.[4] Considering McAteer's involvement in Dublin labour circles, the arms he mentioned, if his account is true, were probably those of the ICA which was now being trained vigorously by James Connolly, the acting general secretary of the ITGWU following Larkin's departure to America in late 1914. The ICA, which had only fifty active members in March 1914,[5] had roughly three hundred by the summer of 1914[6] and, according to the membership rolls, 339 by early 1916.[7] In the first half of 1915 Connolly was lecturing Dublin Irish Volunteer officers in Dublin on the tactics of street-fighting.[8] By the autumn Connolly's demand for armed action became more persistent and the IRB men planning the Rising in secret within the Irish Volunteers were afraid that he would go it alone in a precipitate uprising.[9] The situation was also coming to a head once more on the industrial front, with a long strike on the Dublin docks from September straining the fragile finances of the Transport Union.[10]

The intensification of ICA training in 1915 presumably also involved more focused attempts to acquire rifles and ammunition, thus giving credence to McAteer's putative flight from the RIC. However, he may have signed on as a sailor from Dublin to a port on the north-eastern American seaboard on other grounds: because he had been summoned there by James Larkin. The labour leader had left Ireland for the United States in 1914, ostensibly to recuperate from mental exhaustion, the after-effects of the 1913 Dublin Lock-Out, and to collect funds for the ITGWU. However, once in America, Larkin turned to what he excelled at, agitating on labour and anti-war issues.

The American interlude (1914–23) showed Larkin to be unpredictable and unremittingly abusive towards perceived enemies. His politics at that time have been described as 'an eclectic stew of Christianity, socialism, syndicalism, communism and Irish nationalism';[11] and he could justify working for an Imperialist power as a paid agent. This involvement with the Germans, which probably consisted mainly of anti-war propaganda backed by agitation for strikes, began sometime in 1915. It ended abruptly in Mexico City in November 1917, when Larkin was dumped by his Teutonic paymasters after he had once more refused to undertake acts of sabotage. On his way to Mexico, Larkin met the German agent Carl Witzke in San Francisco. In 1929 Witzke made the following statement to American intelligence:

> Larkin got me several men [...] Levesovski and McIntyre, both of them labor agitators and radicals. As far as I know, both of these men went to Vladivostok. The main idea of going to Vladivostok was to spread radical propaganda [...] and incidentally to blow up the munitions stores.[12]

McAteer did not go as a German saboteur to the Russian Far East, and there is no direct evidence that he met Larkin in the USA or in Mexico, where, according to the British police, the Edentober man had spent some time during his American exile.[13] On landing in New England, McAteer headed for New York shortly before Christmas 1915 and his first contacts there, where he worked as a machinist on the construction of a new subway line, probably included Larkin. Both men arrived in Chicago in April 1916. Larkin was between speaking tours and agitation forays into the Western mining regions, and in the process of setting up the anti-war news-sheet *Irish Worker* with Jack Carney. McAteer worked in a tunnel-gang.

McAteer's peregrinations hither and thither across the North American continent were those of the archetypical 'labor agitator': half hobo, half insurrectionist, riding the rails with his bundle, 'going on to organize' like Joe Hill. He was a militant of the Industrial Workers of the World (IWW), a card-carrying 'Wobbly'. His political beliefs, like Larkin's to a certain extent, were a mixture of Fenianism and syndicalist activism, with little respect for parliamentary democracy and a belief in revolutionary violence. The 'Wobbly', a specifically American variant of syndicalism, fought for the 'One Big Union' and fomented strikes which would lead to a general strike and the capitulation of capitalism. The IWW, however, had shot its bolt by 1914, was against party politics and was riven by contending purist factions – anarchist and syndicalist tendencies.[14] Both wings still found adherents because of the brutal conditions of American capitalism or the reaction to labour unrest by employer-owners backed up by local State authorities: the violence perpetrated by vigilantes, lynch-mobs, policemen (often Irish), 'scabs' and Pinkerton agents with their billy-sticks, black-jacks, whips and shotguns.

McAteer was 'run out' of more than one town. After Chicago he headed for the harvesting fields and thence to Seattle where he signed up as a sailor on a coaster to Anchorage, Alaska. By now an 'unpaid IWW job delegate', McAteer spent two months in the white North and the rest of 1916 in California, as miner, fruit-picker, harvester, often under arrest because of strike activity, and constantly on the move. In June 1917 Seán McAteer, as 'John McEntee', landed in San Francisco. America had entered the war two months previously and the 'Espionage Act' was being debated in Congress, a *carte blanche* for the authorities to stamp out anti-war activity. That same month Larkin, too, was in the Golden Gate city, conferring with his German handlers, so he may have met his younger comrade. After he had read his name on a list of men to be drafted into the US Army, McAteer decided to move to a quieter location down the coast, and worked as a longshoreman.

Back again in San Francisco at the end of 1917, McAteer was arrested when Department of Justice officials, on the trail of draft dodgers, raided a meeting of IWW delegates. He was released after three months' detention on giving a pledge that he would report immediately to Camp Lewis military base. Instead of donning 'doughboy' khaki, he contacted the local IWW secretary and, with false papers making him 31 years of age, betook himself to the mining grounds of Nevada and Arizona.

By 1919 Seán McAteer, like Larkin, had become a fervent adherent of Soviet Russia. The authorities saw this, in itself, as a criminal offence. 'Criminal syndicalism' laws were passed first in California in 1919, and soon afterwards in 23 other states, including Washington and Idaho, both Wobbly strongholds. Following a foiled bomb attack on his house, A. Mitchell Palmer, President Wilson's Attorney General, used the powers invested in his office to launch a concerted attack on the Left. The 'Palmer raids' shocked liberal America, especially the blanket arrests and mass deportations. Even Edgar J. Hoover, Palmer's assistant, and Supreme Court judges held the draconian operations to be unconstitutional, but the 'Red Scare' of 1919–20 found general acceptance, not least because of the sensationalist and uniformly anti-labour press.

It was arguably time to get out and return home, but McAteer stayed at his revolutionary last, signing on in the Hekla Mine in Burke, Shoshone County, Idaho, at the beginning of 1920. Burke was a one-horse town, the setting for a classic Western film, where the railroad, a single-spur track from Wallace, the nearest big town seven miles away, ended. Here was work aplenty in the first years of peace, in the lead, zinc and copper mines, or as a lumberjack in the forests, now National Parks. Gold was discovered near Wallace in 1883, silver one year later in what turned out to be the biggest silver lode in the United States. Shoshone County is in the north of the state, near the border with Washington and the Bitterroot Range of mountains dividing Idaho from Montana.

The IWW was still functioning, kept alive mainly by anarcho-syndicalist 'decentralisers' following the great Chicago trial of the leadership. Over one hundred IWW functionaries had been tried in Chicago in 1918 on charges of sabotage and obstructing the war effort. Fifteen of the core leadership received twenty years, thirty-three others were given ten years, one thirty-five years and the rest shorter sentences. The convicted were released on bail from Leavenworth Penitentiary in July 1919 pending their appeal. When the defence case was rejected and the sentences confirmed in October 1920, nine IWW leaders refused to hand themselves in. Some, like Bill Haywood, fled to Soviet Russia, a move that was seen by many IWW rank-and-filers as 'desertion'. The majority who surrendered to serve their sentences were amnestied during the 1920s. That was to become McAteer's dilemma:

to stand trial, or to abscond – thus forfeiting the expensive bail bond guaranteed by friends or sympathisers.

The IWW was organised in District Organizational Committees with a secretary and a chairman. The shop-steward in the mine or lumber camp, the 'job delegate', reported to the 'stationery delegate' in the nearest town, handed over the union-dues and collected new membership-cards, dues-stamps and IWW literature. Sheriff Jesse Freeman of Shoshone County was tipped off about McAteer's IWW activities and he duly lodged a 'complaint' before a local judge. It was really an application for an arrest-warrant, couched in vague and archaic legalese:

> That on or about 13 day of March 1920 in and at the County of Shoshone, State of Idaho, the crime of Criminal Syndicalism was committed as follows, to-wit, by John McEntee, who being then and there a member of a society, group or assemblages of persons formed to teach and which does teach the doctrines of criminal syndicalism, did then and there wilfully and unlawfully continue and retain such membership in the said County of Shoshone, State of Idaho.[15]

McAteer's own version of his arrest and prison term in Idaho is, like almost everything he wrote or said about himself, inaccurate, since it exaggerates his revolutionary deeds and is vague with regard to geography and dates. In this instance we may doubt his claim that he was arrested at his place of work (the mine) and spent about a year in Wallace Jail. McAteer was duly arrested and brought before the local judge on 15 March, informed of the charge and his right to an attorney. He was told that a preliminary hearing would soon take place and that bail was fixed at $500.

During the hearing on 23 March 'McEntee' was not called to give evidence. The first witness was William Shupp, a 'stationery delegate' of the IWW from Spokane who had been an active Wobbly in a lumber camp near Wallace in 1919. District Attorney Hull asked him to identify IWW booklets, including the *Joe Hill Song Book*, Walker C. Smith's *Sabotage: Its History and Function* and Elizabeth Gurley Flynn's *Sabotage*. It was not established whether the witness owned all these pamphlets or had read them. He was not asked about 'McEntee', but only to identify the Irishman's IWW card, and that it had been transferred by one Joe Doyle from district number 400 (agriculture) to 800 (metal mining) in January 1920.

Mr Polley of Idaho State Constabulary then took the stand, confirming that he and Deputy Sheriff Cook had arrested McEntee 'on or about the 15th day of March, or the 13th day of March'. They first searched the suspect's room in the Burke Hotel in Burke, opening his suitcase and confiscating two books and a receipt. Polley and Deputy Freeman had waited in vain for 'McEntee' to return to the hotel, then driven back to Wallace, spotted their man on a street corner and carried out the arrest. In the protocol of the hearing, these State's exhibits are not described, but were probably nothing more than two IWW membership-cards, and a receipt for union dues. Polley was then cross-examined by Mr Wallace, McAteer's defence lawyer, and had to admit that the only evidence to link 'McEntee' to the IWW were the State's exhibits: the defendant had never been seen 'around any meetings talking the philosophy of the organization or anything of that kind'.

Defence counsel argued that it would be 'a waste of time' to bring the State's case on this kind of evidence before a jury. Judge Weninger disagreed and found that 'McEntee' should be held in the local jail until he could lodge the bail bond of $500. In April the prosecuting attorney filed the charges ('criminal syndicalism') for trial and named twenty-two witnesses for the courtroom session, of whom at least four were Irish – Bryan Murray, Pat Malone, Joseph O'Mara and William Phalon.

In the meantime the IWW had engaged two lawyers for McAteer. In their deposition to the local court they held that the 1919 statutes of Idaho State pertaining to 'criminal syndicalism' were in violation of the US Constitution. They also criticised that the 'sabotage' attributed to 'Mr McEntee', or the 'violence' and 'terrorism' to the IWW, had not been specified. On 2 July three locals ('residents, householders and freeholders') signed the bail bond surety of $500 before the District Court Clerk, who ordered Sheriff Freeman to release 'the said John McEntee'. In all, McAteer was in the Wallace lock-up not more than three and a half months.

At first, McAteer stayed in the area around Wallace, finding work in a mine in Kellog. As many other IWW activists had been arrested in the State, McAteer, according to himself at least, was asked by the North West Defense Committee to return to Wallace, organise the legal representation for his comrades still in gaol and act as local IWW organiser. For this he received a miner's wage, but soon had to relinquish the position after hearing that his second arrest was imminent.

'McEntee' then descended on Butte, Montana, the toughest mining town in America, the scene of major riots in 1915 between the socialist town administration and the militants of the Western Federation of Miners. Most of the protagonists, or antagonists, were Irish, like Acting Mayor Michael Daniel O'Connell, who was trying to restore normality after a period of martial law. The real enemy of the Irish was the Anaconda Copper Mining Company, which was trying to break the power of organised labour by playing the craft unions against the industrial unions. Jim Larkin had arrived in Butte in September 1915 to persuade the local miners to rejoin their union. When McAteer stepped into this miners' rough-house five years later, riots, wild shooting and acts of arson were frequent occurrences. The major source of violence were the agents of the copper company, who were intimidating the miners by firing on pickets and infiltrating the IWW and Butte Miner's Union (BMU) with touts and provocateurs.

The BMU, a conservative, non-socialist trade union, which in both membership and leaders was predominantly Irish, was also under fire from the authorities because of its anti-war stance in 1917–18, especially its rejection of the alliance between the United States and Britain. Anti-British feeling was also high because of the Black and Tan atrocities in Ireland. In Butte, McAteer probably worked in harness with Larkin's closest collaborator, Jack Carney, who, aligning himself with the radical minority amongst the miners, spent over half a year in the town in 1920/21.[16]

By his own account McAteer was elected secretary of the 'Metal and Coal Miners Independent Union 210 and 220', most probably a Wobbly organisation in opposition to the traditionalist BMU. He took up office in January 1921 and was also active in the underground Communist Party, alongside William J. Dunne, later a prominent functionary of the Profintern and twice the representative of the CPUSA at the Comintern in Moscow.[17] However, 'Mr McEntee' was a man 'out on licence', because his trial in Wallace was due to begin on 19 May 1921. The Clerk of Shoshone County Court sent out subpoenas to eighteen witnesses, but seven, English, Irish and Scandinavian miners, had already left the region.

McAteer did not face the judge a second time. He left Butte on 5 May 1921 in the company of Bill Dunne, who was on his way to

Moscow, and both attended an IWW conference in Chicago. Dunne and other leading communists advised 'McEntee' to leave the United States, no doubt arguing that he could be sentenced to a lengthy stretch. That was realistic, for other Wobblies charged with 'McEntee' – Embry, Frazer and Joe Doyle – were sentenced in the Wallace trial to ten years. McAteer laid low in Chicago for a few weeks before travelling to New York to arrange false seaman's papers and an illegal passage home. Using the passport of one 'Leon Rosset' he worked his passage as a sailor on an American ship and disembarked on a Dublin quayside in August 1921.

McAteer found Ireland profoundly changed and still in turmoil. The war against the British had ended a month previously in an unsteady Truce. Back in his home area McAteer learned that the resistance to British terror in Oriel had been sporadic. Dundalk town was a bastion of Redmondism and clericalist influence exerted through the Ancient Order of Hibernians (AOH).[18] Only thirteen local Volunteers remained with the republican faction when Redmond split the organisation in 1914.[19] The men of north Louth, one veteran remembers, had officers 'with feet of clay' and the local IRA had to depend on Volunteers from Down or Armagh to carry out attacks. After one such ambush in Newry in April 1921, the Black and Tans went on the rampage, forcing the people of Ballyholland, home of the McAteer clan, to sleep in the fields.[20] In May 1922 arrest squads of the new Stormont regime carried off known IRA men and let the B Specials loose on Newry and its environs. They attacked McAteer's native hamlet, Flurry Bridge, on 22 June, looting Gallagher's public house before coming under fire from the IRA.[21]

Before he entered the limelight in Dublin in January 1922, the activities of McAteer are not known in any detail. Ireland was undergoing a process of economic austerity: the war boom was truly over, with one hundred thousand registered as unemployed and widespread resistance to wage-cuts. Strikes by engineers, dockers and railwaymen in Dublin in the second half of 1921 all ended in defeat and wage reduction – the shape of things to come in 1922 and 1923.

McAteer rejoined the ICA and the SPI, organisations in a state of flux because of conflicting loyalties rooted in the Irish struggle for independence and the Russian Revolution. ICA men had served as auxiliaries to the Dublin IRA in the War of Independence, gathering intelligence and procuring guns.[22] In the interregnum between the July Truce and the Treaty signed with Britain in December 1921, the ICA acted like the IRA, emerging from illegality to organise training camps and drilling. There were two ICA battalions, north and south of the Liffey, and at least one small unit in the provinces, in Roscrea, Co. Tipperary.[23] The hard core of ICA men remained loyal to the memory of Easter Week and James Connolly, but there was a lot of petty feuding in the ranks between ITGWU and Larkin loyalists.[24]

The 'Bolshevik' faction within the SPI formed the Communist Party of Ireland (CPI) on 28 October. Between October 1921 and the start of the Civil War in late June 1922, CPI leader Roddy Connolly purged the Dublin membership from over a hundred to thirty-six. Outside the capital there were no more than twenty to thirty registered members.[25] McAteer received Party Card No. 36 and was subsequently elected to the Dublin District Committee with responsibility for literature and agitation.[26]

McAteer, now calling himself 'McIntyre', worked closely with two men who later turned to writing: Liam O'Flaherty[27] and Jim Phelan. All three were newcomers in the sense that they were globe-trotters and thus had not taken part in IRA activities in Ireland in the years 1919–21. With their 'propaganda of the deed' view of politics, they soon clashed with the Party leadership. O'Flaherty, a craggily handsome Aran Islander, had left Clonliffe Seminary and University College Dublin to enlist in the Irish Guards in February 1916. Badly injured by shell-fire twice on a single day in September 1917 near Passchendaele, O'Flaherty was treated for shell-shock and melancholia.

After being discharged from the Army with a small disability pension in May 1918, he witnessed the Armistice celebrations in London before sailing from London to Rio de Janeiro. The squalor of trench warfare and meeting men from all walks of life on the battlefields of France and Belgium had radicalised the native Irish-speaker, turning him away from separatist nationalism toward socialism and admiration for the Russian Revolution. His wanderings and experiences resembled McAteer's. O'Flaherty worked on boats in South America and the Mediterranean, tried his hand at a series of labouring jobs in Canada, joined the IWW and crossed the American border to visit his elder brother in Boston. Influenced by Tom, a radical socialist who had joined the CPUSA, Liam followed suit before resuming his maritime life, reaching

Britain by a circuitous route. In the autumn of 1921 he was in Dublin, a member of the ICA and the CPI.

Jim Phelan was far more persistent in his roving ways, even taking to the roads and the seas; and dying, in 1966, a member of the traveller community in England.[28] Phelan was born in 1895 in Inchicore, then a village on the western outskirts of Dublin, where his world-travelled father had found work as a craftsman in the railway yards. Young Jim, 'battering myself against the world', was in constant trouble with his strict, conventional parents, periodically running away from home and school. The ferocious beatings he was subjected to on his rueful return, and the hard life on the street-warrens of Dublin's Coombe district, made him 'able to look after himself' physically from a very early age, prowess he refined as a street fighter against the police during the 1913 Lock-Out. Phelan was an ICA man from the beginning, and like McAteer and O'Flaherty, more interested in class warfare than the struggle for national independence.

His drifting frequently took him away from Dublin, and he never completed his apprenticeship in the blacksmith's forge at Inchicore railway works. Jim Phelan had an intense interest in, and knowledge of, Dublin slum life, especially its argot and street ballads. His first literary efforts were about the population who lived on, rather than in, the streets of the Liberties, colourful characters later to find a wider audience in the plays of Sean O'Casey or in *The Informer* by Liam O'Flaherty. According to himself, Phelan belonged to the secret inner circle of the ICA and was close to the Larkin clan since his sister Maggie and Jim Larkin's sister, Delia, married two brothers named Colgan. By 1921, Phelan concedes, the Liberty Hall men were doubting his loyalty to the cause. As working men with families to support, they probably took Jim's frequent and lengthy absences from Dublin, either as a ham actor in travelling fit-up companies or as a metal worker in the British Tank Corps in Dorset, as proof of a feckless and disreputable nature. In early 1922 Phelan was back in Dublin after months on the road, leaving the navvy gangs on the Roundwood Reservoir for his native city, where he soon met O'Flaherty and McAteer ('McIntyre').

O'Flaherty was by now the CPI's best-known member, a striking figure in proletarian cap and throat muffler, sitting at his box beside Nelson's Pillar in Dublin's Sackville St (now O'Connell St) selling copies of *The Workers' Republic*. The CPI had called for action on the unemployment issue as early as December 1921,[29] launching a campaign of street agitation early in the New Year by holding open-air meetings on Sundays in Beresford Place beside Liberty Hall. O'Flaherty's oratorical gifts and mischievous nature appealed to Phelan, who ambled up to the speakers afterwards and joined the workless army. On 9 January 1922, the day following the successful meeting, a committee of the unemployed, with the sanction of the CPI leaders, was formed to press the cause of the jobless to Dublin Corporation. O'Flaherty acted as chairman, McAteer as his assistant, in a deputation to the Lord Mayor in the Mansion House. The Corporation listened sympathetically to the demands of the five men. The aldermen could hardly provide public works at trade union rates, but at least one aim of the manifesto, provision of 'a permanent meeting place' for the unemployed, was achieved.[30]

This was the Rotunda Concert Hall (now the Gate Theatre), where O'Flaherty's committee was allowed to stay daily until 5 p.m. On Wednesday, 18 January, they refused to quit the building, staying until the Saturday, when they were forced out by threats of violence. The occupation was the talk of the city, a well-planned operation justified in a manifesto posted all over Dublin and signed by O'Flaherty and McIntyre, who now gave the Irish version of his name, Seán Mac an tSaoir. The initial response to the coup was not negative, with local shops and a bakery supplying the 120 occupants with free provisions and tobacco.[31] O'Flaherty formed his men into companies, appointing officers and guards. On the Thursday night a hostile crowd gathered outside, protesting at the Red Flag draped from a window and firing stones and bottles at the building. The trouble began with the ejection of a drunken 'officer' from the occupying garrison and was sustained by the presence of members of Catholic Action among the unruly crowd outside. On the Friday night the mob dragged down the red banner and fought their way into the hall. The police and the IRA kept the hostile groups apart and cleared the building the day after.[32]

In persuading the unemployed to vacate the premises, the Communist Party effectively deflated a crisis which might have led to armed clashes with the Provisional Government and the IRA which, in the absence of a State police force, was still operating in the name of the Dáil. Officially, the Party stated that it had not kept 'closely enough in touch' with the Unemployed Council, which 'was ridiculous in allowing any one member [O'Flaherty] to become a dictator and to appoint officers'.[33] Internally, however, Connolly and other leading communists ascribed the Rotunda confrontation to 'premature' action orchestrated by two ex-Wobblies, O'Flaherty and McIntyre, who were also accused of dividing among themselves funds which had been collected for the unemployed.[34] A committee of enquiry subsequently found that the charge had little substance because of the chaotic nature of the withdrawal from the Rotunda, but one problem remained: the attitude of the two men, who shared the view 'that no proper Communist Party had any leaders at all, all must be rank-and-filers'.[35]

Despite such un-Leninist statements, neither man was expelled from the Party. O'Flaherty skimmed over the Rotunda affair in his autobiography, adding that he had been 'driven out' of Dublin and had fled to Cork with two companions.[36] In the immediate aftermath of the Rotunda incident, O'Flaherty was still Dublin's most popular communist, praised in the Party press for his rousing speeches at Beresford Place, or in Finglas in support of farm workers. He was rescued from eviction by a jobless crowd led by Roddy Connolly.[37] Sometime in March 1922 he went to Cork with McAteer and Phelan. The latter describes the short trip as 'lively', before he got itchy feet once more, returning to Dublin and thence to Liverpool to work metal again.[38] McAteer's version of what the trio was up to in the southern capital is prefaced with the fantastic statement that the Rotunda had been evacuated owing 'to the bombardment of the building with bombs and machine-guns'. In Cork, the account continues, 'I with the other two [i.e. Phelan and O'Flaherty] formed a communist group in the city and collected money for the relief of the famine raging in Russia.'[39] This is the 'nucleus of a branch' which Connolly mentioned to Comintern emissary Borodin some months later.[40]

The southern mission of the trio had also a hidden agenda: to form new branches of the ICA before the tension between the IRA and the new Free State Army after the acceptance of the Treaty by the Dáil erupted into open warfare. Connolly, if we read between the lines of his missives to Moscow, had probably given up hope of bringing over the ICA men to communist positions and formed 'a military Section' instead – which O'Flaherty and McAteer refused to join, allegedly because they were not to lead it. When O'Flaherty desisted from any further part in the agitation work of the Dublin Branch, he was suspended for three months.[41] He continued to push for the recruitment of ICA men to the CPI, writing articles for a journal of the CPGB, thus prompting a protest from Connolly to the Comintern.[42]

There were other efforts to take over, or neutralise, the 200-odd ICA men at large, who were predominantly anti-Treaty. The Transport Union or ITGWU, and organised labour as a whole, wanted to stave off the impending fratricidal strife and put the ICA under the direction of the trade unions. This move would have meant the liquidation of the autonomous workers' militia, removing the control of its Army Council and detaching its soldiers from the republican IRA. Some leading ICA officers went along with the proposal initially, but most of the rank-and-file sympathised with the IRA and stayed with their Commandant, John Hanratty. Hanratty, like McAteer and Phelan and many ICA activists, was influenced by Delia Larkin and against the sitting ITGWU leadership.[43] Delia had been ousted from Liberty Hall, as had the old Larkinite loyalist P.T. Daly; they and their supporters felt that too much power rested in the hands of William O'Brien, from 1919 treasurer and practically the secretary of the ITGWU, secretary to Dublin Trades Council and vice-chairman of the Irish Trades Union Congress (ITUC).

Meanwhile McAteer, by his own account, was in the south: 'I was called back to Dublin and sent to Tipperary to re-organise our units and help in the organisation of the seizure of the Soviet Creameries.' The 'units' involved were probably a handful of communist sympathisers and tearaways. The resumption of factory occupations, starting on 13 May 1922, had nothing to do with the CPI, being organised by the ITGWU officials Hedley, McGrath and Dowling. The creameries belonged to the Cleeve family, who had threatened to close all their plants (in the counties of Tipperary and Limerick) if the workers did not accept a one-third reduction in wages.[44] This time the farmers, in contrast to the creamery seizures of 1920, were on the side of the owners, and the strikes dragged on. Perhaps McAteer was to the fore in Tipperary town, the centre of the labour troubles and in rebel hands in the first weeks of the Civil War. The Red Flag flew over the Cleeve's property, and over the local gas works. The Bank of Ireland branch had been relieved of £42,000, and Lord Barrymore of his coal stocks in order to fire the boilers of the 'sovietised' gas works. In another operation which bears the adventurer hallmark of McAteer, the manager of Cleeve's, James Reidy, was kidnapped in Mallow and brought to Tipperary.

The Free State Army took the town after heavy fighting, but not before the retreating republicans had burned Cleeve's factory, the workplace of four hundred locals, to the ground.[45] This wanton act of destruction, one IRA participant remembered, 'ruined us in the locality'.[46] What McAteer wrote about his next Munster exploits is pure fantasy:

> I was in Cork and was instructed to seize all the land belonging to the aristocrats, which I did and signed my name for the seizure. I was appointed Commandant of the 1st and 2nd Division of the Irish Citizen Army and fought against the Free State Government.

The 125 men and nineteen women of the ICA who took part in the early stages of the Civil War did so in Dublin, under the direct command of the IRA leader Oscar Traynor. Their fighting ground was Sackville (now O'Connell) Street and nearby, in barricaded hotels and offices. The military tactics of the rebels, or 'Irregulars', as the government named them, were inane. Instead of concentrating defensive positions on the west side of O'Connell Street, forming a link to the IRA garrison in the Four Courts, the rebels occupied the eastern side of Dublin's main thoroughfare.[47] O'Flaherty was with the ICA men holding Vaughan's Hotel in Rutland Square (now Parnell Square), but his unit and the few CPI members taking up arms, including young Connolly, were withdrawn before government forces assaulted the Sackville Street hotels, thus ending the fighting in Dublin on 5 July.[48] O'Flaherty, disillusioned but with enough fresh impressions for his first short story ('The Sniper'), slipped through the armed cordons and embarked for Liverpool. He was in two minds about what he should do next: join a flying column in the hills south of Dublin, for the defeated 'Irregulars' the obvious next move, or return to America. In the end he did neither, going to ground in London to write at a feverish pace.[49]

His initial urge in Liverpool, however, was to go back to the fighting in the company of his friend Jim Phelan. Phelan, now in a steady job, refused and, although he is characteristically vague in his memoirs on the long discussions with O'Flaherty, he possibly felt he could be of more use to the 'movement' doing what he had done periodically in the past – smuggling revolvers to Ireland on the North Wall boat for the ICA.[50]

After one week's combat in Dublin, the Free State Army captured almost every active member of the Citizen Army. Individual ICA men took to the flying columns in mountainous terrain. McAteer was possibly with the Tipperary men whose columns were more or less intact when they took to guerrilla warfare following the loss, in August, of all towns in the county to the Free State Army. At the end of the year McAteer returned to Dublin, in his own grandiose phrase 'to take charge of the Brigade' and be 'elected Commandant of the Irish Citizen Army'.[51] His contact there was with Pat Colgan, husband of Delia Larkin. In their house he deposited his CPI and IWW membership-cards and an American Merchant Marine Passport. He later wrote that he was 'out leading a column in Wicklow'.[52] It consisted of about twelve ICA men who fought the last battle of the workers' militia – against a Free State Army round-up in Glenasmole. After a day's desperate fighting, the group broke through the armed ring and headed north.[53] McAteer went to Liverpool and renewed old contacts.

NOTES

1. The scanty biographical data to hand is taken from the following sources: Derzhavnyi Arkhiv Sluzhi Bezpeki, Kyiv (Archive of the Ukrainian Security Service, Kiev), Investigation File No. 5572, David Ivanovich Twist; RGASPI, f. 17. o. 98, d. 4566, ll. 17–19 (Autobiography, 20 March 1925); *Newry Reporter*, 16 June 1923, p. 3 and 21 June 1923, p. 5; *Dundalk Democrat*, 16 June 1923, p. 4.
2. Darach McDonald, *The Chosen Few. Exploding Myths in South Armagh* (Cork and Dublin 2000).
3. Emmet O'Connor, *James Larkin* (Cork 2002), pp. 3, 90.
4. PRO, CO 904/97.
5. National Library of Ireland (NLI), William O'Brien Papers, Ms 15673(1), information from Capt. Jack White.
6. Samuel Levenson, *James Connolly. A Biography* (London 1973), p. 260.
7. NLI, William O'Brien Papers, Ms 15672.
8. National Archives of Ireland (NAI), Bureau of Military History (BMH), WS 261, statement of General Piaras Beaslai. The talks were given on 23 January and 6 March 1915.
9. Levenson, *James Connolly*, pp. 259–82.
10. C. Desmond Greaves, *The Irish Transport and General Workers' Union. The Formative Years: 1909–1923* (Dublin 1982), pp. 150–56.
11. O'Connor, *James Larkin*, p. 64.
12. Emmet Larkin, *James Larkin. Irish Labour Leader, 1876–1947* (London and Henley 1997), pp. 217–18.
13. *Newry Reporter*, 16 June 1923, p. 3.
14. See Patrick Renshaw, *The Wobblies. The Story of the IWW and Syndicalism in the United States* (Chicago 1999).

15. The account of the prosecution against McAteer is taken from court files, kindly copied for the author by Penny Fernquist, Deputy Clerk of Shoshone County Court, Idaho.
16. Richard Hudelson, 'Jack Carney and the *Truth* in Duluth', *Saothar*, 19, 1994, pp. 129–39.
17. Harvey Klehr, John Earl Haynes and Kyrill M. Anderson, *The Soviet World of American Communism* (New Haven and London, 1998), p. 360.
18. NAI, BMH, WS 260, statement of Hugh Kearney.
19. NAI, BMH, WS 353, statement of James McGuill.
20. NAI, BMH, WS 1148, statement of Patrick J. Casey.
21. NAI, BMH, WS 634, statement of Jack McElhaw.
22. Unless otherwise noted, the history of the ICA is based on the official history commissioned by its veterans – R.M. Fox, *History of the Irish Citizen Army* (Dublin 1943).
23. NLI, O'Brien Papers, Ms. 15673 (1).
24. For an innovative study of the ICA after 1916, see Brian Hanley, 'The Irish Citizen Army after 1916', *Saothar*, 28, 2003, pp. 37–47.
25. RGASPI, f. 495, o. 89, d. 13, l. 7.
26. RGASPI, f. 17, o. 98, d. 4566, ll. 8, 17–19.
27. See Peter Costello, *Liam O'Flaherty's Ireland* (Dublin 1996).
28. See Jim Phelan, *The Name's Phelan. The First Part of the Autobiography of Jim Phelan*, London 1948 (Belfast 1993).
29. *The Workers' Republic*, 10 December 1921, p. 5.
30. *The Workers' Republic*, 14 January 1922, p. 6; *Dublin Evening Mail*, 12 January 1922, p. 6.
31. *The Freeman's Journal*, 19 January 1922, p. 3; *Irish Independent*, 19 January 1922, p. 11.
32. *The Freeman's Journal*, 21 January 1922, p. 5; *Dublin Evening Mail*, 21 January 1922, p. 3.
33. *The Workers' Republic*, 28 January 1922, p. 5.
34. RGASPI, f. 495, o. 189, d. 16, ll. 133–34.
35. Ibid., l. 53.
36. Liam O'Flaherty, *Shame the Devil* (London 1934), p. 22.
37. *The Workers' Republic*, 25 March 1922, p. 3; Paddy Bergin, 'Liam O'Flaherty', *Labour History News*, no. 6, Summer 1990, p. 7.
38. Jim Phelan, *The Name's Phelan* (Belfast, 1993), p. 275.
39. RGASPI, f. 17, o. 98, d. 4566, l. 18 (reverse).
40. RGASPI, f. 495, o. 89, d. 13, l. 8.
41. RGASPI, f. 495, o. 89, d. 16, l. 54.
42. RGASPI, f. 495, o. 89, d. 12, ll. 17–18.
43. Arthur Mitchell, *Labour and Irish Politics 1890–1930. The Irish labour movement in the age of revolution* (Dublin 1974), pp. 162–64; Fox, *Citizen Army*, pp. 214–17.
44. Greaves, *The Irish Transport and General Workers' Union*, p. 312.
45. *Tipperary Star*, 5 August 1922, pp. 2–3.
46. Michael Hopkinson, *Green Against Green. A History of the Irish Civil War* (Dublin 1988), p. 168.
47. Fox, *Citizen Army*, pp. 218–22.
48. Mike Milotte, *Communism in Modern Ireland. The Pursuit of the Workers' Republic since 1916* (Dublin 1984), p. 59.
49. O'Flaherty, *Shame the Devil*, pp. 24–39; Costello, *Liam O'Flaherty's Ireland*, pp. 40–49.

50. Phelan, *The Name's Phelan*, pp. 278–79.
51. RGASPI, f. 17, o. 98, d. 4566, l. 18 (reverse).
52. RGASPI, f. 495, o. 218, d. 21, l. 3.
53. Fox, *Citizen Army*, p. 225.

'Going up' in Liverpool

In 1923 Liverpool was a tough place, Britain's second busiest seaport and home to a large Irish community living in appalling slum conditions like their Dublin cousins. It was an important destination and point of departure for two revolutionary organisations – the IRA and the Communist International. Comintern officials were hidden in the city and then given forged seamen's papers for the next leg of the journey overseas. Until they left the CPGB in 1924, Bessie and Jack Braddock were the leaders of Scouse Bolshevism, organising the unemployed, in a mass movement that won new relief-rates and led a Hunger March to London in 1922, the first of the famous inter-war treks of the jobless. In the Braddocks' joint biography, published in 1963, Jack omits to mention his involvement with the IRA, or his acquaintanceship with Seán McAteer or Jim Phelan.[1] The Braddocks' break with Communism is described in some detail, a plausible retelling of trust betrayed and inner-party machinations which persuaded them that their political home was in the Labour Party, for which Bessie was a forthright and popular MP from 1945. The first biography of Bessie Braddock, a hagiographic portrait of a hard-nosed proletarian mother-figure with a heart of gold, published in 1957, does mention husband Jack's involvement with the IRA, and the trouble he brought upon himself by consorting with Phelan and McAteer.[2]

Liverpool was also a conduit for smuggling arms to Ireland during the War of Independence. The shipments were small and brought on the short crossing by sympathetic seamen, while the bigger shipments, German in origin, were transported to Ireland direct and landed only after the Truce.[3] Arms procurement in Britain was often carried out with the assistance of communists close to the IRA. One such raid, on the Hay Mills factory in Birmingham in April 1922, was foiled by the police, who arrested twelve Irishmen and the local communist street orator H.M. Emery. Emery subsequently jumped bail and fled with his wife to the USSR, acquiring there the status of a political immigrant. The CPGB leadership, angry about the affair since it had not been consulted beforehand, blocked the Emerys' return to Britain for some years because of Scotland Yard's interest in the case.[4] Emery's involvement with the IRA, which is probably typical of CPGB collaboration with Irish Republicans, was either his own or a local initiative. He had not informed Party headquarters in London in 1921 of his intention to work with the IRA's Supply Department, thinking it was sufficient to divulge his illegal involvement to two members of the Party's Central Committee, who advised him to quit the position of Birmingham Party secretary.[5]

Pressure on Irish republicans in Britain increased during the Irish Civil War, since many of the activists were known to the Free State authorities, who were now using their own agents in Britain and cooperating closely with the police there. On the basis of evidence that the Anti-Treaty IRA was reorganising its structures in Britain, Dublin urged Scotland Yard to act. A total of 140 republicans were seized and deported to Ireland, where they were interned, a sweep that effectively destroyed the cross-channel IRA. The House of Lords found that the deportations were illegal and requested that the men be sent back to Britain.[6] With the Civil War almost at an end, the Free State government complied. The British police re-arrested nine of the deportees and charged them with attempting to overthrow the Dublin government by force of arms. At least two of the defendants, Patrick and Dennis Fleming, had lived at a Liverpool address where detectives found correspondence addressed to 'O/C Liverpool'.[7]

In a separate trial, held at Liverpool Assizes in June 1923, William Horan and John Finn, both Irish-born, were sentenced to five and three years' penal servitude respectively. Horan, the local IRA commander, according to Liverpool CID, was charged with possessing explosives, while Finn had kept 3,500 rounds of revolver ammunition and machine-gun parts at his address.[8] Following the mass arrests of March–April and the seizure of Horan in May 1923, the remnants of the Liverpool IRA command felt cornered. When the Irish Civil War ended that month with the 'dump arms' order of the IRA, the efforts of republican sympathisers perforce turned from gun-running to collecting funds for the families of the 12,000 republicans interned in Ireland. Such monies were distributed by the 'Republican Prisoners' Dependants Fund', under the supervision of Kathleen Barry, the sister of the republican hero Kevin Barry. The

Irish Communists had set up their own prisoners' assistance scheme in January 1923 for the nine members of the CPI still in Free State custody. 'Cross-channel comrades' were also urged to donate.[9]

Fund-raising for the 'cause' or the 'movement' by illegal means, usually armed robbery, was commonplace in Ireland during the Civil War. Indeed, so widespread was crime at that time that it is impossible to distinguish an IRA 'job' from just another case of desperadoes taking advantage of a general break-down in law and order. And even if the robbery was for 'the lads', could some of the booty be kept for 'expenses'? We cannot say with any certitude whether this question was uppermost in the minds of the duo who carried out the post-office robbery on 11 June 1923, in Liverpool's Scotland Road – Seán McAteer and Jim Phelan.[10]

Phelan had been in the city since March 1922, working as a blacksmith in a firm in Roscoe Street, and he seems to have settled down to family life with Dora, his Dublin wife. McAteer had arrived in Liverpool around March 1923 and both men frequented the 'International Club' at 52 Byrom Street, a stronghold of various shades of left-wing opinion. CID officer Moore kept an eye on the place and knew Phelan by sight. The detective inspector held Phelan to be an important IRA man and warned him 'to keep out of trouble' when he met him prowling around the docks. At the time Phelan was being unusually sedentary by his own standards; he states he was considered by the local IRA to be 'a capable and active conspirator'.[11] Probably closer to the truth than Phelan's partially dissembling memoirs is a description of Phelan and McAteer from the lore of Liverpool docklands:

> The Irish refugees had to be fed and someone had to find the money. Phelan was a man who grieved because he trod on a kitten. M'Ateer was not unknown to banks; he had a habit of withdrawing £1,000 at a time without telling the teller, of tossing notes across the table and then asking someone to loan him a cigarette.[12]

Shortly after his arrival in Liverpool in March 1922, Jim Phelan was approached by James Cully and Joseph Kennedy, IRA operatives, to assist them in a 'hold-up'. They trawled the Scotland Road area and decided on two potential targets, Higgins' butchers or the post office near St Martin's Hall. Observing the butchers for two or three nights, they moved off, possibly because the cash-van did not arrive. On one evening they did go to the post office, but it was closed. Indecision being his second name, Phelan backed out of the harum-scarum plan. He was constantly in two minds: whether to stay or take to the roads again, work at his craft or explore once more the dosshouses ('paddincans') of the tramping folk, the vagrants who peopled his first stories. He was also impressionable and loyal to his friends to an inordinate degree.

Cully and Kennedy also pressed McAteer to carry out a robbery. By May 1923 he had decided that he and Phelan 'would have to stick-up some place'. The weaponry was provided by Jack Braddock, Liverpool's best-known communist and a member of the Control Commission of the Central Committee. He had known Phelan for about a year and a half, McAteer for a shorter period, probably from the Byrom Street club. They hardly differed in their politics: both were communists and Braddock had attempted to establish a branch of the IWW in Liverpool during World War I, with little success. And he contributed, with other Liverpudlians, to the press fund of the CPI weekly.[13]

Phelan talked to James Cully on 2 June 1923 about holding up Higgins' butchers and the IRA man replied that 'the only way for us fellows was to go out and take something'. The impetus, then, seems to have come from the IRA and, with so many republicans in gaol, Phelan, who had not taken part in the Irish Civil War, maybe felt it was time to show his mettle. For the more politically active McAteer, the need to help the dependants of his comrades in the flying columns of Tipperary and Wicklow became a duty. After approaching Braddock for guns on 3 June, Phelan received a package two days later in Hardman Street from Jimmy Horan, a local communist. The parcel contained a .22 automatic pistol with some rounds and a .32 revolver without ammunition. Phelan had told Braddock that they needed the firearms for 'a job', weapons that were to be returned 'unless there was an accident'.

On 8 June Phelan and McAteer moved into a lodging-house owned by Thomas Gowland at 97 Byrom Street. Gowland knew Phelan by sight, thought his name was Shamus (Séamus, the Irish form of James) and had also heard him being called Finchley. McAteer told the landlord that his name was McGinty. It is likely that the move to the lodgings was in anticipation of a quick exit from the city and an attempt to cover tracks – in order not to jeopardise their relatives, whom they may have told that they were leaving Merseyside. Now there was a third man in the gang, Augustine Power, a 20-year-old sailor close to Braddock. On 11 June the trio sauntered along Scotland Road, for McAteer was to point out the post office to Phelan, but they went past without noticing it and continued up Stanley Road where, Power said, there were some banks. They hung around one bank branch for a while, then crossed the tram lines and walked back to the corner of Great Homer Street. McAteer was in charge, telling Phelan to get the car and look at one of the smaller banks in Musgrave Street.

Phelan rejoined his companions in crime at 1.30 p.m. in John's Gardens. If their minds were made up to do something, only McAteer knew it. When Power was about to leave, McAteer told him to bring a gun. Phelan asked why and the Edentober revolutionary said: 'One of them post offices has to go up.' He repeated the sentence when telling Phelan to go to Jimmy Cully's house (51 Eldon Place) to collect the 'stuff'. Phelan had dumped Braddock's parcel there and he duly collected it. Cully also gave Phelan a .38 revolver and ammunition, and a certain Joe Kennedy completed the Inchicoreman's arsenal with the gift of a lead pipe.

Phelan then went to the lodging-house where McAteer was waiting. He kept the .22 automatic and put six bullets in the magazine. McAteer took the heavier weapon, the .38. The .32 revolver from Braddock was useless without bullets and it was given to Power with an instruction to meet the other two at Scotland Road at twenty minutes to seven.

Power never appeared, but his comrades did not hang around.

Phelan asked McAteer where the post office was, and they went there: Hopwood Street Sub-Post Office, 360 Scotland Road. A policeman was patrolling the vicinity, so the two decided to kill time by having a drink in a pub. When they came out, the bobby had left, but they were still indecisive. Standing in the street, Phelan felt it was his last chance to talk, saying 'It's a bad chance.' McAteer gave him the tired answer: 'Well, something has to be done.' The two men crossed over to the shop, the idea being that McAteer should ask for a penny stamp. They realised this wasn't going to be a big coup, a huckster's shop selling sweets, lemonade and stationery, with a post-office grille and counter at the back beside a public telephone booth. The business was run by Mrs Lovelady, a widow who was away visiting relatives in North Wales that day, and her assistants were her daughter Annie and Jane Heery.

The young women were balancing the day's takings, silver and coppers from post-office transactions, when two men entered the shop minutes before the closing time of 7 p.m. The taller of the men, Phelan, closed the door and fastened it; his smaller, thinner companion moved towards the post-office counter.

For a few seconds the girls, immersed in their calculations and agreeing that 'it has gone quiet', did not notice that McAteer was at the customer side of the post-office counter with a gun in his hand. He told them to be quiet 'for a few minutes' and that he wanted the money. Annie Lovelady ran towards the telephone booth, while Miss Heery screamed, 'Oh, no!' McAteer warned her to stay where she was. She made a dart for the door into the kitchen and screamed 'Jim!', the name of the eldest of Mrs Lovelady's sons, who was upstairs at the time.

At this stage Phelan ran out of the premises, while McAteer walked through the open flap of the counter to the private area and warned Miss Lovelady to drop the telephone. As McAteer was scooping up the assorted coins, Thomas, the youngest Lovelady son, ran out of the kitchen and tackled the robber, pulling him out from behind the counter. There, in the open shop space, McAteer took a step back and discharged one shot. Thomas slumped to the floor, where his brother James found him seconds later while the blue smoke of the detonation was still in the air. As Miss Heery was phoning for an ambulance, James and Annie, who had picked up Phelan's cap from the floor, ran out of the shop and saw two men disappearing around the bank at the corner into Newsham Street. James Lovelady lost sight of McAteer after he had disappeared into Harper's Stables.

Meanwhile, Phelan, who had been overtaken at the beginning by the swifter McAteer, had a crowd, alarmed by James Lovelady, chasing him through Great Homer Street, up Opie Street and through the entry into Arkwright Street. James Cunliffe, a labourer standing at the corner of Mellor and Arkwright Streets, caught Phelan's coat, but the Irishman pulled free after firing over his assailant's shoulder. Cunliffe continued the chase up Mellor Street and Phelan fired another shot in his direction, aiming at the ground. At the corner of Mellor and Anthony streets the plucky Cunliffe brought the big Dublinman to the ground – Phelan was five foot eleven and weighed thirteen stone. Two policemen were on the scene before the crowd could give Phelan a worse pummelling. He was taken to Rose Hill Bridewell.

The victim, Thomas Lovelady, was an 18-year-old general labourer and half-blind since a childhood accident. A policeman on duty, seeing the crowd before the Post Office, investigated and accompanied Thomas in the ambulance to Stanley Road Hospital. The House surgeon, Dr Woodeson, examined the abdominal wound and found a lump at the patient's back – the bullet, which had not penetrated the outer skin. Thomas Lovelady was operated upon that night but died the following evening, after 'a turn for the worse'. The post-mortem, carried out on 13 June, found that Lovelady had bad lungs and was very thin. The bullet had travelled through the whole thickness of his body, rupturing many small blood vessels. Singed holes were found in the victim's coat and waistcoat, evidence that the .38 bullet had been fired at a distance of no more than six inches. The cause of death was exhaustion due to haemorrhage of the abdominal blood vessels.

Detective Inspector John Kearns and Detective Sergeant David Senogles were in charge of the murder case. Kearns examined Phelan's pistol, discovering four bullets in the magazine and a spent cartridge in the breech. Phelan was tight-lipped after Senogles charged him with shooting with intent to murder James Cunliffe in Arkwright Street the previous evening. Phelan asked where the street was, and, on hearing the answer, denied the charge. He maintained that he was Albert Finchley, a native of New Orleans, a fireman who worked on ships trading with England. For the past two years, he said, he had moved between London, Liverpool, Hull, Glasgow and Southampton. He reserved his right to stay silent about his missing companion. At the proceedings at Dale Street Police Court the same morning, Phelan refused to answer questions, save that he was Albert Finchley from New Orleans. He was remanded in custody for seven days.

At this stage – while Thomas Lovelady was still alive – the police thought the fugitive gunman was another American, aged about 30 years, height five foot six or seven inches, medium build, pale complexion, clean-shaven and with very dark hair brushed back. The description from Detective Sergeant Senogles also stated that the man was dressed in a blue serge suit, with collar and tie, and was in possession of a revolver he would not hesitate to use. The police carried out an exhaustive search of local boarding-houses and watched the exits of the city. Two suspects were arrested in Liverpool, one in Manchester, but were soon released.

Wednesday, 13 June, was a bad day for Phelan. Lovelady had died the previous evening and now he was before the stipendiary magistrate again in the forenoon and remanded until Friday, the date of the inquest. Phelan denied the charge of wilful murder, calling it 'a deliberate malicious falsehood' and pleading that he had not been in the shop at the time the shot was fired, which was strictly true. He stuck to his version of events in the afternoon when Senogles visited him in his cell in the Main Bridewell and charged him with the murder. That was at 4.10 p.m.

Scarcely back in his office, Detective Sergeant Senogles returned at the request of the prisoner. Phelan now made a lengthy statement, maintaining that the shots he had fired were aimed (over the head, into the ground) to scare off his pursuers. Giving McAteer's proper name and Dublin address, Phelan insisted that he did not believe 'that McAteer would shoot at anybody', only 'to frighten people with the same as I did'. He completed his voluntary statement with a detailed account of how he had obtained the firearms. Phelan asked to see Senogles again on the Thursday, saying he 'was desirous of turning King's Evidence' and wished 'to explain everything'. His confession was a supplement to what he had disclosed the previous afternoon: details of the bungled raid, the involvement of Cully and other IRA men, and more damning evidence against Jack Braddock and Gus Power.

Jim Phelan had two court appearances on 15 June. The first was obligatory, in the police court to hear the charges proffered against Braddock and Power under the Explosive Substances Act. Power had made a statement about how he had disposed of the ammunition and the .32 pistol, which police had found in the meantime. Braddock strongly denied that he had anything to do with the 'raid episode'. Both were kept in custody. Phelan was then brought into the dock and formally charged with Lovelady's murder. The Public Prosecutor asked for a further remand of seven days in Phelan's case. The Judge requested the accused whether he had anything to say against a further remand. Phelan answered in the negative, adding that he wished to attend the inquest.

The inquest was a short affair, adjourning until 28 June because the evidence was not yet complete. After listening to the witness James Lovelady, the jury left to view the body. The proceedings were really over when a squad of policemen and the handcuffed prisoner entered the court. Phelan was given pencil and paper to take notes while the depositions were read out to him. However, he wrote nothing, declined to comment and thanked the court. Liverpool CID then issued a 'Hue and Cry' for the 'wanted gunman', which was disseminated locally and in the North of Ireland:

> John McAteer, soubriquet M'Ginty, a native of Newry Ireland, aged 28 years, 5 ft. 8 in., medium build, blue-grey eyes, dark brown hair, clean-shaven face, sallow complexion, old scar on upper lip (believed right side), dressed in grey or navy blue suit, dark shoes, black socks, and felt hat, soft collar and tie, or white silk muffler. He has been a seaman and has visited the USA and Mexico. He is known to be a dangerous gunman and has worked with the IRA. His brother is now interned in Mountjoy Prison, Dublin. He filled a prominent part in the unemployed demonstration in Dublin in February 1922, and his photograph is believed to have appeared in the Dublin papers about that time. He is believed to be known at the following addresses:
> 18 Connaught Street West, Hyde Park, London
> 10 North [Great] Clarence Street, Dublin
> 17 Gardiner Place, Dublin
> Flurry Buildings, Edenstadder [Edentober], Newry, Co. Down [Co. Armagh]
> Crowban [Crowbane], Newry, Co. Down.
> He also has relatives in this city.
> Please have every possible enquiry made at all likely places with a view to his arrest. It is particularly requested that watch should be kept on outward bound ships, as he may endeavour to leave the city.

The police later offered a reward of £50 for information leading to McAteer's arrest.[14] That was a lot more than the Liverpool GPO had established was missing from the Sub-Post Office till: £3.5s.4½d. And a man had to die for it.

One week after the inquest, Phelan, Braddock and Power were again in Liverpool Police Court, at a sitting to hear evidence with the view to committing Phelan for trial at Manchester Assizes. He was charged with the wilful murder of Thomas Lovelady, with the intent to murder James Cunliffe and with being in illegal possession of a firearm and explosive substances (bullets). The prosecution against Braddock and Power was confined to explosives; they were not accused of being accessories to murder. The local men who had downed Phelan in the street during the chase were called to the witness stand, as were the young ladies from the sub-post office. Miss Lovelady did not recognise the bulky figure of Phelan in the dock as being one of the robbers, but because he was identified by other witnesses and had made a full confession himself, that part of her statement was of no consequence.

The Public Prosecutor drew attention to a particularity of English law: that if two or more persons set out with an unlawful intention, and in carrying it out cause the death of a person, they are all equally responsible. Phelan, then, had to carry the can and was therefore a candidate for the gallows. He was again remanded, whereas Braddock and Power were released on bail. During his last court appearance in Liverpool, on 28 June, Phelan was incriminated by witnesses and by Detective Sergeant Senogles, who read out the long depositions he had taken at Phelan's request. The accused did not question any of the witnesses or make a new statement, merely asking that part of his deposition be read a second time to the jury. The jurymen found him guilty of the charges and he was committed for trial at Manchester Assizes.

At the one-day jury trial on 9 July, prosecuting counsel argued strongly that, with bank raids rife in the country at the time, there was no political motivation for the crime, 'a common murder committed by desperadoes'. Interestingly, in his autobiography published a quarter of a century later, Jim Phelan wrote that the botched hold-up 'had no connection with Irish politics, was an armed robbery (of four pounds, I believe)'.[15] This question of motive did not detain the court, which heard several witnesses. The defending counsel, Mr Maxwell Fyfe, made the submission that there was no case to go before the jury, but was overruled by Justice Branson. That the fugitive McAteer was acting separately in firing the shot *after* Phelan had fled the scene had no relevance in English Law. The German phrase *mitgefangen, mitgehangen* (caught together, hanged together) seems apt and with McAteer still at large, Phelan would have to carry the full responsibility alone. No witnesses were called for the defence. The jury needed only 30 minutes to pronounce their 'guilty' verdict. Justice Branson then placed the black cap on top of his wig and sentenced James Phelan to death by hanging. The condemned man had nothing to say. As he was being led down to the cells, 'an audible sob' was heard from the body of the court.

It was Phelan's first serious offence and he was to be hanged for it. In Manchester's Strangeways Prison there was time to reflect, for example, on the personal details of the prisoner on the index-card in the slot of his cell door, which gave his bodily weight as 13 stone 4 lbs. That was a vital piece of information for the King's Hangman, for he tied a sack of sand, approximating to the weight of the prisoner, to the other end of the rope, to break his fall and his neck, neatly. Knowing he was for the Big Drop, Phelan's main feeling, initially, was not anger, but sorrow: a 28-year-old looking older than his years, with enough experience of 'life-battering' to outdo the misdeeds of ten Dublin tenements he knew so well and no more roads to wander. He was, in his own words, 'dying but not sick', hurrying, with each passing day, to the 'mist at the end of the bog road'.

A glimmer of hope remained: his application to the Court of Criminal Appeal in London, which examined the case on 27 July. His counsel, Mr Maxwell Fyfe, did his best, submitting that it was unproven that the two men had entered the sub-post office with 'a common design to overcome resistance'. He argued further that the carrying of a revolver in order to frighten people was not sufficient evidence to condemn a man for murder, especially since Phelan had drawn it *after* he had left the shop. Fyfe's strongest point, that the appellant had made good his escape when McAteer fired the fatal shot, made no impression because both men had come for the same illegal purpose and the act of one would fix the guilt of both. The Chief Justice reiterated this cornerstone of English law in his judgement, dismissing the appeal since he saw no reason to interfere with the sentence.[16]

The hanging was scheduled for 15 August. The warders were friendly on this last leg of the legal drama. They were often older men, who told Jim Phelan of previous hangings and how the condemned had gone to their end, peacefully in the rarest of cases. Phelan did not speak openly of his fears, preferring to play the good-humoured Dublinman, reading Cervantes or playing cards with another ex-seaman, a young warder who talked at length about his garden. Phelan was pleased to read that there was no mention of 'perturbed behaviour' on his part in the occurrence book kept by the head warder. The volume chronicled the last days of candidates for the rope, in order that prison staff would be prepared for violence in the last minutes. As the date drew near, Phelan was determined that he was not going to walk to his death, like the cattle in Dublin's Prussia Street being led to the axe on a rope. No, he would attack the first of the squad to enter his cell and take the hangman with him, at least. He knew that all objects or furniture which could be used in a struggle would be removed on the night before a hanging. Still, he had a metal bar hidden, the kind of weapon he had used against the Dublin Metropolitan Police in 1913.

As a lover of song and Dublin city lore, Phelan may have mused over the words of that wistfully defiant ballad, 'The Night Before Larry Was Stretched', the tale of another hanging, written in Dublin's Newgate Gaol chant of the 1780s. Phelan wanted no truck with the clergyman offering him solace, just like Larry in the ballad:

> Then clergy came in with his book,
> He spoke him so smooth and so civil:
> Larry tipped him the Kilmainham look,
> And pitched his big wig to the devil;

And Phelan had decided his ending would not be so sad and expected:

> When he came to the old numbing chit,
> He was tucked up so neat and so pretty,
> The rumbler jogged him off from his feet,
> And he died with his face to the city;

But Phelan did not meet the hangman, nor did he have that ultimate round of man-to-man brawling which was his second nature. On 10 August the Home Secretary in the Bonar Law cabinet, W.C. Bridgeman, commuted two death sentences to penal servitude for life. The more prominent case concerned Alexander Mason, who had shot and killed a taxi-driver in Brixton and on whose behalf a public petition was organised and supported by several MPs.[17] Jim Phelan was also 'respited', presumably because he had not fired the fatal shot, unlike the murderer Mason. Phelan had no sympathising circle in the outside world, his crime had no Irish republican tag to it and he had not used the courtroom as a political platform. He had been in political movements but was never of them, too much of an individualist 'not to recognise the court', as the IRA canon demanded. Nonetheless he did the communist movement one service before starting his prison stretch.

After Phelan's confession to Detective Sergeant Senogles in June, Detective Inspector Moore interviewed Jack Braddock at his home in Fell Street and had the house searched. Neither ammunition nor weapons were found. At the assizes trial of Braddock and Power after the commutation of Phelan's capital sentence, the following dialogue took place between the 'lifer' and prosecuting counsel:

> Did you say to the police on June 13, 'I have previously borrowed a .22 pistol from John Braddock'?
> I did not.

By withdrawing his 'King's Evidence', Phelan destroyed the prosecution case. He went back to Strangeways, while Braddock and Power walked out of the court as free men.[18]

The press titled Jim Phelan 'the silent witness', a soubriquet which gained him some credit among the professional criminals he met in his gaol odyssey before being released in 1938: Strangeways, Maidstone, the chain-gang in Dartmoor, Parkhurst on the Isle of Wight, Winson Green in Birmingham and London's Wormwood Scrubs. To his surprise he found he had considerable kudos among the 'wide men' because he had 'taken the rap' for McAteer, 'a big shot among the wide men'. In his sociological sketch of prison inmates, Phelan distinguished between the 'mugs' or 'steamers', the small-time or incidental criminals who were forever bewailing their ill-luck at being caught and treated unfairly by the courts, and the 'wide men', the professional thieves, confidence-tricksters, bank-robbers and safe-breakers, who took their time in the 'stir' (prison) as a risk of their trade. They made sure they got 'cushy' jobs inside, in the library or the kitchens, 'counting down the calendar' as best as the conditions would allow. His friendship with this clientele, Phelan insists, 'saved my life and my reason'.[19]

On his release in 1938 Jim Phelan rented a bed-sit in Camden Town, and took to writing. He published over twenty volumes of short stories, an autobiography and pastiches from the world of long-term prisoners, tramps and travelling folk. Towards the end of his life, he was a well-known script-writer and radio personality. References to McAteer or Braddock in his writings are oblique, for he was not going to let the authorities know anything as long as his 'mates' were still alive.[20]

NOTES

1. Jack and Bessie Braddock, *The Braddocks* (London 1963).
2. Millie Toole, *Mrs Bessie Braddock M.P.* (London 1957).

3. Emmet O'Connor, 'Waterford and IRA Gun-Running, 1917–22', *Decies*, 57, 2001, pp. 181–93. See also, idem, 'Communists, Russia and the IRA, 1920–1923', *The Historical Journal*, 46 , 1, 2003, pp. 115–31.
4. C. Desmond Greaves, *Liam Mellows and the Irish Revolution* (London 1987), pp. 327–28; Barry McLoughlin, 'Visitors and Victims: British Communists in Russia between the Wars', in John McIlroy, Kevin Morgan and Alan Campbell (eds), *Party People, Communist Lives. Explorations in Biography* (London 2001), p. 212.
5. RGASPI, f. 495, o. 100, d. 225, ll. 2–3.
6. Eunan O'Halpin, *Defending Ireland. The Irish State and Its Enemies since 1922* (Oxford 1999), pp. 20–22.
7. *The Times*, 31 May 1923, p. 11.
8. *The Times*, 19 June 1923, p. 16.
9. *Workers' Republic*, 3 February 1923, p. 1.
10. The account of the botched hold-up is based on press reports and the court file – PRO, ASSI 52/345.
11. Phelan, *The Name's Phelan*, pp. 277–80.
12. Toole, *Mrs Bessie Braddock*, p. 90.
13. *The Workers' Republic*, 29 April 1922, p. 2.
14. *The Newry Reporter*, 16 June 1923, p. 3; 21 June, 1923, p. 5.
15. Phelan, *The Name's Phelan*, p. 281.
16. *The Times*, 28 July 1923, p. 4.
17. *The Manchester Guardian*, 11 August 1923, p. 7.
18. Toole, *Mrs Bessie Braddock*, pp. 88–90.
19. Jim Phelan, *Meet the Criminal Classes* (London 1969), pp. 13–29.
20. See Jim Phelan, *Nine Murderers and Me* (London 1967).

Sailor's Friend

The Liverpool CID, Scotland Yard and the Royal Ulster Constabulary (RUC) clung to the outside chance that Seán McAteer might return to his native place of Flurry Bridge on the new state border or perhaps visit his relatives in County Down. They thought they had their quarry when, on 1 August 1923, the RUC arrested a returned native with an American accent in Dromore. The man said his name was Samuel Magennis, a sailor who had been to Liverpool quite recently. The suspect was charged in a special court and brought to Belfast for interrogation by the Liverpool CID. Exhaustive enquiries were made which confirmed the statements made by Magennis and he was released from Crumlin Road Gaol on 10 August.[1]

It is highly unlikely that McAteer visited his home or Dublin, for the trail was too hot and he could expect no refuge from the Free State authorities. On 15 June, four days after he had fired the lethal shot, he was issued with certification by Tom Bell, Political Secretary of the CPGB. The typewritten piece of cloth, which McAteer probably had sewn into the collar of his overcoat, confirmed that he was a political refugee from Ireland and was being commended to the Moscow headquarters of International Red Help by the British Communist leadership.[2] McAteer must have made his way to London and met Bell in order to arrange for his passage to Soviet Russia and to agree on his new identity. The new name, David Twist, sounded very English, Dickensian in fact, and may have been the idea of Bell, an older man and self-educated labour veteran.

Most visits by British communists to Moscow at that time were clandestine affairs without official documents. The route was by ship to a north German port, usually Hamburg, and then on to Berlin in order to receive a visa from the Soviet Embassy. In the German capital McAteer met Elena Stasova, Lenin's ascetic former secretary, known as 'Comrade Absolute'. At that time she was in charge of the Women's Department of the Comintern, based in

Berlin. Her name, however, came to be associated more with the organisation she had co-founded in December 1922 to help revolutionaries all over the world – International Red Help, which was known in Russia under its acronym MOPR.

By mid-July McAteer was in Moscow, where the Comintern supported his application for political refugee status.[3] Since the 1917 Revolution a government commission had allowed roughly 100,000 persecuted revolutionaries, in the main Russian repatriates, to settle within Soviet borders. In 1923 MOPR set up its own commission for political asylum-seekers, granting 3,700 official status that year. The political refugees, mainly Poles, Germans, Hungarians and Bulgarians, were distributed to official homes in Moscow, Minsk, Leningrad and Odessa. The last city had two buildings, with living space for 230 persons, for incoming refugees.[4]

Odessa, McAteer's home for the next fourteen years, was a vibrant city on the north-west coast of the Black Sea, a cosmopolitan twin to Marseilles or Naples. The city was an imperial idea, not an old urban settlement but a fort ceded by the Turks in 1792. The Russian outpost was built and planned for Catherine the Great by French aristocrats, who ran the city's affairs until 1814. In the early years of the ice-free port, the commercial language was Italian and most of the shipping business was in the hands of Greeks. Odessa became a Russian-language enclave surrounded on three sides by Ukrainian peasants, a city living from the wheat it exported from as far away as Poland, and from the foreign capital it attracted in the last quarter of the nineteenth century. The Belgians had established sugar refineries and a modern tramway, the Germans had provided gas lighting and the British had built a new waterworks. What gave Odessa its distinctive stamp was also the large Jewish population which had fled south to avoid the trade restrictions imposed on them in the Russian Empire by the 'May Laws' of 1882. A census of native languages spoken in the city in 1897 revealed that almost a third of the inhabitants spoke Yiddish, which is akin to German; one-half spoke Russian, with only one in every twenty speaking Ukrainian as a native tongue. That percentage was almost as high as those speaking Polish as their first language and, as in many Russian regions, there was also a German minority engaged in model farming.[5]

Most of Odessa's Jews were poor, living in their ghetto, the Moldavanka. Many Jewish families hoped their progeny could also become world-famous musicians, like the Odessa child prodigies Jascha Heifetz or Efrem Zimbalist, but gifted offspring were as likely to turn to politics, like Lev Trotsky and the militant Zionist Vladimir Jabotinsky, or to writing, like Isaac Babel. The sequence with the runaway pram trundling down the Odessa Steps in Eisenstein's *Battleship Potemkin* is the best-known visual image of the seaport, while Babel's short stories with their inimitably colourful prose are Odessa's most famous literary tribute to itself. Babel's tales about his native city recount his break with the strict Jewish Orthodox education imparted in the Talmud Torah and the teeming life of the Moldavanka, especially its Jewish gangsters. In the aftermath of the abortive 1905 Revolution, there were widespread pogroms in the city and workers' unity remained a fragile concept.

The Bolsheviks did not establish an organisation in Odessa until June 1917. Their subsequent seizure of power was an alliance of Jews and Russians against Ukrainian nationalism as represented by the new State parliament, the Rada, in Kiev. The multi-ethnic Red Guards of Odessa, who for a while were relatively independent of the local Soviets and the Bolshevik Party, prevented pogroms against the Jewish sector of the population during the revolutionary and Civil War periods. In those heady days, even Odessa's underclass, the soldiers' widows, the professional criminals and the jobless, formed their own Soviet and were prominent in the Red Guards.[6] This anarchic element, paired with the mixed ethnic composition of the population, gave Odessa a special disreputable flair often found in important ports. The local dialect was a mixture of capriciously ungrammatical Russian and Yiddish with many foreign loan-words. As late as the 1990s, shoppers at Odessa's markets were delighted to be still greeted by the respectful *monsieur* or *madame*.[7]

Seán McAteer was fortunate to have been sent to such an exotic and climatically attractive part of the USSR. His first job, however, as a machinist in the docks, was probably seen as a waste of his talents and he was soon taken on as a propagandist in Odessa's International Seamen's Club (Interklub). The clubs were an idea of the communist trade-union international, the Profintern, which established International Propaganda Committees (IPK) to recruit foreign sailors for communism. The local IPKs had another function, namely to employ communist activists as smugglers of propaganda, secret correspondence and Party cadres from one continent to another. These committees therefore collaborated closely with OMS, the courier and communication service of the Comintern, and perforce also with representatives of the Soviet secret police GPU (later NKVD).

The business of the seamen's clubs was – on paper at least – supervised by the local Port Bureau, which consisted of a party nominee and a delegate each from the three Russian transport unions (transport, waterways, railways). However, because the clubs were seen as a creation of the Profintern, which coordinated the activities of the Port Bureaux, the interest of local trade unions in the clubs was often perfunctory. After approximately a year as an instructor for English-speaking sailors at Odessa's Interklub, McAteer was posted as manager to the newly established Sailors' Club at Nikolaiev, a Black Sea port on the estuary of the Bug about 100 kilometres north-west of Odessa. His workplace was very near the harbour, in a run-down building owned by the port authority. McAteer was in charge of a cleaning woman and an Italian-born instructor, who spoke Greek. The club was financed in the usual way, with Profintern headquarters in Moscow providing about 60 per cent of the wage-bill and the local transport unions a further third. The remainder came from the port authority, as the club had a right to a tenth of the profits accruing to the Soviet Merchant Marine (Sovtorgflot) by its sale of provisions to the foreign ships docked at the port. An internal report of the Profintern on the Nikolaiev club (May 1925) was mainly positive ('no disagreements among the staff'), but criticised the shabby state of the club and the lack of funds for propaganda, factors which allegedly had led to a drop in visitor traffic. McAteer, the organiser of excursions, concerts and evening get-togethers with the foreign seafarers, was held to be valuable:

> Comrade Twist is an energetic Irishman and a member of the Party. He is fully capable of coping with his work and with fostering relations with local Party organisations.[8]

By contrast, the investigating commission was totally dissatisfied with the Odessa Interklub, which probably explains why McAteer was soon sent back there. The club premises consisted of four rooms and was about a twenty-minute walk from the shipping berths. The deputy secretary of the Port Bureau and the *de facto* manager of the club, Tsesarsky, was held to be politically illiterate and was accused of running the place for profit. Other members of the Port Bureau showed no initiative and had come together only once in two years to discuss the club's affairs. There was no buffet, Tsesarsky did not get on with the Italian instructor Polano and closed the club every evening at 9 p.m., far too early for *matelots* out on a spree. Polano was also hampered in his work by the Italian consul, who threatened Italian sailors, the biggest sailor contingent visiting the port, with reprisals on their return to fascist Italy should they visit the club or take part in any of the concerts or excursions it organised. The commission recommended Tsesarsky's removal and the recruitment of communists with foreign language skills.[9]

Seán McAteer's main difficulty in 1924–25 was one which plagued every Soviet citizen at one time or another – lack of documentation. In order to join the Soviet Party he had to prove that he had been a member of the Communist movement in Ireland. As a Profintern employee he was expected to join the VKP(b), but was hindered initially by the fact that the old CPI was dissolved in early 1924. Letters of recommendation by Peter and Jim Larkin were mislaid by Bob Stewart, the CPGB representative at the ECCI. Only after his successor, Ernest Brown, and Jim Larkin had intervened for McAteer (by certifying his revolutionary credentials) was 'Comrade Twist' accepted as a member of the Soviet Communist Party, as and from 23 May 1925, with membership acknowledged since 1921. This length of service (*stazh*) was just as important as the new Party card, a recognition that its holder was an experienced and trusted cadre. McAteer was a committed communist, but he also knew he would never gain the trust of the Soviet authorities or hold down an important job unless he could join the VKP(b). Hence his three, increasingly urgent, applications for membership.[10]

Around the time of his admittance to the ranks of the Bolsheviks, McAteer met his future wife, Tamara Terletskaia, a hospital physician. Their daughter Maria was born in 1927. From 1925 the popularity of the Seamen's Clubs rose, owing to more focused policies and the practice of meeting the sailors, when possible, on their ships and inviting them to a club evening. In 1925 over four thousand sailors visited the Interklub in Odessa's Sailors' Palace, one-half of whom were Italians and one-quarter from British-owned ships.[11] For the following year the figures for Odessa fairly plummeted since McAteer, 'who had carried out the work successfully in the first half-year was transferred to Nikolaev'.

Tsesarsky, still closing the club between eight and nine in the evening and sending the curious sailors out on the street, was seen as the biggest hindrance to agitation among the foreign crews. He was accused of running the club in a high-handed bureaucratic fashion, and as a commercial enterprise. The Moscow IPK Executive was powerless since the local unions had refused hitherto to sanction Tsesarsky's dismissal.[12]

The chairman of Odessa's Waterfront Union stated that the unions provided funds and the club premises, but had no control over Tsesarsky's conduct, which, it admitted, was scandalous since prostitutes were now frequenting the premises. The blame, the chairman wrote in an incoherent letter to the Central Committee of his union in Moscow, lay really with the Profintern, which had sent an inspection team to Odessa in October 1926, persons more interested in an 'away match' work assignment (*komandirovka*) at the balmy seaside than setting things right. The case was typical of the infighting between Soviet institutions in apportioning blame when two or more bodies were responsible. Tsesarsky and Polano were fired at the end of 1926, to be succeeded by a new manager who had to run operations on his own since 'Twist' was in Nikolaiev.[13] The man in charge of Odessa Seamen's Club for the next decade was Levio Amadei, an Italian political immigrant who had joined the Italian CP in 1921, the French section of the Comintern in 1922 and the Soviet Party (like McAteer) in 1925.

Amadei's report on the club's activities during January 1927 showed that he unleashed a veritable storm of activities for the incoming sailors, including a boxing match between German and Italian seamen. His countrymen asked him the usual questions: Why were there homeless children on the streets? Why was there private trading in the USSR? Why does one see well-dressed people and beggars? Why are the German colonist-farmers emigrating to America? He believed that the number of sailors from British ships visiting the club had fallen because these were of Chinese, Indian or Arab origin and easily intimidated by their white Anglo-Saxon officers. The intimidation of Italian sailors was far worse, with the Consul visiting the Italian ships and holding assemblies where the crew members had to solemnly promise not to visit the Profintern club. If they did, he often forced the captain to withdraw their seamen's papers, which had led to several threats of strike. Another factor affecting the organisation of excursions and visits to the Red

Army Club was the decision of the Waterfront Union to halve the monthly subsidy to the Interklub.[14]

Amadei, whose knowledge of English was almost non-existent, had to do without his 'English instructor', Twist-McAteer, for the greater part of the next two years. On 5 March 1927 McAteer received a telegram at his flat from Achkanov, head of the IPK in the Profintern, summoning him to Moscow as soon as possible. The Irishman was to be sent to Vladivostok with a certain Comrade Alex and from there to Shanghai. McAteer received the necessary certification from Achkanov, who requested the Interklub in Vladivostok to afford the emissary every assistance. The aim of the mission, initially at least, was to supervise the printing of the Japanese edition of the Profintern propaganda sheet *Krasnyi Moriak Azii* (Red Seaman of Asia) and have it smuggled from the Soviet Far East to Japan. The Japanese CP had been illegal since its foundation in 1922 and Shanghai was the next station after Vladivostok on the smuggling route for Russian agents and communist literature destined for Japan.

McAteer wrote to Achkanov that the Vladivostok Interklub was too far away from the docks, with room for only twenty visitors. This made his work or agitation and political discussion almost impossible. He and others considered the Japanese editor of the fortnightly news-sheet to be 'politically unfitted for the work' but, as nobody else knew Japanese, McAteer wanted to know how one could examine that its contents were in line with Profintern policy and who, in the last resort, was responsible for the paper. He ended his first report with a complaint ('most annoying') that the Profintern in Moscow had issued him with such a shoddy false passport that his departure for China was being delayed by at least ten days.[15]

Vladivostok was but an interlude for McAteer. With the prospect of the Kuomindang achieving full military victory in China on the strength of its alliance with the Comintern, which provided the 'national-revolutionary' Chinese forces with arms and Soviet military advisers, the propaganda apparatus of the Soviets for Japan would be moved to Shanghai.[16] In expectation of that victory, the official Soviet agents were concentrated in early 1927 at the seat of the Guomindang government in Wuhan, or in Shanghai, the destination of 'Twist' and 'Alex', where they would meet the emissaries of the Comintern's Eastern Bureau.

On McAteer's arrival in Shanghai, the official Kuomindang-Communist alliance was already breaking down. Chiang Kai-shek, the most successful of the nationalist Chinese generals, was confronted by communist uprisings in the wake of his successful offensives against the provincial warlords. Before he entered Shanghai, a general strike had broken out. Factories were occupied and the police disarmed by the workers, who attempted to attack the colonial enclaves in the city. Chiang Kai-shek, who wanted to free himself from dependence on the Soviets, needed recognition by the Western powers. He was not prepared to tolerate a repeat of the attacks on foreigners, as in Nanking in March, when a British cruiser had to rescue the white colony under fire. The Comintern, still hoping that the united front with the Chinese nationalists could hold, ordered the Shanghai strikers to avoid conflict with Guomindang troops entering the city and to bury their weapons. Chiang turned on his erstwhile allies, taking decisive action against communist organisations and striking workers, of whom thousands were shot out of hand. The Shanghai catastrophe played a part in the last round of the power-struggle between Stalin and Trotsky. The latter, a vociferous opponent of the Russian-backed alliance of nationalists and communists in China, felt vindicated, while Stalin, in a typical manoeuvre, plagiarised his opponent's policy and ordered a purely communist uprising in Canton in December 1928, another fiasco, which ended in a bloodbath and a victory for Chiang.[17]

Seán McAteer's wife stated that her husband had spent the years 1927–29 on 'illegal work' in China. Since there is documentary evidence that he was again working in the Odessa club in September 1928,[18] his commission may have been a roving one, with lengthy stays in Vladivostok. That port regained its status as a relay station for the Communist International in respect of transporting literature and agents to Asia following the bloody disasters in China.[19] With the 'White Terror' still raging in Shanghai, McAteer hardly resided there but may have been employed by Comintern's communications service (OMS) as a courier. A letter of recommendation by Tom Bell, written in March 1929, suggests that McAteer was 'taken on' by some clandestine Soviet institution.[20]

To further complicate the scanty facts of McAteer's 'secret' career, 'Comrade Alex', the other emissary sent by the International Propaganda Committee (IPK) to Shanghai, ended up working for

Soviet Military Intelligence (GRU). Alexander Ulanovskii, two years older than McAteer and a native of Odessa, was gaoled as a teenager for anarchist activities. He subsequently emigrated, returned to Russia and, after taking part in the Revolution and the Civil War, worked for Soviet espionage in Berlin. At the beginning of the 1920s he again changed agencies, becoming one of the main organisers of the seamen's clubs and running the IPK network from Hamburg, the most important European base for dispatching secret Soviet correspondence and agents overseas. Although sent to China in 1927 on Profintern business, he joined GRU one year later and was *rezident* in China in the years 1929–30.[21]

According to the scattered and imprecise data available, Seán McAteer, now once more David Ivanovich Twist, returned to Odessa, his family and his old job at the Interklub before moving on to a higher post in the port in 1932. He might have ended up in Moscow, as permanent representative of James Larkin Snr's Irish Worker League at the ECCI. In March 1928, a year before he cut all formal ties with Moscow, Larkin had nominated 'John Twist' for the post. The Edentober man was a friend of the Larkin clan, one of the few people Larkin Snr trusted to put his standpoint to the Moscow bureaucracy. Having a man on the spot, Larkin felt, would counteract the influence of the CPGB in Irish Communist affairs. The suggestion was not acted upon.[22]

The 1929–31 period was interspersed for McAteer by short transfers to clubs in Mariupol (Sea of Azov) and to Poti in Georgia, or by a semester studying Economics at the Transport Academy in Leningrad. The Interklub in Odessa was still being managed by Amadei. He was often at daggers drawn with the local unions, who wanted to replace him with a Russian but, as he was obviously efficient, he kept the post.[23] In the late 1920s his more formidable enemy was the Italian Consul, Meriano, who was as assiduous as ever in preventing Italian sailors visiting the club premises. Those Italian sailors who wanted to contact their Russian class brothers had to do it on the street or at secret meetings organised by activists of the VKP(b) or the Komsomol. Amadei held Meriano to be behind the smashing of the newspaper kiosk in front of the club and the recruiting of agents from among the Italian political refugees living in the port. Following another case of imprisonment in Italy of a sailor who had dared to frequent the Interklub, the secret police (GPU) arrested three Italian refugees, but one managed to escape abroad and write about the club in Italian newspapers. Other Italians protested against the arrests to a Profintern investigator, who recommended they be expelled from the city.[24]

The work of the sailors' clubs in the USSR was increasingly orientated towards topical themes (defence of the Soviet Union, propagating the industrialisation programme). The ulterior motive, however, was to establish as many IPK cells as possible on the visiting foreign vessels in order to organise strikes for political motives or against the wage-reductions being imposed during the slump. A strike organised by the Hamburg IPK in autumn 1931 spread to the USSR, where German crews struck with the assistance of Interklub personnel in the Black Sea ports.[25] In Odessa, Amadei and his staff succeeded in setting up over forty cells on foreign ships in 1930, but that was due to intensive campaigning by 'brigades' organised by the VKP(b) since the interest of the local unions in internationalist propaganda remained minimal.[26] In the following year Amadei reported that he had recruited over four thousand foreign seamen for the IPK and organised excursions to Odessa factories (273) and discussions at the club (154) between the seafarers and local workers.[27]

This level of activity fell drastically in 1932, owing to factors which throw an interesting light on the competing interests of the Soviet State and the social reality it had created but sought to hide from foreign eyes. The problem was that the Interklub now had two competitors, both of which were foreign-currency bars open until 3 a.m. and offering all kinds of hard drinks to seafarers out on the town. One of these dens was run by a local character who had been the landlord of a brothel – house of indulgence (*dom terpimosti*) was the Russian euphemism – in pre-1917 Odessa. He had nothing to fear since he was manager of an outlet of the nationalised food consortium. Neither had his main competitor managing the second watering hole for thirsty foreigners. He was employed by TORGSIN, the shop and bar chain set up by the government and selling goods against foreign currency only. International solidarity as exemplified by the Interklub came a poor second to the priority of accruing scarce foreign currency which would be used for importing machinery during the First Five-Year Plan. The GPU tried to stop the traffic in foreign currency by forcing the captain to deposit the purser's cash in a sealed box, which was opened by a GPU officer at sailing time. But frequently the captain of a vessel tricked the Chekists and, using his own funds, bought tokens for himself and his crew from a TORGSIN representative who visited the ships with the pilot. Those sailors, who had neither tokens nor foreign currency, were accosted by the crowd of mostly young toughs congregating outside the bars who were interested in the sailors' clothes or shoes and offered cigarettes, food, TORGSIN tokens and the addresses of prostitutes in exchange.

Once inside, the sailors found plenty of 'girls' to dance with and enough hard liquor, while the officers stayed in a separate lounge. Seamen sympathetic to communism were shocked by the open pimping and trafficking in foreign currency and complained to Amadei at the Interklub. Amadei was the initiator of a commission of enquiry comprising representatives of the local Party committee and club staff, which found that the bars were discrediting 'Soviet power'. However, the local Party grandees, probably beneficiaries of kick-back payments, and the badly paid police (*militsiia*), turned a blind eye to the scenes of haggling and drunkenness outside the nightspots. Amadei had little on offer to tempt the carousing crewmen away from these dens of iniquity, as the assortment of food and drink on sale in the Interklub buffet, despite directives from on high, remained unattractive. The 'shortages economy' in 1932, the year of widespread famine in southern Russia and the Ukraine, was evident where the rouble, and not the dollar or the Reichsmark, changed hands.[28]

That year McAteer took a new job, becoming a white-collar employee of the port authority, first as senior reception officer for foreign ships and later as deputy administrative manager in the freight office. It was certainly a career advancement from being Amadei's English-speaking assistant in a dingy dockland club visited more by Italian and German sailors than British or American ones. Because of his forthright attitude, Seán Twist was also making enemies and lost his job with the Merchant Marine in December 1935.

Believing that his dismissal from Sovtorgflot was due to an intrigue, he appealed to the Control Commission of the Odessa Party organisation. As Party credentials were being scrutinised at the time ('verification of Party documents') – Part I of the Party purge which was to last until 1938 – Twist-McAteer's Communist biography was examined. The Comintern confirmed his years in the CPI and his admittance to the Soviet Party in 1925.[29] While his loyalty to Bolshevism was therefore not in question for the time being at least, he, as a foreigner, had no chance against native Russians or Ukrainians in what would now be called a clash of personalities or a mobbing confrontation at the workplace. The decision to strike him from the port authority payroll had probably little to do with his work record, but was a sign of the times: the suspicion generated by the Party leadership and encompassing all spheres of Soviet life since the Kirov murder of 1 December 1934 affected foreigners disproportionately, especially soft targets like this fugitive Irishman with a Soviet passport.

NOTES

1. *Liverpool Daily Post*, 3 August 1923, p. 7; *Newry Reporter*, 4 August 1923, p. 7; *The Times*, 11 August 1923, p. 5.
2. RGASPI, f. 539, o 4, d. 143, l. 7.
3. RGASPI, f. 17, o. 98, d. 4566, l. 16.
4. GARF, f. 8265, o. 1, d. 1, ll. 60–61.
5. Neal Ascherson, *Black Sea* (New York 1995), pp. 136–41.
6. See Tanja Penter, *Odessa 1917: Revolution an der Peripherie* (Cologne 2000).
7. Robert A. Rothstein, 'How It Was Sung in Odessa: At the Intersection of Russian and Yiddish Folk Culture', *Slavic Review*, 60, no. 4 (Winter 2001), pp. 781–801.
8. RGASPI, f. 534, o. 5, d. 161, ll. 37–38.
9. RGASPI, f. 534, o. 5, d. 167, ll. 68–70.
10. RGASPI, f. 17, o. 98, d. 4566; f. 495, o. 218, d. 21.
11. RGASPI, f. 534, o. 5, d. 179, ll. 6–11.
12. Ibid, ll. 160–61.
13. RGASPI, f. 534, o. 5, d. 187, l. 14.
14. Ibid, ll. 24–30.
15. Ibid, ll. 103–4.
16. Ibid, ll. 108–9 (Achkanov to Vladivostok, 29 March 1927).
17. Michael Weiner, 'Comintern in East Asia, 1919–1939', in Kevin McDermott and Jeremy Agnew, *The Comintern. A History of International Communism from Lenin to Stalin* (Houndmills 1996), pp. 163–79. See also Margarete Buber-Neumann, *Kriegsschauplätze der Weltrevolution. Ein Bericht aus der Praxis der Komintern 1919–1943* (Frankfurt 1973), pp. 86–131.
18. RGASPI, f. 534, o. 5, d. 199, l. 47 (request to Moscow for receipts).
19. Ibid, l. 5 (Vladivostok Seamen's Club to Profintern, 13 February 1928).
20. RGASPI, f. 495, o. 198, d. 896, l. 2.
21. A. Kolpadiki and D. Prokhorov, *Imperiia GRU. Ocherki istorii rossiiskoi voennoi razvedi. Kniga vtoraia*, Moscow 2001, p. 422. The British secret service had been trailing Ulanovskii since 1925 and documented his arrest and sentencing in Copenhagen in 1935. See PRO, KV2/1417.
22. RGASPI, f. 495, o. 89, d. 49, ll. 12–16.
23. RGASPI, f. 534, o. 5, d. 187, l. 118 (Amadei to Achkanov, 31 July 1927).
24. RGASPI, f. 534, o. 5, d. 199, ll. 69–72.

25. RGASPI, f. 534, o. 5, d. 227, l. 31. For details of the Hamburg initiative, see Ernst von Waldenfels, *Der Spion der aus Deutschland kam. Das geheime Leben des Seemans Richard Krebs* (Berlin 2002), pp. 106–18.
26. RGASPI, f. 534, o. 5, d. 227, ll. 3–5.
27. RGASPI, f. 534, o. 5, d. 233, l. 35.
28. Ibid, ll. 35–37.
29. RGASPI, f. 17, o. 98. d. 4566, ll. 3, 4, 12, 13.

Last Twist

How does one defend oneself in a totalitarian environment, as a foreigner without allies, an outsider from an entirely different political culture? Seán McAteer was certainly somebody who did not suffer fools gladly, most probably irascible when confronted with incompetence and conceit, and evidently – and recklessly – persistent in combating injustice. He had been, after all, a revolutionary since his teenage years, a member of the Communist Party by choice and not, like many of his colleagues, the holder of the Party card (*bilet*) to further social mobility.

Many of the misunderstandings between McAteer and persons more powerful than himself in Odessa had to do with the interpretation of language. What is uttered by an Anglophone in a spirit of gentle ridicule ('the wind-up') or pure spleen may be taken literally, as an indication of a hostile attitude, and all the more serious for the offended listener because the perceived slight is unexpected since the coded nuances are outside his ken.

Dealing with seafaring folk off the boats or with Odessa's dockers and carters in their own argot was hardly conducive to linguistic differentiation in either Russian or English. Added to that was probably the 'tough guy' way of speaking which McAteer had picked up in the United States (his letters are studded with Americanisms). As a republican from the Louth-Armagh border area, McAteer may have harboured a deep-set bias towards the English. That they showed interest in the internationalist propaganda he was thrusting upon them hardly lessened such a prejudice: the seamen's section of the communist-run Minority Movement in Britain had a low reputation in the Profintern since it was unable to organise IPKs like the Dutch and the Germans and had squandered Moscow funds to feather the nests of CPGB officials.[1]

McAteer's confrontation with his bosses in Odessa, however, went far beyond such suppositions about mentalities or abrasive vocal exchanges. In combating behaviour he saw as unjust and deleterious to the communist cause, McAteer employed topical motifs, Stalinist Newspeak, the epigonal language of Satan (Stalin) to drive out Beelzebub (Trotsky). That was playing with fire, for to accuse superiors or colleagues in 1937 of 'Trotskyism' was tantamount to calling for their permanent removal from society. The February–March 1937 Plenum of Stalin's Central Committee had promulgated that 'Trotskyists', in league with foreign intelligence services, had penetrated all Soviet institutions and were responsible for sabotaging (railway accidents, mine disasters, the drop in industrial output, shortages in raw materials) the 'successes' of the Second Five-Year Plan. Not surprisingly, those feeling themselves threatened by McAteer replied in kind.

The storm that broke over the Irishman's head in the first half of 1937 had been gathering force for years.[2] The instigator of the long intrigue against McAteer was Mordio Piorun, a native of Odessa born in 1884, who worked in the counter-intelligence department of the secret police as an agent and translator. In 1931 the Odessa OGPU, hearing from Moscow that Scotland Yard was interested in 'Twist', ordered Piorun to investigate the foreigner. For the next six years Piorun was McAteer's sinister shadow, but the enquiries produced no evidence of political dissent. According to Piorun, Amadei at the Interklub had complained to him of McAteer's 'arrogant' attitude towards English sailors and that he was not a diligent worker. Because of his commission to unmask political undesirables and 'operatives of foreign spy networks', Piorun was a constant visitor to the offices of the port authority, where McAteer now worked. His superiors there – according to Piorun's testimony – held McAteer to be politically reliable but 'arrogant'. Years of observation on Piorun's part had therefore produced nothing of substance, merely the contention that 'Twist was a quarrelsome character'.

Piorun, having himself appointed to a responsible post at the port authority (manager of the sector for special projects) in March 1935, then undermined McAteer's position from within. In protesting against his sacking, McAteer appealed to his employers, and later to the local Party organisation. He based his case on the fact that Piorun, the man who had taken his job, was not a member of the VKP(b), whereas he was, and of long standing.

The dismissal stood. McAteer was most likely the victim of a whispering or blacklisting campaign preventing him from getting a job where he could have kept his head down – at the shipyards in his own trade, for example. The only employment he could find, and for which he was not qualified, was as an English-language teacher in the Odessa *kombinat* for foreign languages. That institute offered foreign-language courses for many kinds of third-level curricula. In early 1937 McAteer was allotted extra teaching hours at the teacher training college (*pedtechnikum*). Piorun was never far away. In fact, the sleuth's career path followed that of McAteer: instructor (later inspector) of the regional educational department and, from January 1937, teacher of French at the *kombinat*.

McAteer, by self-definition an 'outspoken person', discovered that corruption was rife at his workplace. He made a report on his findings to the VKP(b) City Executive in October 1936. At his insistence a commission was formed. McAteer was a member of it and he succeeded in having the accounts system at the *kombinat* examined. The results exposed: misappropriation of funds, manipulation of the budget balances and having relatives of the *kombinat*'s leading personnel on the payroll who never entered the school. The cultural officer at Party headquarters said the whole business was a personal quarrel, while the investigator of the VKP(b) Control Commission in Odessa wanted to know from Twist what he expected to gain from the whole affair. The commission's chairman, Stepanov, offered the complainant another job, but McAteer refused, saying the protest was not about material things but about morals.

What McAteer had unearthed was probably typical of any Soviet institution since 'achieving' or 'over-achieving' the 'plan' inevitably encouraged 'cooking the books' all the way up the line of command, until the bloated statistics reached the ministry in Kiev or Moscow. His accusations were not made in secret, for he first aired them at a meeting of the Party cell at his workplace. The director, McAteer alleged, had forged a teacher's name on the payroll, pocketing the salary of the fictive pedagogue, and attempted to force his secretary to have sex. That was the last straw: the director and some teachers told McAteer he would 'get it in the neck'. Piorun grimly told the trouble-maker to his face that he would 'fix' him.[3] The exchange of niceties probably occurred when McAteer curtly told Piorun to leave his class, for, as a teacher of French, the inveterate bloodhound had no right to be there.

It was easy to find a pedagogical pretext to discredit teacher Twist. McAteer's formal schooling had ended in his mid-teens. The extant documents in English from his own pen show that he was not good at prose. Against that he was probably under pressure to get through the system (the plan!) students who had no previous knowledge of any foreign tongue and he thus felt that he had to cut corners. In early February 1937 McAteer set papers for eleven students for the semester just ended. Piorun, and a female colleague who taught English, were commissioned by the director of the *kombinat* one month later to examine the marking. Both were of the opinion that McAteer had been too lenient, because his total of mistakes marked on the papers was about 40 per cent beneath theirs.

Perhaps McAteer questioned their findings; in any case Piorun dug deeper, widening the charges from favouring students to one of ideological deviancy. The second report (21 March) alleged that McAteer had passed his students into the next course before the written examinations in February, giving them all the result 5, at the top of the five-point marking system. As regards the written tests, McAteer was accused, either through ignorance or intent, of overlooking mistakes so that all eleven students passed the written exam (1×5, 4×4, 6×3, i.e. no student received the 'failed' grade of 1 or 2). Twist was the head of the English Department, but Piorun, with the help of the Irishman's fellow teachers, questioned his competence:

> These [overlooked] errors belong to the gravest in the English language, for example, the unused gerund and the incorrect use of the definite and indefinite articles and the incorrect sequence of words in a sentence, for without the correct word sequence it is impossible to understand English phrases.

Piorun proceeded to criticise McAteer's use of Charles Kay Ogden's *Basic English: A General Introduction with Rules and Grammar* (London 1930). Ogden (1889–1957) had studied at Magdalene College in Cambridge and translated books from French and German before becoming an editor at the publishing firm of Kegan Paul. His system of teaching English in seven weeks was based on a core vocabulary of 850 words and the general elimination of verbs: 100 'operations', 400 'things', 200 'picturable' words, 100 general 'qualities' and 50 'opposites'. *Basic English* became a world bestseller and was commended for use by the British government of the day and later. Its weakest point is that English relies heavily on up to 4,000 idioms which require the use of nearly 2,000 words, i.e. far more than the vocabulary of *Basic English*. From the start, the scheme, linked to Ogden's plans for 'world peace', was seen by some as a form of linguistic imperialism to keep the 'natives' comically communicative in order to perform their lowly tasks. In Piorun's words, *Basic English* was 'a language created for slaves'. This accusation against the Irishman concerned past behaviour because, as Piorun mentioned in his report, some students had objected to Ogden's scheme, and at a sitting of the English teachers 'Twist was forced to declare that it was necessary to stop teaching this type of English.'

Perhaps there was no primer for teaching English at all at the *kombinat*, either because none had been published in the USSR (Odessa was and is largely russophone) for a student age-group or was not available in such numbers that students and teachers could obtain copies without difficulty. But that did not detain Piorun, who devoted his 'textual analysis' to a dog-eared English schoolbook Twist used and had recommended to his colleagues, the *Royal Readers*. That was the series produced by the publisher Thomas Nelson and Sons (Edinburgh and New York) for use in schools in Great Britain and, with some modifications, in the colonies as well, but not in Ireland where the *Irish National Reader* was the main school primer. The descendants of the original Thomas Nelson (b. 1780), founder of the eponymous publishing house, which has kept its Christian orientation over the years, specialised in cheap Bibles and books for 'the common man', including translations from French and German classics.

McAteer possibly found the book in a second-hand bookshop or in the library of his institute, which still held volumes published in the Tsarist era. It is unknown which volume of the *Royal Readers* he worked through with his students, possibly Volume V, published in 1889. The series were graded as regards tasks to be practised and the degree of difficulty, with the fifth volume revising the contents of earlier ones and offering dictation exercises taken from Civil Service examinations. Each chapter was followed by a vocabulary giving meaning and accentuation and there were set questions after each chapter to test whether or not the student had comprehended the text. The fifth volume offered articles in the natural sciences, geography, poetry, the biographies of 'great men' and verse or rhetoric for recitation. This product of the late Victorian era contains, besides favourite poems from Goldsmith ('The Deserted Village') and Byron ('Waterloo'), pieces from Victor Hugo and the Hungarian revolutionary Lajos Kossuth.

McAteer, unsure of his pedagogical suitability, owing to his early school-leaving age and lack of teaching experience, was embarrassed by the book's title and appearance, tearing out the title page with its image of the coat of arms of the British Royal Family. Arguably, he might have done the same had he lived in Flurry Bridge and taken care over what his daughter Maria was reading at her school. Piorun concluded his prosecution case by stating that the *Royal Readers* volume was 'ideologically harmful' and that its disseminator Twist had urged colleagues to teach from it.

Piorun and *kombinat* director Gorin were not finished yet. They questioned Twist's students and scrutinised their written work, especially what the teacher had actually taught about the economic geography and history of the British Empire. Order No. 43 of 4 May 1937 issued by the *kombinat* and signed by Piorun, Gorin and his secretary Kopelman commenced with the political charge that Twist had falsified English history by imparting it 'in the spirit of bourgeois-reactionary historiography'. Since this was 'a political crime unworthy of a Soviet pedagogue', the accused was to be banned from teaching socio-economic subjects; because he was a member of the VKP(b), Twist's 'unworthy behaviour' was to be referred to his Party organisation. The incorrect method of marking students' exam papers, the Ukrainian text continued, demonstrated that they had been badly prepared for their examinations; since that was attributed to the bad quality of Twist's teaching and proved his unsuitability for the post, 'pedagogue Twist' was to be dismissed forthwith.

Three days later McAteer penned a long letter of complaint to Elena Stasova, the chairwoman of MOPR in distant Moscow. For him she represented the highest ideals of the Revolution and the internationalist spirit of the world movement. He had probably met her only once (1923, in Berlin, on his way to Moscow), but had corresponded with her previously, perhaps in connection with his dismissal from the Soviet Merchant Marine. He now wanted her to know what he had experienced in his teaching career. McAteer was undoubtedly aware that there was little the old revolutionary icon could do, and his letter was as much a call for action against the politics of local cliques as a plea for individual help.

The missive, a mixture of denunciation and pathos, told of the machinations at the *kombinat* and the authorities' inaction (even that of the public prosecutor), but with two self-critical admissions – that he had taught the history of England only to the Stuart period and had 'artificially' allowed students to pass into the next class. He justified his address to Stasova with the argument that 'it is difficult to get any kind of action in this town', hence the long catalogue of incidents and their instigators (Piorun), who were described either as 'Trotskyists' or persons working in their remit:

> My honest opinion is that this town is the base of Trotskyism and notwithstanding many have been arrested, hundreds are still at large, doing their work of robbery, disorganisation and political wrecking of Party work. [. . .] I sincerely trust that you will believe in me, it may be strange that I am always in trouble, but the class struggle is far easier in capitalist countries to combat than in our [Soviet] Union and what I have written is honest and truthful.[4]

Stasova answered by return, reassuring Comrade Twist that he was not disturbing her, informing him that she had turned his letter over to 'the proper organisation' [the NKVD] and encouraging him to write again if he needed assistance.[5] She sent a Russian translation of McAteer's letter to NKVD Commissar Ezhov, but did not comment on its contents in her covering letter.[6]

Following his dismissal from the *kombinat*, McAteer was isolated and awaiting the handling of his case by the Odessa Party organisation. A kangaroo court packed with local functionaries would probably expel him and send the minutes of the sitting to the NKVD. His arrest was the likely outcome, with no prospects of a lucky flight abroad, as in 1923. An outside chance did exist, in colluding in the downfall of those more powerful than himself. The February–March 1937 Plenum of the VKP(b) had made such scenarios permissible, as the published speeches of Stalin and Zhdanov (Party Secretary in Leningrad) revealed: too many regional Party structures were run by potentates who rarely held elections but had their friends, cronies and even family members coopted to leading bodies; in future, secret-ballot elections to all Party posts would be held and the general membership given an opportunity to criticise the work-record of the incumbents.

In April–May 1937 the Party press was full of exhortations to take part in this democratic process, to avail of 'criticism from below'. And McAteer would have read of the much-publicised and, for him encouraging, case of Mrs Nikolaenko, a rank-and-file Communist in Kiev who had protested that there was too much applause when the Ukrainian Party leader Postyshev spoke publicly. Postyshev duly expelled her as a 'counter-revolutionary' but she was reinstated after appealing to Stalin.[7] At 'electoral-reporting' meetings held in April–May 1937, many Party officials were hauled over the coals by the aggregate membership and voted out of office. Countrywide, 55 per cent of the sitting Party committees lost power. In the Odessa region, just over a third of all secretaries and organisers in the VKP(b) cells were removed, and one in five of the newly elected officers was a newcomer.[8]

McAteer could not have known that this participatory democracy was a ruse to deflect pent-up anger from the Politburo, or that it was merely an intermezzo, for most leading Party committees were exterminated in the autumn of 1937. As a good Party member with a sense of grievance, McAteer took *Pravda* at its word. At an aggregate meeting of the Kaganovich City District sometime in May, he attacked Evgenii Veger, the First Secretary of the Regional Party Committee, for protecting 'Trotskyists' (reinstating them in their jobs or giving them new posts in distant regions). In following the 'lessons' of the February–March Plenum, McAteer also alleged that the followers of Trotsky held all important posts in the economic, educational and political life of Odessa and were so strong that 'only complaints to the centre can dislodge' them. He reiterated the scripted plot of the show-trials of August 1936 and January 1937, that enemies wanted to re-establish capitalism in the USSR: Veger was doing nothing about the black-market bazaar which sold everything that was not available in State shops, because 'responsible workers [managers] are working in collaboration with the speculants [speculators] to show the working class the failure of the socialist economy'.[9]

Comrade Twist was thereby risking his own downfall. But these were extraordinary times, with the local *nomenklatura* unsure of itself and the whole country in the midst of a denunciatory hysteria encouraged and driven by initiatives of the Kremlin. On 12 June, Seán McAteer suffered a nervous breakdown. What set it off? Months of harassment and the loss of employment had undermined his emotional stability. He could expect no succour from abroad: he was a Soviet citizen, wanted by the British authorities for murder, and the only person of note who could have intervened, Jim Larkin Snr, had discarded communism years previously. Even if Larkin had been in the good graces of Moscow, any intervention on his part would have been ignored, as Harry Pollitt, leader of the CPGB, discovered when he tried to find out what had happened to the prominent British communist Rose Cohen in 1937–38.[10] Seán McAteer had now nowhere to flee to.

Two more immediate events may have led to McAteer's emotional crisis. First, and more importantly, his wife, Tamara, and daughter, Maria, had left for a two-week holiday, thus depriving him of support he would have badly needed. Second, on 11 June 1937, *Pravda* announced that the case of the 'military conspirators', the marshals of the Red Army, was nearing completion. In fact, their trial behind closed doors ended that evening and the accused were shot in the early hours of 12 June. Public meetings to 'greet' the verdicts were held in every city, on the orders of the Politburo. One of the prominent victims was Iona Iakir, who had started his revolutionary career as a fitter in Odessa and served as Commander of the Kiev Military District between 1925 and 1936. He was highly respected as an expert in military theory and presumably had a sizeable following in Odessa. The arrest and execution of the elite of the Red Army shocked the country.[11]

Seán McAteer, although believing that much was wrong in the Soviet Union, may have looked on the Soviet military command as the last, and incorruptible, bastion of the 1917 Revolution. But now the generals and marshals around Tukhachevskii and Iakir were portrayed as vile plotters linked to the German Army. McAteer, with a military career of sorts to his credit, may have felt that his world was collapsing around him, in a bedlam of conspiracies, subversion and corruption. He probably did not know what or whom to believe any more.

On 12 June McAteer began a drinking bout and made a public nuisance of himself before taking to his bed on 15 June. He wandered around Odessa, sometimes needing help to stagger onwards or homewards. In a bar he foolishly confided in a Party member called Kovalenko that Odessa was in a bad state of affairs and that Veger, the VKP(b) grandee running the city, was a 'Trotskyist'. Kovalenko denounced McAteer to Party headquarters and, on the morning of 15 June, the Irishman, after one hour's leaden stupor, was summoned to the Control Commission of the VKP(b). Still in a drunken state and very vociferous, McAteer repeated his accusation against Veger and was relieved of his Party card. He then made his way to the NKVD building to make a statement, demanding to see an officer from the Foreign Section whom he knew from his dockland years. Probably not making much sense there either, McAteer demanded he be arrested as a foreign spy. His acquaintance told him to go home and 'sleep it off', but kept McAteer's attaché case.

Efrim Chechelnitskii, director of the foreign language courses at the *pedtechnikum*, sent Feldman and Spasov, two teacher colleagues, to McAteer's flat. Finding him loud, abusive and incoherent, they soon left. For the next week Comrade Twist stayed in bed, recovering from his vodka binge and too 'ashamed to look people in the face'. By 23 June he had recovered his equilibrium, writing again to Stasova, to notify her of his 'disgraceful conduct'. Like its predecessor, this letter, really an act of contrition interspersed with denunciations against 'Trotskyists' (including NKVD officers), was an exhortation to have party cadres in Odessa investigated by Muscovite plenipotentiaries. McAteer concluded his rambling text with an apology for his 'scandalous behaviour' and a pathetic avowal of loyalty: 'I shall not be found wanting when the day comes to shoulder a gun to defend our fatherland.'[12]

Stasova handed the missive to William L. Patterson, an Afro-American Communist lawyer with a leading position in MOPR and the CPUSA. He advised that the letter, and its Russian translation, be sent to the secret police, for the 'statements should be followed up'. Stasova's assistant duly sent the documentation to Ezhov on 2 July.[13]

This correspondence had no influence on McAteer's situation since his last letter to MOPR took five days to reach Moscow. In the meantime, the NKVD had issued an arrest warrant. McAteer's seizure was probably only a matter of time since most of the foreigners he knew were subsequently arrested. What precipitated his arrest was the drunken bout and two persons he had most likely abused during his four-day 'batter' – Feldman from the 'special· department' of the *pedtechnikum*, a police informer, and his 'handler', First Lieutenant Gaiderov of the NKVD.

The indictment was as yet unclear and the arrest illegal. The warrant was issued on 23 June to an officer of the 3rd (counter-revolutionary) Department of the NKVD Administration called Aronovich, ordering him to search the apartment of the suspect David Ivanovich Twist and then take him into custody. 'Order No. 607' was valid for two days only, but Aronovich did not perform the task until 26 June. Nobody objected to the invalid arrest warrant during the search of McAteer's rooms on the second floor of Ulitsa Karla Marksa 48. Sergeant Aronovich arrived in the company of the house janitor and two officials of the housing trust. Twist offered no resistance and made no complaint about the search, which unearthed nothing sensational – just his Soviet passport, letters and school notes. The short interrogation in Odessa Prison was simply a registration procedure, the answering of twenty questions about social origin, education, political affiliations and family status. Twist gave his real name and nationality, but did not mention his Irish family when filling in the space about relatives and their employment. Neither then nor later did the circumstances of his flight to the USSR in 1923 (the Liverpool hold-up) interest the secret police.

Usually, the document entitled 'resolution to arrest' preceded the issue of the arrest-warrant. In McAteer's case, the order was reversed. The justification for taking Twist into custody, signed by Gaiderov on the day of arrest, was that the Irishman was probably a spy. The 'investigation' would be on a surer footing – being drunk and disorderly was not a crime against the *State* – if and when the Party organisation responsible for McAteer expelled him. It complied on 27 June.

At a closed meeting of the VKP(b) group at the *pedtechnikum*, Chechelnitskii opened the proceedings and summarised the case to date (expulsion from the school, Twist's drunkenness and his 'intrigues'). Calling for Twist's expulsion from the VKP(b), Chechelnitskii had to explain why this had not been done earlier, hence the self-critical remark:

> We are guilty in that we dragged on his case up to now and the reason for that was that there was nobody here at the time to examine it. We did not have people with a knowledge of the English language.

The next three speakers, although knowing what was expected of them (voting for the expulsion), were relatively restrained. Spasov said that Twist had passed the Party review of 1935, carried out all Party tasks and unmasked people in the *kombinat* who were subsequently dismissed. After seeing Twist in a drunken state in his flat, however, 'everything became clear' to Spasov, especially the statement Twist had made in his presence – he had started to drink in order that attention be given to his case and it be cleared up. Comrade Smirnova remembered that the bout of criticism and self-criticism unleashed by Twist at his workplace had 'offended' his colleagues, but members of the Bolshevik party, she added, 'cannot be friends'. Sukman concurred, adding that even if Twist was reserved ('It was difficult to know him'), he did not think that the Irishman had a bad side. Having seeing Twist tottering drunk through Odessa, Sukman felt that this was cause enough for expulsion, but he did not believe Twist was guilty of any counter-revolutionary crime because of his teaching methods: 'He does not know History and does not have sufficient education, can only make a mess of things, but that was unintentional.'

Feldman, the NKVD informant, then took the floor. He had no reservations:

> He committed forgery, tore out certain pages from the book 'Royal Reader'. In recent times he began to drink and discredit Veger. Went to the NKVD and stated that he was a foreign spy and asked to be shot, created a public nuisance on several occasions before complete strangers.
>
> Our great fault was that we did not reveal his countenance. The directorate should have attended his lectures and examined his teaching. We'll have to contemplate the matter more deeply – why he began to drink precisely on 12 June, the day on which the verdict was announced in the case of the military-fascist spies Tukhachevskii and others. I tried to find out from him what had induced him to drink but he did not give me an answer to that question. He'd have to be expelled even if he had not been arrested.

Vorborev, the director of the *pedtechnikum* and chairman of the session, closed the tribunal with an argument which could be applied to almost any Party member: Twist had a suspicious biography and his 'mask' was that of a Communist who had performed Party tasks; the party organisation did not unmask him in time, but would do so now, by expelling him from the ranks.

The resolution, drawn up and passed unanimously, contained a battery of charges:

Twist had received his post by false pretences since he had no pedagogical qualifications;

he had falsified English history (bourgeois historiography) by not analysing the rise and fall of feudalism;

he had intrigued against his colleagues and repressed criticism against himself;

he had not carried out his party tasks;

he attempted to deceive the party organisation by tearing out the title page of Royal Readers;

he was often drunk and appeared in an intoxicated state in the offices of the party's control commission;

he had joined the party for egotistical motives, without sharing its aims, and by his deceit had discredited it.

The resolution was sent to the next higher party body, the Kaganovich District Committee. It confirmed the expulsion on 4 July. The protocol of the kangaroo court at the *pedtechnikum*, and the resolution it passed, were transmitted to the NKVD. The most incriminating passages were underlined in red pencil and the documents added to the thin file. The first lengthy questioning of the prisoner took place on 4 July. On that day McAteer's statement dealt largely with his sojourn among the cowboys and miners and ended with his return to Ireland in 1921. At the end of the protocol, just above the standard sentence signed by McAteer confirming that what was written down corresponded to what he had said, are the words 'Confession interrupted'.

The note could mean that the interrogator was called away to another case, or that McAteer stopped talking. We can never know because NKVD interrogation protocols at that time (1937) rarely reflect what was actually said but rather what the interrogator thought worthy of putting to paper to underpin the trumped-up charges. The four-page protocol of 4 July may have been a summary of what the NKVD had extracted from McAteer to date. It is also possible, of course, that the suspect was unable to continue his statement because he had collapsed or had been physically attacked. The relatively uncontested content of Seán McAteer's disclosures up to and on 4 July, which must have struck his questioner as the outline of a revolutionary thriller, would indicate rather that the 'investigation' had not as yet gone into any real depth and was interrupted by 'other business'. The fact that the next (minuted) protocol dates from early October also suggests that the interrogating team had other cases to attend to. On the other hand, McAteer may have held out under torture and refused to incriminate himself, which could also explain the gap in the documentation – at the time the NKVD did not protocol 'unsuccessful' interrogations.

The hiatus may also have occurred because of a vastly increased workload for the NKVD: the prisons were filling up with the victims of a three-pronged offensive launched in late summer 1937 against 'inveterate' enemies, against foreigners and non-Russian ethnic groups and against the elite. Confirming to the pattern in all parts of the USSR, there was a huge rise in 'political' arrests and executions in the Odessa Region: 537/2 in 1936; 8,351/3,416 in 1937; 5,352/4,512 in 1938.[14]

Any foreigner arrested at the time was accused of espionage for a foreign power. Confessions of 'spying' were extracted by all imaginable means, usually by protracted beatings. On 5 October Seán McAteer was accused of being involved in a spy-ring, which he denied. Six days later the questions centred on his work for the port authority, whether he knew the employees of the Lloyd-Triestino Shipping Co. Kigerl and Benisovich, or the Turkish sea-captain Dugo. McAteer acknowledged that he had had business with these persons in the course of his work. Benisovich had been arrested in July and was forced to mention a certain 'Twis' during an interrogation in September. The NKVD officers were fabricating the existence of an Italian espionage organisation in Odessa and adding 'confederates' to the network as they thought fit.

On 5 November McAteer admitted his 'counter-revolutionary' behaviour as a teacher, the details of which were taken directly from the resolution of 27 June expelling him from the *pedtechnikum* cell of the VKP(b). That confession sufficed for an indictment under § 7 or §9 ('wrecking') of Article 58 covering 'counter-revolutionary crime'. The last recorded interrogation is from 13 November, when McAteer twice denied that he had links to international espionage or had been recruited for counter-revolutionary aims. His file contains three interrogation protocols of the same day, from his erstwhile colleagues Piorun, Chechelnitskii and Feldman. But these, as with the record of the interrogation with Benisovich (29 September), may have been forged by the NKVD team.

The indictment, drawn up on 15 November and signed by four officers, contained three points: that he carried out 'subversive-wrecking activities' and 'cultivated counter-revolutionary bourgeois thoughts' in his lectures to the students; that he had been recruited for the Italian Secret Service by Benisovich; and that he was linked to other intelligence services. The recommendation to try Twist's case before the local *troika* was 'supported' by a confession, which McAteer had never made: 'subversive activities in connection with foreign intelligence agencies'.

The *troika* was a three-man board, consisting of the NKVD Commander, the local Party Secretary and the Public Prosecutor. The secret policeman was the most important member, chairing the nightly sessions behind closed doors. It was a perfunctory business, with no time to examine each file. The case of David Ivanovich Twist was decided on 16 November in his absence and the verdict was death by shooting. The sentence was carried out, probably in the prison, during the night of 28–29 November 1937.

Benisovich had been executed in early October. Evgenii Veger, Odessa's leading communist, a member of the Central Committee of the VKP(b) and the target of McAteer's letters to Moscow, had been arrested a day before the Irishman. Because of his prominent function, Veger was transported to the Soviet capital and shot there in late November on the orders of the Politburo. His remains were cremated with hundreds of others and thrown into an unmarked grave in Donskoi Cemetery. The extermination of Veger had most probably nothing to do with McAteer, being part of a general purge of the Central Committee – of the 139 members and candidate members elected at the 17th Party Congress in 1934, one hundred had been annihilated by 1939.

In October 1937, an investigation commission from the Moscow headquarters of the Soviet trade unions swept down on the Interklub and removed Amadei and his assistants. The petty charges included his moving the new radio-set bought for the sailors to his apartment upstairs, or that he had not offered ice-cream in the buffet during the hot summer weather. Of a more serious nature was that the library contained works of 'enemies of the people', or that some of the Party activists engaged in club activities were already in prison. Amadei was held responsible for matters over which he had no control: that many female factory workers were part-time prostitutes, soliciting sailors visiting the club premises during the Spanish Civil War.

Although the local police had sent over 170 prostitutes into banishment or to the Gulag in the first ten months of 1937, the sex industry was booming. It was also frustrating that the propagandists of the Party could make no headway against the Spanish seamen, who, as anarchists, rejected the Soviet dictatorship.[15] Levio Amadei, his German assistant, Becker, and his fellow-countryman, Sepich, the club carpenter, were arrested and shot in 1938.

German and Romanian military forces captured Odessa in October 1941. During their reign of terror, over 280,000 civilians were massacred or deported to a concentration camp. McAteer's family survived. Tamara, his wife, probably sensed that he was no longer alive when she took advantage of 'the thaw' after Stalin's death to make enquiries about her spouse. Daughter Maria wrote the first family letter to the Military Prosecutor of Odessa District in November 1955. After outlining his biography, Maria requested confirmation of whether her father was alive or dead, and that his case be reviewed for rehabilitation purposes. She concluded by professing her belief in his innocence – 'an honest, principled and devoted Party Communist'. Within a few days she was informed that the file had been found and was being examined.

Tamara Twist probably accelerated the enquiry in Odessa by writing to the Main Public Prosecutor of the USSR in Moscow. The wheels of justice ground slowly, for in 1955–56 the military jurists were overwhelmed with appeals, which were subject to a complicated and time-consuming process. Part of that work was to question witnesses who had known or incriminated the victim. In August 1956 Colonel Bystry interviewed Chechelnitskii, now a civil servant, who went to great pains to explain his dilemma in respect of Twist. He held him to be a good communist and had never heard any complaints about him from the students, but was forced by the director of the *pedtechnikum* and Feldman, the police agent, to stage the expulsion assembly. Chechelnitskii denied that he was ever questioned by the NKVD subsequently, voicing the opinion that the protocol of his interrogation (13 November 1937) in Twist's prosecution dossier was a forgery.

Bystry then sought out Piorun and placed him under oath. The ex-NKVD agent turned teacher now worked as a statistician, despite his 72 years. When summarising his clashes with Twist, Piorun ascribed the negative opinion of the Irishman to others, saying that he had never noted anything 'counter-revolutionary' about the person he had hounded for seven years. His negative remarks about Twist's teaching abilities were now factual (lack of education). The *Royal Readers* volume was no longer anti-Soviet, it merely contained 'bourgeois ideology'. Since he had never visited Twist's lectures, he did not wish to say anything more.

The investigators were coming close to a decision in early 1957. Since 'Twist' had been incriminated by Benisovich, the military jurists examined their dossiers in tandem. Bystry discovered that Benisovich had mentioned an Englishman 'Twis', whom he had 'recruited' in 1930 to collect data on port traffic. Bystry included such inaccuracies and fantasies in his summary of the David Twist case, arguing that, since Twist had never confessed to spying, the shooting verdict must be declared null and void, as must Benisovich's. He referred to his interviews with Piorun and Chechelnitskii, and their view that Twist may have been a bad teacher but was never against the Soviets. The three-man senate of the Odessa Military Tribunal accepted Bystry's report on 1 March 1957, finding that 'the guilt of Twist cannot be confirmed by objective evidence and that there were no grounds for repressing him'.

With the verdict struck out, Seán McAteer was rehabilitated in the eyes of the Soviet State. Tamara Twist was immediately informed, but she still wanted to know where her husband was and, if he were dead, where he was buried. That only became possible after the political system which murdered John McAteer and other countless victims had collapsed. In full realisation that openness (*glasnost*) about the crimes of Stalin would irreparably discredit communism, the secret police kept on lying until 1990, directing the local registrar of births, marriages and deaths to issue false certificates.

Tamara received the officially forged document on 24 April 1957: David Ivanovich Twist had died from stomach typhus on 6 May 1944. The place of death was omitted on forms pertaining to the executed victims, for the relatives might go there and lay flowers, thus creating an 'anti-Soviet disturbance'. And if the bereaved knew exactly where the loved one had expired, they could also deduce the cause of death. McAteer's family was hardly fooled by this shabby manoeuvre, knowing that 'ten years without the right of correspondence' – the cryptic communication Tamara received from the NKVD in November 1937 – was a synonym for death by the bullet.

Four years later, in 1961, an enquiry from abroad caused the Odessa KGB to send a lengthy memorandum about McAteer's biography, including his rehabilitation, to the archival department of the KGB in Moscow. The enquirer was James Larkin Jnr, secretary of the Workers' Union of Ireland. He may have met Seán McIntyre, as he called him, at Aunt Delia's before or during the Civil War or heard his father, Big Jim, speculating on the further adventures of his Edentober comrade. But neither father nor son went public on the issue. The Soviet Red Cross was directed by the KGB to inform the Ministry for Foreign Affairs to draft a reply to Larkin. It was another falsehood:

> That Twist David Ivanovich (i.e. Sean McIntyre) was living in Odessa during the occupation and that after the liberation of the city by Soviet troops, nothing could be established as to the fate of David Twist.

When Soviet communism was on its last legs, in January 1990, the CPSU in Odessa finally rehabilitated Twist 'in party matters and posthumously', thus nullifying the expulsion resolution of June 1937. The party notables could have done so in 1957 and given his family some belated satisfaction. They probably passed the meaningless resolution so late in the day because they were under public pressure from the local branch of *Memorial*. Local historians had located a mass grave from the 1930s at km 6 on the Ovidiopol road. In a field near the present airport site, a cabin was erected in the late 1930s for gravediggers. They dug pits at night, which were soon filled with the bodies of those executed in the city; in the morning the rubbish carts from Odessa arrived and the refuse was dumped on the corpses. When a trench for cable was being dug in 1961, the mass grave was discovered. A delegation from the KGB ordered that the skeletons be reburied. In late 1989 the KGB was still refusing to meet Memorial-Odessa to discuss the killing field.[16] In 1996 a monument was erected to the victims in Odessa's Second Christian Cemetery.

NOTES

1. See Jan Valtin (Richard Krebs), *Out of the Night* (New York 1940); Waldenfels, *Der Spion, der aus Deutschland kam*, pp. 139–46.

2.   The basis for this chapter is the prosecution-file of David Ivanovich Twist held in the archive of the Ukrainian secret police in Kiev.
3.   GARF, f. 8265, o. 4, d. 57, ll. 175–178.
4.   Ibid.
5.   Ibid, l. 172.
6.   Ibid, l. 170.
7.   J. Arch Getty, *Origins of the Great Purges. The Soviet Communist Party Reconsidered, 1933–1938* (Cambridge 1985), p. 250.
8.   Ibid, pp. 158–60.
9.   GARF, f. 8265, o. 4, d. 57, ll. 192–93.
10. Francis Beckett, *Stalin's British Victims* (Stroud 2004), pp. 54–72.
11. *Isvestiia TsK KPSS*, no. 4, 1989.
12. GARF, f. 8264, o. 5, d. 57, ll. 192–95.
13. Ibid, ll. 191, 196.
14. L.V. Koval'chuk and G.A. Razumov (eds), *Odesskii Martirolog, tom 1* (Odessa 1997), p. 670.
15. RGASPI, f. 534, o. 5, d. 244, ll. 32–48.
16. *Moscow News*, no. 48, 1989, p. 15.

Index